GAGE
SCHOOL ATLAS
OF
CANADA

Cover by Fortunato Aglialoro

Design by G. Cluett and Jean Galt

Gage Publishing Limited wishes to thank the following individuals and organizations for the use of photographs in this book. Page 1, courtesy of the Scarborough Board of Education, Scarborough, Ont., and Paterson Photographic Works Inc., Toronto. Page 30, National Film Board Photothèque, Ottawa. Page 32, Bill Brooks Photography, Scarborough, Ont. Page 46, (top) Bill Brooks Photography, (centre) Ontario Ministry of Industry and Tourism, (bottom) Bill Brooks Photography. Page 58, courtesy of Robert Waldock, Scarborough. Page 62, (top) National Film Board Photothèque, (centre) National Film Board Photothèque, (bottom) courtesy of the Ministry of Forests, Province of British Columbia. Page 76, (top) National Film Board Photothèque, (middle) International Nickel Company of Canada Limited, (bottom) Bill Brooks Photography. Page 85, (top) Bill Brooks Photography, (middle) National Film Board Photothèque, (bottom) Bill Brooks Photography. Page 92, (first and second) Bill Brooks Photography, (third) J. K. Smith, Toronto, (fourth) Ontario Ministry of Industry and Tourism. Page 102, (top) Bill Brooks Photography, (middle) Travel Alberta, Edmonton, (bottom) Bill Brooks Photography.

ISBN 0-7715-8260-9 hb.
ISBN 0-7715-8263-3 pa.
8 9 10 11 12 BP 91 90 89 88 87
Written, printed and bound in Canada

GAGE SCHOOL ATLAS OF CANADA

A Skills-building Atlas

Edited by G. Cluett, N. Scrimger, and J. K. Smith

Consultants: James A. Carroll and Irene Richmond

Artwork by James Loates illustrating

gage EDUCATIONAL PUBLISHING COMPANY
A DIVISION OF CANADA PUBLISHING CORPORATION
TORONTO ONTARIO CANADA

CONTENTS

THE GAGE SCHOOL ATLAS OF CANADA

An atlas is a collection of maps. In this atlas of Canada, there are maps of the whole country, maps of the provinces and territories, and maps of sections of Canada—the Atlantic Provinces, Central Canada, and Western Canada.

Using the maps in this atlas, you can learn all kinds of things about Canada, or about a section of Canada, or about a province or territory. You can even find out about a particular city in Canada. Let's take Vancouver as an example.

- Where in the world is Vancouver located?
- In what province or territory is it located?
- Is it a capital city?
- Is it a big city?
- How does it compare in size with other cities?
- What makes it important as a city?
- How do people there make a living?
- What is the climate like?
- What is the land like around Vancouver?

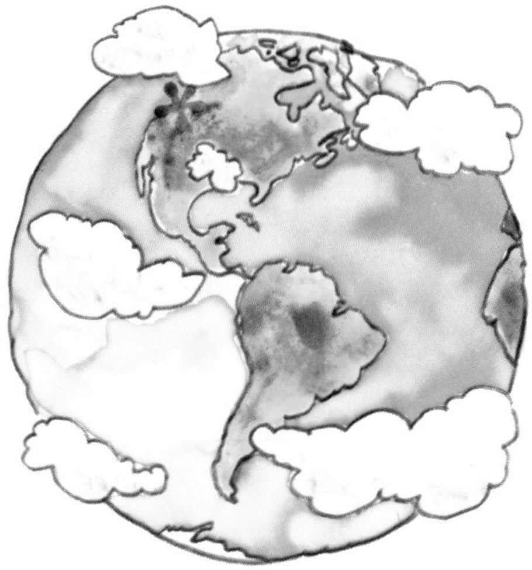

You can find the answers to all these questions about Vancouver by reading maps in this atlas. And you can find the same kind of information about other places in Canada.

In fact, you can use this atlas for all kinds of social studies projects about Canada. There are maps that show farmlands and the crops that are grown and raised on them. There are maps that show forests and how we use the trees that are chopped down. There are maps that show mines and oil wells and railways and automobile factories, and many, many, other things.

Special Features of This Atlas

With so many maps showing so many different things, how will you know which maps to use? How will you know where to find them? How will you know what is shown on the maps? There are special features in the *Gage School Atlas of Canada* that will help you to use the maps to find out the things you want to know.

CONTENTS

If you look at the *Contents* on pages iv and v, you will see that the maps in this atlas have been grouped in sections. Each section deals with a particular topic. One section, for example, contains maps showing how land and water are used in each of the provinces. These maps show farming, fishing, logging, mining, manufacturing, and other land and water uses. The climate section contains maps showing ranges of temperatures and amounts of rainfall across Canada. The maps in the people and places section show the size of towns and cities in each of the provinces. There are other topic sections as well. Check the *Contents* to find out what these are.

So, if you want to do a report on land and water uses in New Brunswick, or transportation in Central Canada, or some other topic, check the *Contents* to find the section dealing with the topic you want. Then look up the maps listed there and read them to find the information you need.

Or, if you want to do a project on a province or region in Canada, check each of the sections in the *Contents* to find all the maps of that particular province or region.

HOW TO READ A MAP

You can't find out very much just by *looking* at a map. You have to be able to *read* a map. This part of the atlas will show you *how to read a map.*

- You will learn about the signs and markings that tell what things are shown on a map.
- You will learn about direction on a map.
- You will learn how to measure distance on a map.
- You will learn how to locate places on a map.

Once you have learned these map-reading skills, you will be able to read any of the maps in this atlas.

PHOTOGRAPHS AND QUESTIONS

The atlas contains another feature that will help you use the skills you have learned in reading maps. At the beginning of each section, there are photographs and questions that deal with the topic of the section. The photographs will give you a picture of what is shown on the maps in the section. The questions will guide you to find the information shown on the maps by using the map-reading skills you have learned.

GLOSSARY

Some things that are shown on the maps may be unfamiliar to you. You may not have a clear idea of what "minerals" and "metals" are, for example. Or you may not know what "metal refining" is. Or you may want to know what a certain metal, like copper, is used for.

In the box below each map, unfamiliar words or terms have an asterisk (*) beside them. If you want to find information about any item that has an asterisk, look it up in the *Glossary*, on pages 114-117.

GAZETTEER

The *Gazetteer* is an alphabetical list of all the places that are shown on the maps in this atlas. Beside each place name is the page number of every map on which that place is marked. If you want to find the maps that show Kapuskasing or Kelowna, Cape Race or Vancouver Island, or any other place in this atlas, just look in the *Gazetteer*, on pages 120-132.

The *Gazetteer* also tells you where a place is located on each map. This will help you to find places quickly and easily. To find out how to do this, read *How to Use the Gazetteer*, on pages 118-120.

You can use the *Gazetteer* for more than just finding the location of places on a map. Let's say you want to do a project on a particular place — for example, Victoria or Calgary or Montreal or Toronto. Look up that place in the *Gazetteer* to find all the maps on which it is shown. Then read the maps to get information about the climate of the place, its size, its industries, the roads and railways that connect it to other places, and so on.

You can see that the *Gage School Atlas of Canada* is much more than a collection of maps. With all the special features, it's a geography book and an atlas rolled up in one. If you read the maps, using all the special features, you'll learn a lot about Canada and the people who live there.

MAPS AND YOU

You use maps every day. Without maps, you could not do all the things you do every day. You would not be able to travel to and from school. You could not go on errands or visit friends in your neighborhood. When you do these things, you don't follow a map drawn on a piece of paper. You use one of the maps in your head! That's right! You have a whole collection of maps — *an atlas* — in your head.

Just think of all the places you have been today. How did you know how to get to these places? How did you know whether to walk or take a bus? How did you know where to get a bus? You *must* have been using mental maps — maps in your head.

When you go someplace that is familiar to you, you don't think about the route because you know the way. So, you are not aware that you are using a map. But when you want to go someplace new or unfamiliar, you have no mental map to follow. What do you do then? What do you do if you are invited to the home of a new friend and you don't know the way? Your friend will either have to tell you how to get there — or else draw a plan of the route.

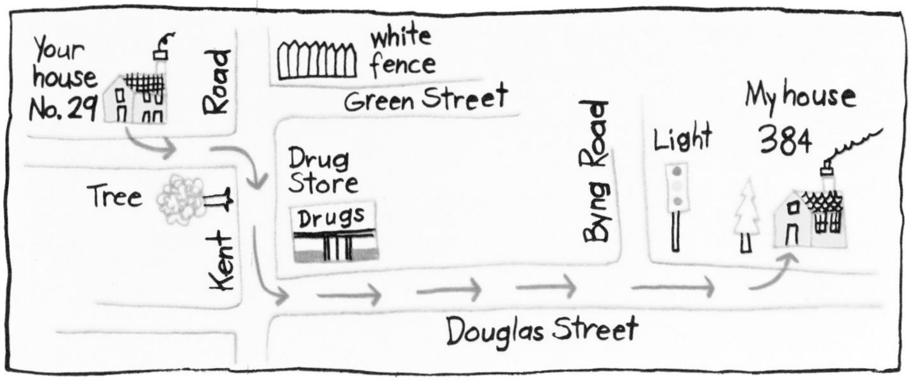

This plan is really a map. It is a map of that part of the earth between your house and your friend's house. That's what maps are.

Maps are plans of the earth's surface, or of any part of the earth's surface.

They can be plans of a very small part of the earth — a map of your neighborhood or town. Or they can be plans of a larger part of the earth — a map of your province or country. Or they can be plans of the whole earth — a globe map.

When we think of maps, we usually think of maps printed on paper. However, maps have been drawn on almost every kind of material. People have drawn maps on clay, bone, leather, stone, wood, cloth, or any other suitable material that was handy.

The oldest map that we know of is on a clay tablet that is about 4000 years old. It shows a piece of land between two hills, with a river running through the land. The tablet is probably a map showing the boundary lines of somebody's property.

Another old map is on a piece of silk. It shows a city in China about 2000 years ago.

Indians in North America drew maps on birchbark and deerskin.

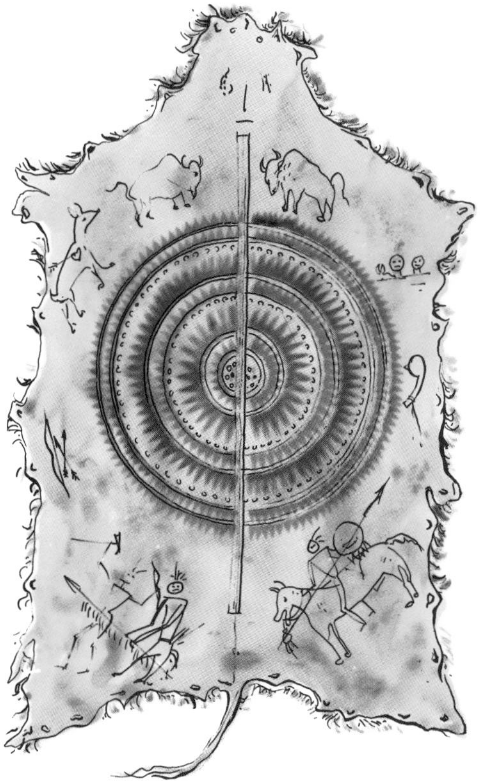

Inuit carved maps out of wood. They carved the edges of flat pieces of wood to represent islands, bays, and harbors.

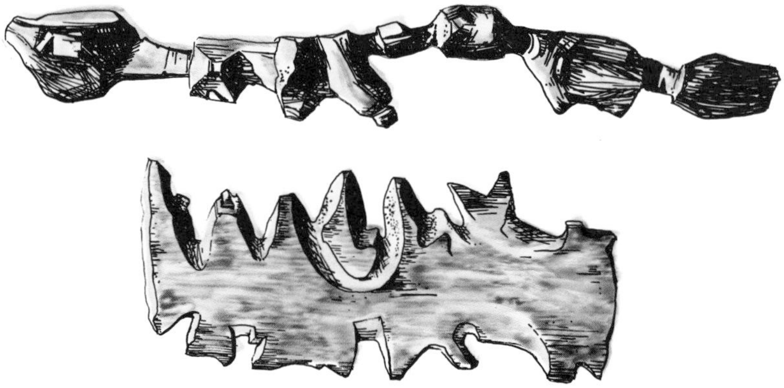

Today, most of the maps we use are printed on paper. Some maps are very large, as big as a wall. Others are quite small. The size depends on what the maps are used for. There are many kinds of maps, because we use maps for many different purposes.

DIFFERENT MAPS FOR DIFFERENT PURPOSES

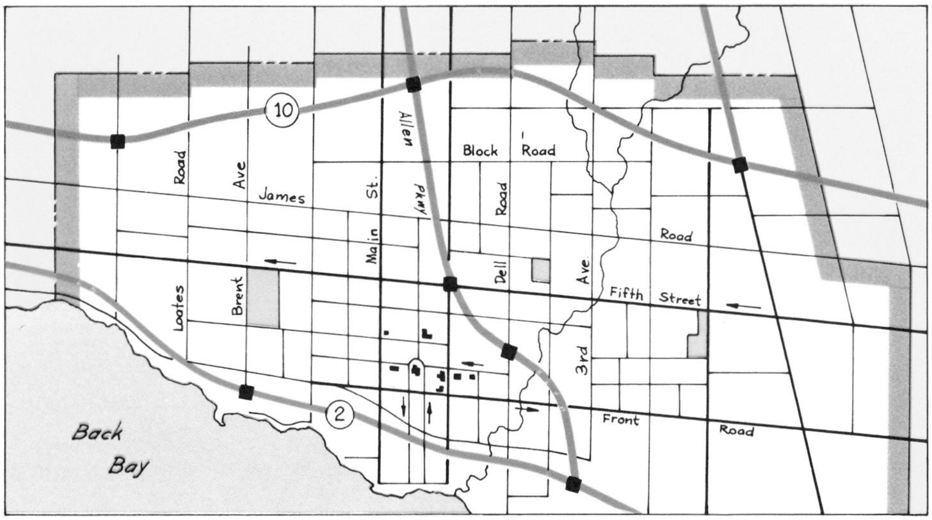

City maps show where the streets are. If we know the address of a place, we can find the street on a map of the town or city. Then we can choose what route we want to take to get there.

Road maps show where the roads and highways are. They tell where places are located and how far apart they are. We use road maps to help us decide which route to take to go from one place to another.

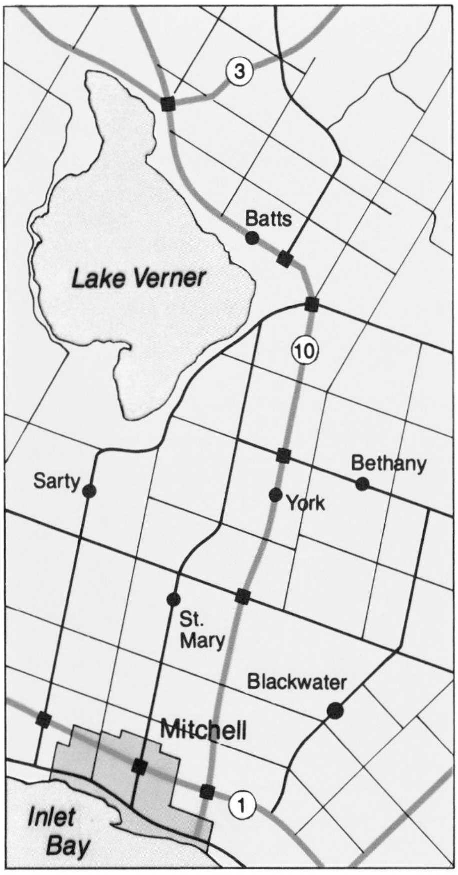

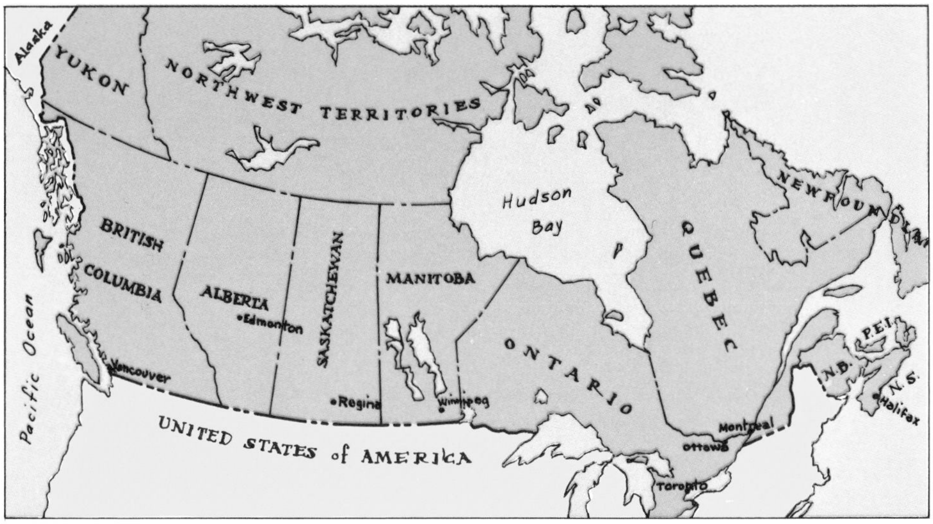

Political maps show towns, cities, provinces, territories, and countries. So if we want to know where the boundary is between two countries or where a town is located in a province, we look at a political map.

Tourist maps tell where parks, picnic grounds, swimming areas, zoos, and other tourist attractions are located.

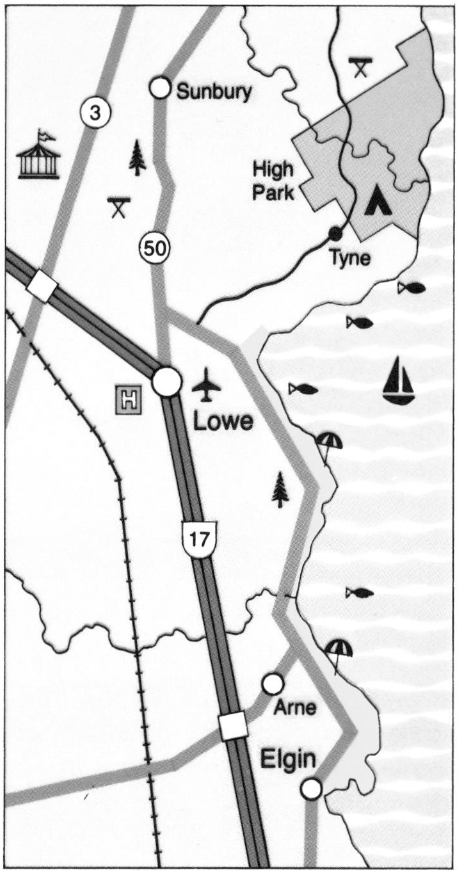

Population maps show where people live and how big towns and cities are.

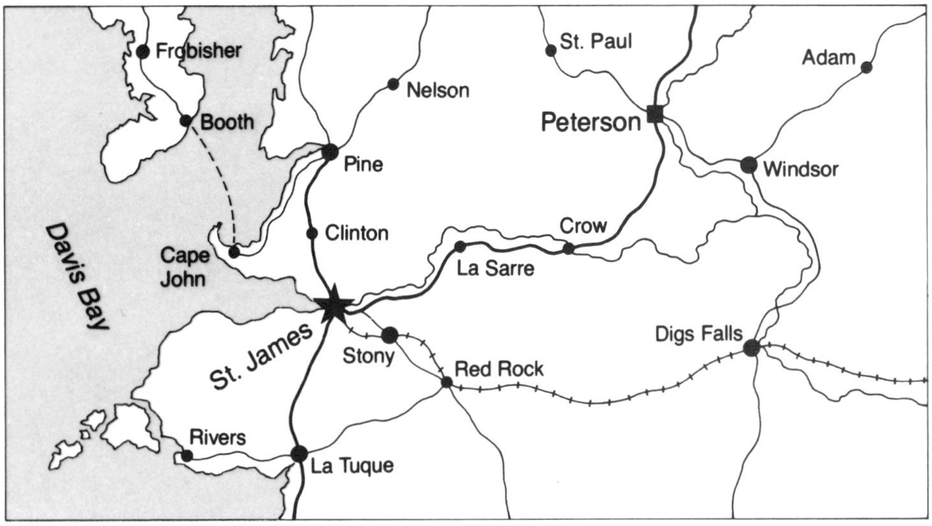

Agriculture maps show where there are wheat farms, cattle ranches, orchards, and other kinds of farms.

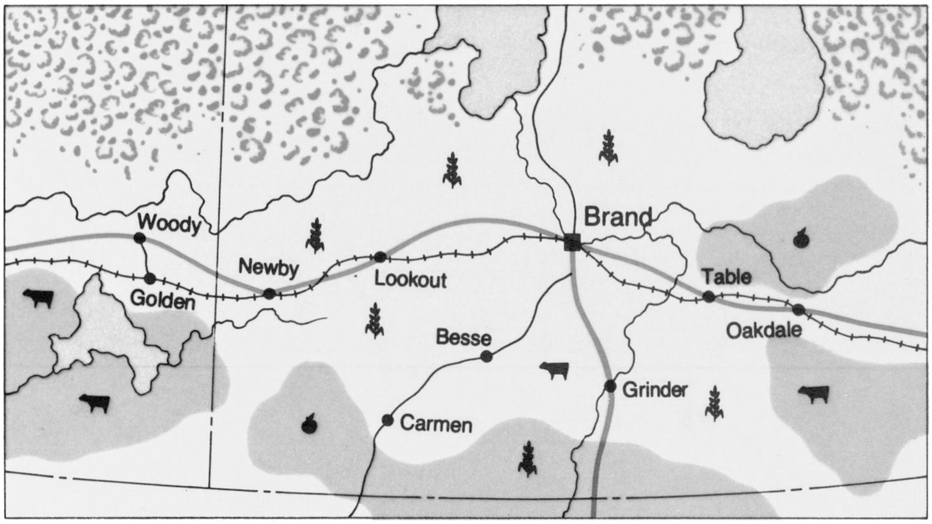

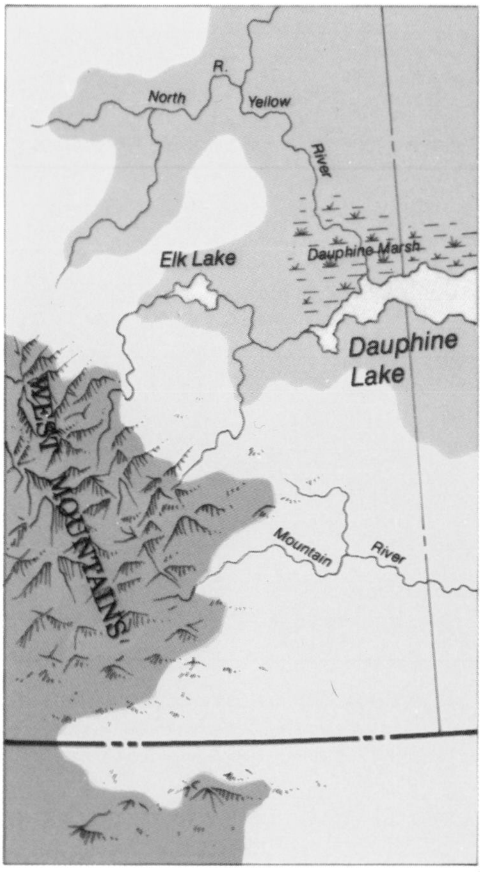

Physical maps show lakes, rivers, mountains, valleys, and other natural features of the earth's surface.

These are just a few of the different kinds of maps we use. There are many, many more. So you can see that we can find out a lot of things from maps.

The maps in this atlas tell where people live in Canada and what kind of work they do. They show what parts of Canada have high mountains, what parts have thick forests, and what parts have a lot of lakes and swamps. By learning to read the maps in this atlas, you will learn a great deal about Canada and Canadians.

HOW TO READ A MAP

Symbols

Here is a *photograph* of a classroom in Donwood School.

What things do you see in the photograph? What is behind the chair? Where is the chalkboard? Where is the bulletin board? What object is farthest away from the chalkboard?

Here is a *picture* of a classroom in Donwood.

What things do you see in the picture? Do the photograph and the picture both show the same classroom? How do you know?

Here is a *drawing* of the classroom that a pupil made.

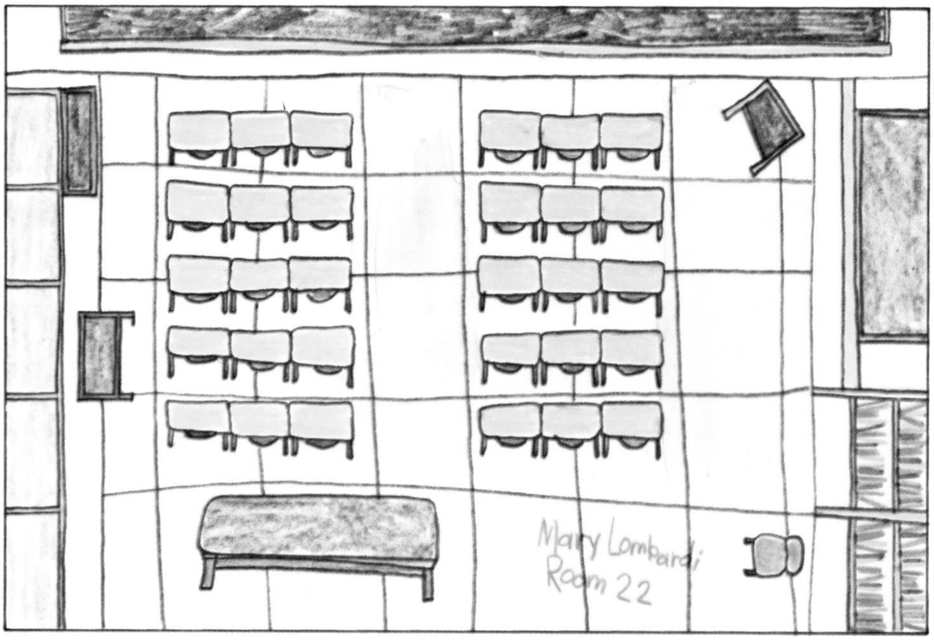

What things do you see in the drawing? Are they the same things that were in the photograph and picture? How do they look different? What is  a drawing of? What is behind the  ? What is  ? What object is farthest away from the 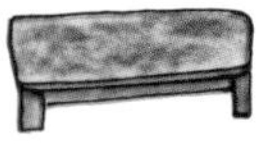 ?

Even without looking at the photograph and the picture, it's still easy to identify the things in the classroom, isn't it? That's because the drawings look like the real objects.

Can you name the objects in these drawings?

What is this? 

That's right, it's a drawing of the sun. But when the weather reporter on TV draws  on the weather map, it isn't *really* just a drawing of the sun, is it? The  stands for or means something else. It means that the weather is going to be sunny. So on the weather map  stands for or represents "sunny weather."

When the weather reporter draws  on the weather map, what does the drawing *really* stand for or represent?

Something that stands for or represents something else is called a *symbol*.

When you see this sign  you know it's not really a picture of an arrow. What does the symbol 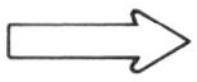 stand for?

When you see  on a label, you know it's a warning. What warning does this symbol represent?

Some symbols look like the things they stand for. Here are some symbols you see on road signs or in buildings. What does each symbol represent?

But

Symbols do not always look like the things they stand for. We use lots of symbols that don't look like the things they represent. The symbol $ doesn't look like  . The symbol ¢ doesn't look like  .

Arithmetic signs are other symbols that don't look like the things they stand for. What do the arithmetic symbols + and – represent?

What do xxoo on a Valentine or birthday card stand for?

Here are some other symbols that don't look like the things they stand for. What does each of these symbols represent?

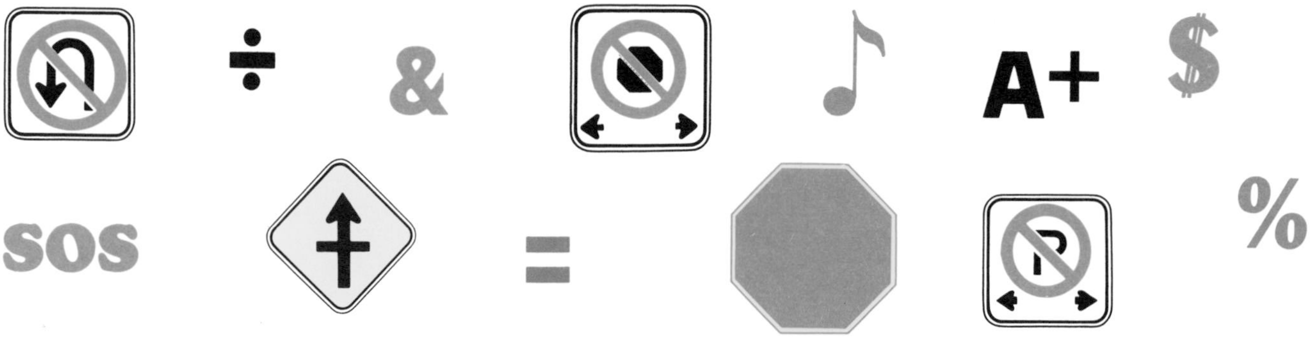

You can see that symbols can be any size or shape. They can even be any color. What does a red traffic light stand for? What does a green traffic light represent?

When we see a red or green traffic light, we know what they represent. But what do we do if we don't know what a symbol stands for?

What do we do if we don't know what these symbols on road signs represent? How can we find out?

We can ask a police official or some other person who would know. Or we can look up the symbols in a driver's manual. In the driver's manual, there is a table or chart that explains symbols on road signs. This kind of table or chart is called a *key*.

Here is a plan of Room 22 in Donwood School.

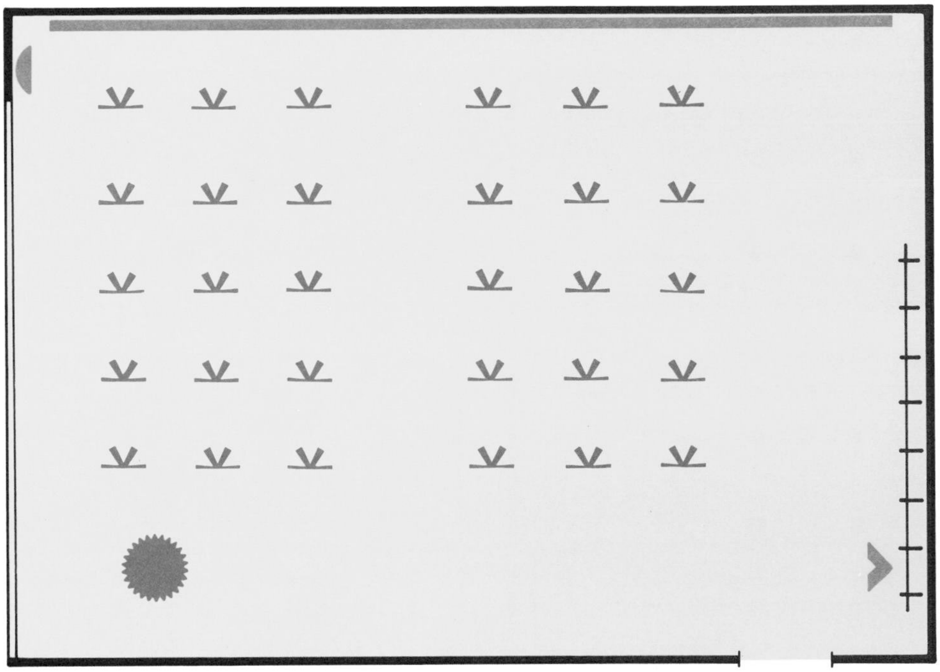

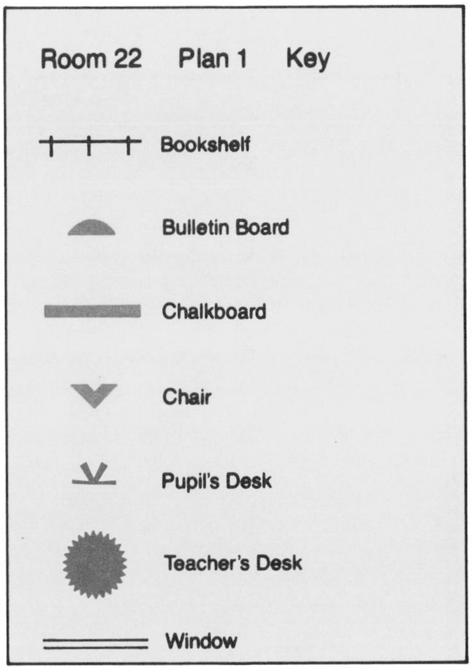

Look at Mary Lombardi's drawing of Room 22 and then look at the plan. How is the plan different from the drawing?

Instead of drawings that look like the objects in the classroom, symbols are used to *represent* the objects. These symbols don't look at all like the things they represent. Can you identify the objects in the classroom? Try to read the plan, without looking back at the drawing of Room 22.

If you couldn't identify some of the objects, look at the right of the plan. There is *a key that explains what the symbols stand for*. Now, look at the key and try to read the plan.

Where is the chair? Is it closer to the teacher's desk or to the chalkboard? What is behind the chair? What is farthest away from the teacher's desk? What is closest to the teacher's desk?

REMEMBER

1. Plans don't have to use drawings that look like real objects. Plans can use symbols that don't look at all like the things they represent.
2. Symbols don't always stand for the same things on all plans. The symbol  doesn't represent a pupil's desk on all plans.  doesn't always stand for a bulletin board.
3. To read a plan, you have to look at the key to find out what the symbols represent on that particular plan.

Here is another plan of Room 22 in Donwood School. This plan uses completely different symbols.

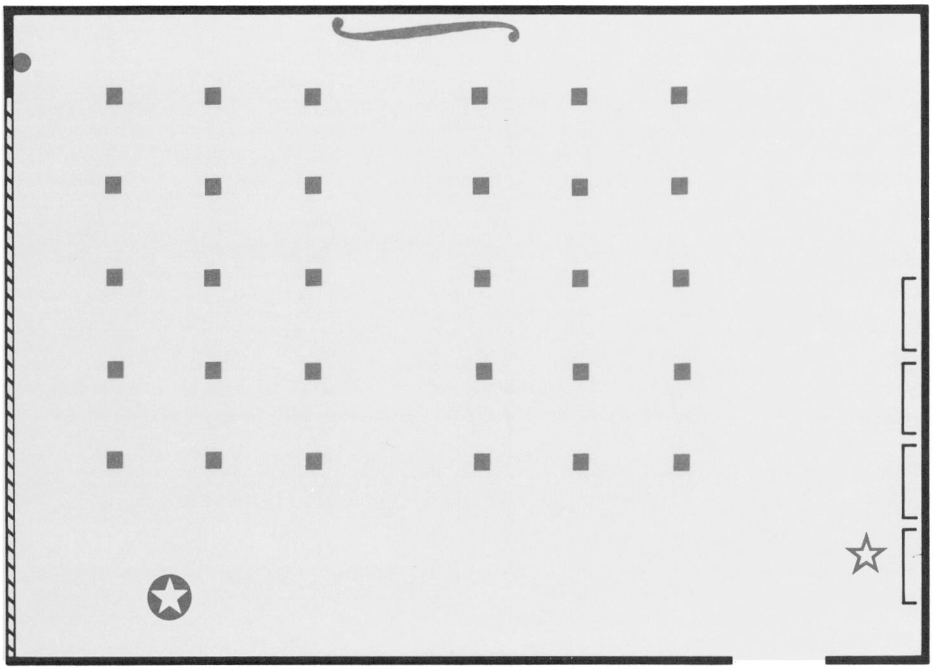

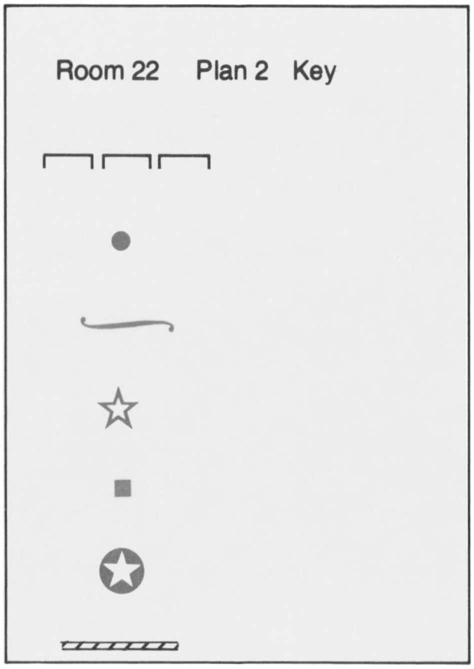

This time, the key has not been completed. If you compare this plan with Plan 1 of the same classroom, you can figure out what the symbols stand for in Plan 2.

Copy Plan 2 in your notebook. Make a key for the plan that tells what the symbols in Plan 2 represent. Exchange plans with a classmate. Did you both agree on what the symbols stand for?

Now, draw a rough plan of your own classroom. Decide what objects you are going to put in your plan and make up symbols to represent them. *Remember to make a key.*

When you have finished, exchange plans with a classmate. Did the keys help you to read each other's plans?

Maps, you remember, are plans of the earth's surface, or of any part of the earth's surface. Maps use symbols, too. And like symbols on plans, map symbols do not always stand for the same things on all maps. So maps also have keys.

On maps, the key is called a *legend*.

Here are some symbols you may have seen on maps.

One symbol that is used on a lot of maps is a dot. Dots are often used for towns and cities. But they may also represent oil wells or silver mines.

The color blue is also used as a map symbol. Blue often represents water. But not always. On some maps, blue may be used to represent low, flat land. On other maps, it may be used to show where there are a lot of factories.

REMEMBER

1. Map symbols do not represent the same things on all maps.
2. To read a map, you have to look at the legend to find out what the symbols stand for on that particular map.

ARCTIC OCEAN
PACIFIC OCEAN
ATLANTIC OCEAN
ATLANTIC OCEAN
YUKON TERR.
WHITEHORSE
NORTHWEST TERRITORIES
YELLOWKNIFE
BRITISH COLUMBIA
ALBERTA
EDMONTON
VICTORIA
SASKATCHEWAN
REGINA
MANITOBA
WINNIPEG
ONTARIO
OTTAWA
TORONTO
QUEBEC
QUEBEC
NEWFOUNDLAND
ST. JOH
N.B.
FREDERICTON
P.E.I.
CHARLOTTETOWN
N.S.
HALIFAX
N

Population of Capital Cities

- 5 000-10 000 People
- 10 000-100 000 People
- Over 100 000 People
- Over 1 000 000 People

- Fishing
- Wheat Farming
- Trapping
- Logging and Lumbering

National Capital: OTTAWA (population over 100 000)

Look at the map of Canada on page 8. Use the legend to read the map and answer these questions.

1. What is the capital of Canada?
2. What is the capital city of Ontario?
3. What is the capital city of Manitoba?
4. What are the capital cities of the two territories?
5. What is the capital city of your province?
6. In which province are there two capital cities?
7. Which capital cities are located on islands?
8. How many provinces are there in Canada?
9. How many territories are there in Canada?
10. Which capital city has the fewest people?
11. Which capital city has more people, Fredericton or Edmonton?
12. In which provinces do people earn a living from fishing?
13. In which provinces are there wheat farms?
14. Is there lumbering in Manitoba? How do you know?
15. In what provinces and territories is there trapping?
16. What is the largest capital city?

Direction

Look back at the plan of Room 22 on page 5.

- What direction do the windows face?
- Is the teacher's desk at the north end of the classroom or the south end?

You can't answer these questions because an important piece of information is missing from the plan. The *direction* is not marked. There is no way of knowing which way is north or south or east or west.

North, south, east, and west are *directions*.

Most plans and maps show only the direction of north, because if you know where north is, then you know where the other directions are, too. If you face north, south is in the opposite direction, east is to your right, and west is to your left.

These are some symbols that might be used to show north.

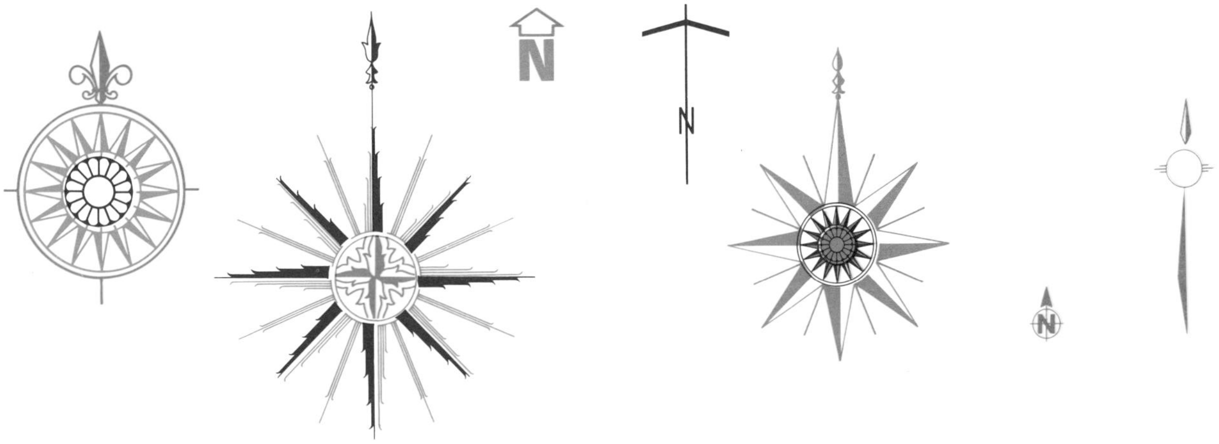

Let's add the symbol  for north to the plan for Room 22.

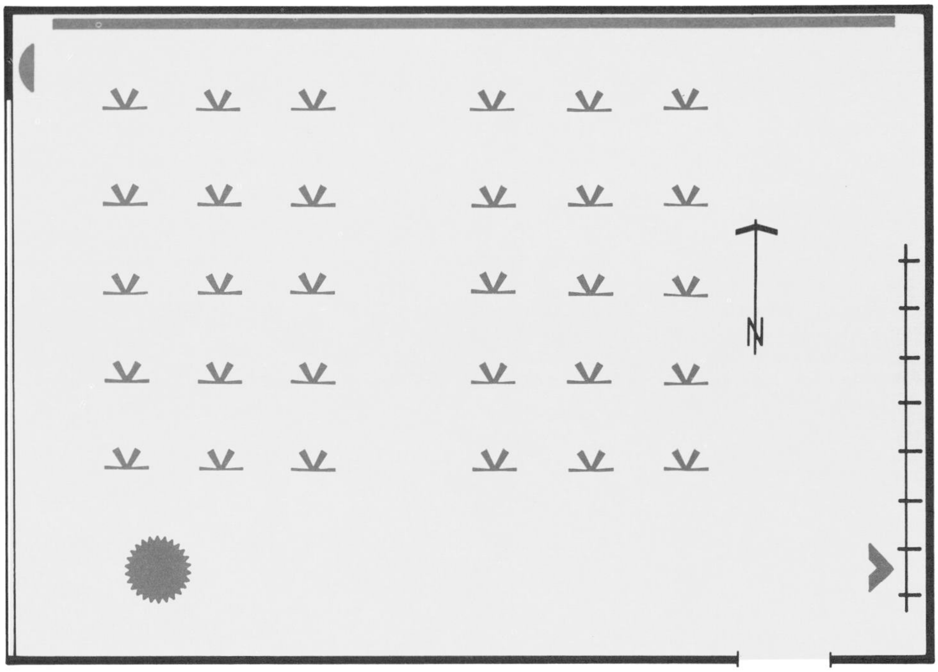

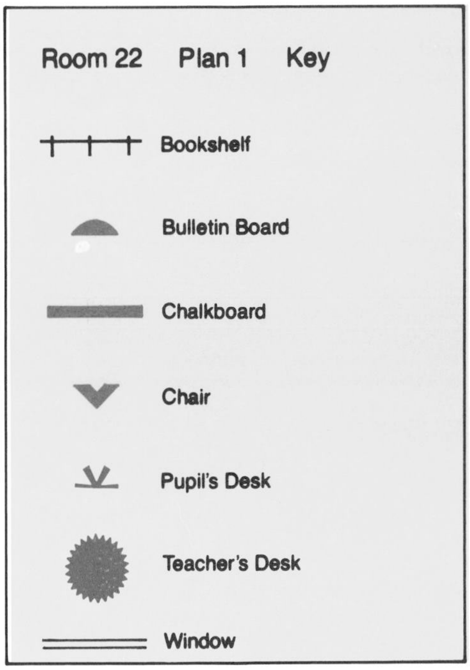
Room 22 Plan 1 Key
Bookshelf
Bulletin Board
Chalkboard
Chair
Pupil's Desk
Teacher's Desk
Window

Now see if you can answer these questions.

- What direction do the windows face?
- Is the teacher's desk at the north end of the classroom or the south end?
- At which end is the chalkboard?

Find out what direction the windows in your classroom face. Decide where north is. Now add a north marker to the plan you made of your classroom.

Direction must be marked on a plan or map. If it is not marked, you don't know whether a place is north or south or east or west of another place. If you want to go from one place to another, you won't know in which direction to travel.

When you're going from one place to another, you don't always travel *directly* north or *directly* west. Sometimes you travel in a direction that is *between* north and west. This direction is called *northwest*. The direction between north and east is *northeast*. What is the direction between south and west? What is the direction between south and east?

One symbol that shows all the directions might look like this:

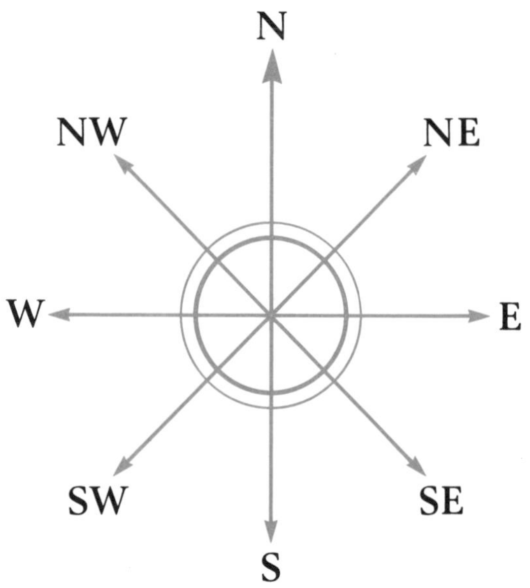

Look back again at the plan on page 5.

The top left-hand corner of Room 22 is the northwest corner. Name the other corners in the classroom.

Donwood School is in a neighborhood called Donwood Heights. Here is a map of the neighborhood.

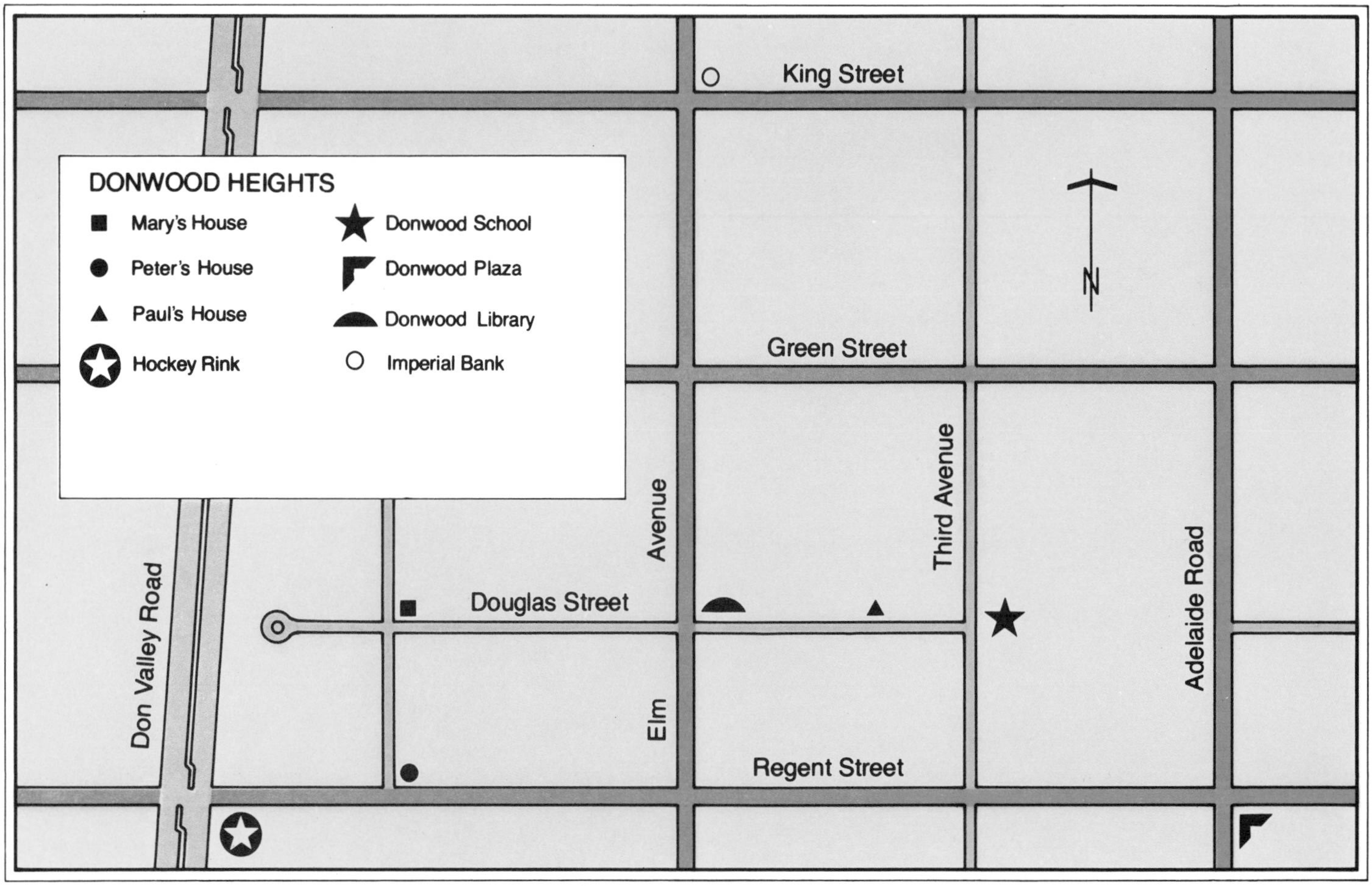

Use the legend and direction on the map to answer these questions.

1. What street is farthest north in Donwood Heights?

2. What street is farthest south?

3. In what part of the neighborhood is the hockey rink?

4. In what part of the neighborhood is the shopping centre?

5. What building is on the northeast corner of King Street and Elm Avenue?

6. What building is on the southeast corner of Regent Street and Don Valley Road?

7. Is Mary's house on the north or south side of Douglas Street?

8. In what direction does Mary go to get to school?

9. In what direction does Peter go to get to the hockey rink?

REMEMBER

1. To know direction on a map, you have to check the marker for north.
2. Maps are usually drawn with the symbol for north pointing toward the top. But not always! North can be at an angle, like this 

or like this 

.

Trapping

Mountains

Wheat Farming

Here is a chance for you to practise reading symbols and direction on a map. Each sentence below needs a direction word. Complete the sentences and write them in your notebook.

1. The province that is farthest ______ is Newfoundland.
2. The province that is farthest ______ is British Columbia.
3. Prince Edward Island is off the ______ coast of Canada.
4. Vancouver Island is off the ______ coast of Canada.
5. Ontario is ______ of Manitoba.
6. Calgary is ______ of Winnipeg.
7. The city that is farthest ______ on the map is Whitehorse.
8. Wheat is grown in the ______ part of Saskatchewan and there is trapping in the ______ part.
9. Toronto is ______ of Montreal.
10. If you live in New Brunswick, you travel ______ to go skiing in the mountains.
11. St. John's is ______ of Halifax.
12. Lake Superior is ______ of Hudson Bay.

Scale

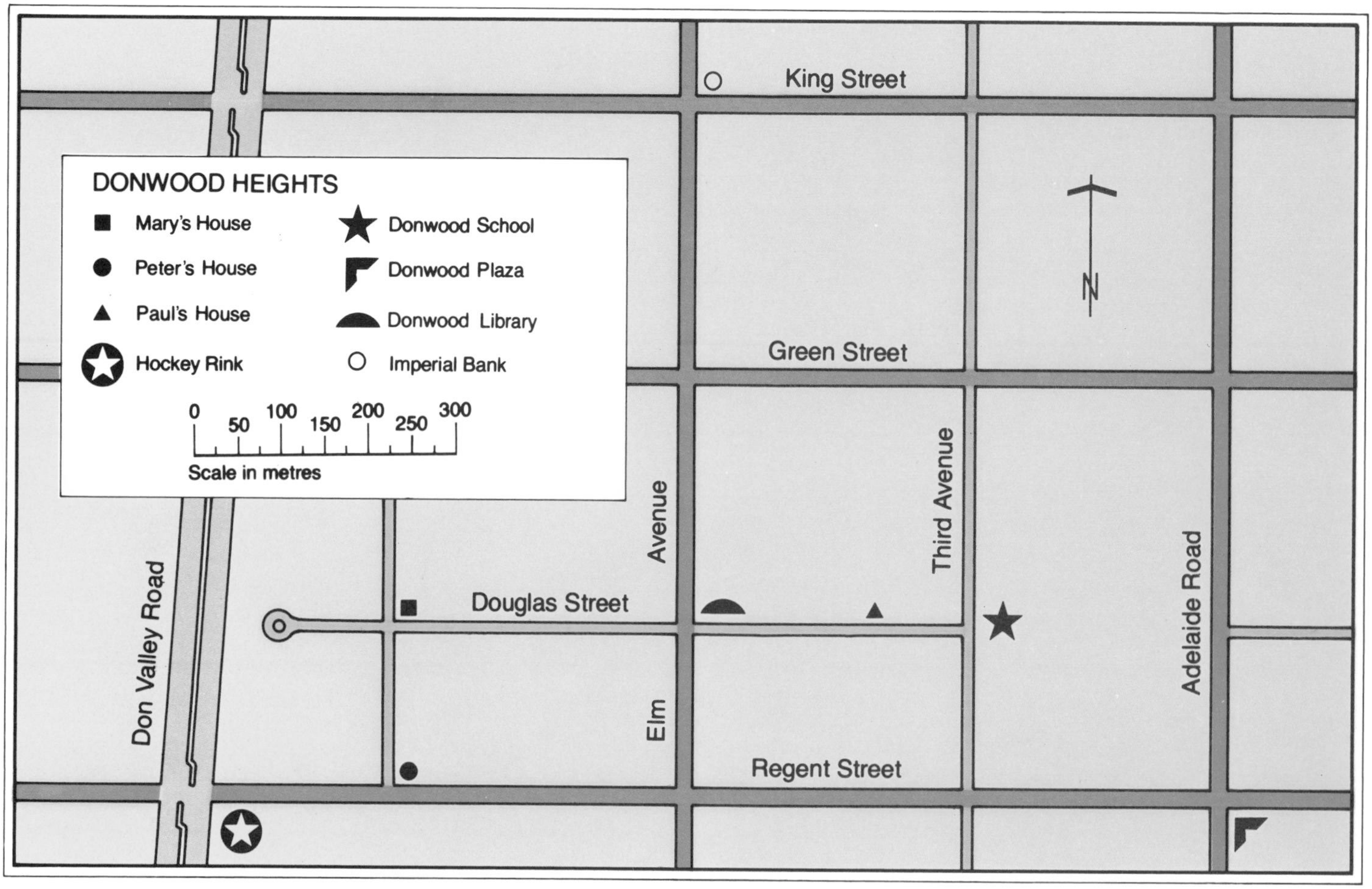

You can find out many things by reading this map of Donwood Heights.

You can check the legend to see what things the symbols represent. Then you can find Donwood School, and the hockey rink, and the shopping centre, and all the other things that are shown on the map.

You can check the marker for north and know in which direction to go if you want to buy something at the shopping centre. You can also find out which side of the street the hockey rink is on.

You can tell just by looking at the map that Paul's house is closer to Donwood School than Peter's house is. You can see that Mary's house is closer to the hockey rink than to the school.

But

You can't tell *exactly* how far it is from Paul's house to the school. You can't tell the *exact* distance between Mary's house and the hockey rink.

You can measure the distance on the map, but that obviously isn't the *real* distance. Mary's house isn't really 4 cm from the hockey rink! Paul doesn't actually live 2 cm from the school! And the real distance from one end of Donwood Heights to the other is certainly not 15 cm!

If the distance on the map were the same as the real distance, the map would have to be the same size as the Donwood Heights neighborhood. Imagine drawing a map on a piece of paper big enough to fit over a whole neighborhood!

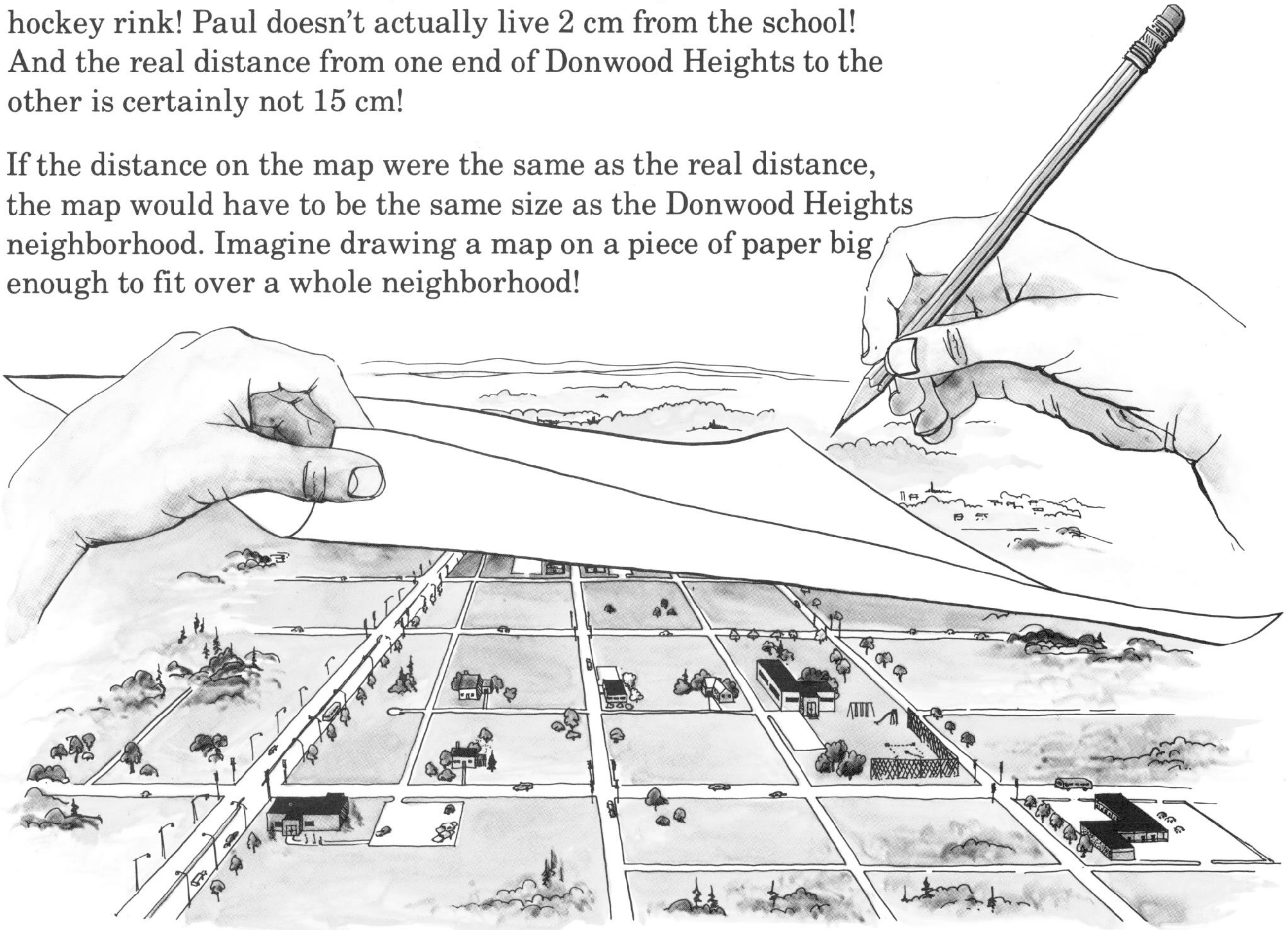

It's impossible to draw a map the same size as the real neighborhood. So, how would a map of such a large area be drawn? There must be some way of showing a large area in a smaller size. There must be some way of representing the real neighborhood on a map small enough to fit on a piece of paper. And there must be some kind of clue on a map that tells what the real size of the area is.

The way real size and distance are shown on a map is called *scale*. The scale marked on a map tells the real size and distance represented on that map.

Look at the map of Donwood Heights and find the scale in the legend. It looks like this.

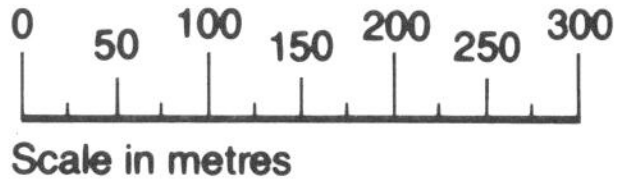
0
50
100
150
200
250
300
Scale in metres

Notice that the line scale is marked 0 at one end and 300 at the other end. This tells you that the length of this line represents a real distance of 300 m. This means that places that are the same distance apart on the map as the length of the line scale are actually 300 m apart in Donwood Heights.

Each of the numbers on the line scale tells what the real distance is in Donwood Heights. Find the 50 mark on the line scale. Places that are this far apart 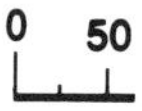

on the map are really 50 m apart in Donwood Heights. Now find the 100 mark on the line scale. Places that are this far apart 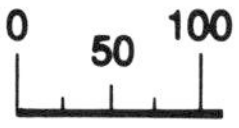

on the map are really 100 m apart in Donwood Heights.

Between 0 and 50 there is a mark that isn't numbered. This mark is halfway between 0 and 50, so the number for this mark would be 25. Halfway between 50 and 100 there is another mark that isn't numbered. What would be the number for this mark? What would be the number for each of the other unnumbered marks on the line scale?

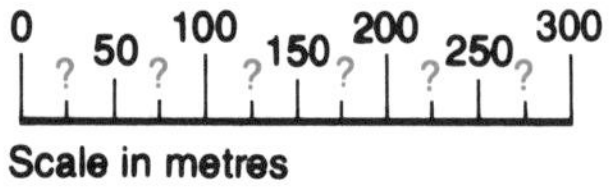

Let's use the line scale to find the real distance from Paul's house to Donwood School.

1. Place a strip of paper on the map so that the straight edge touches both Paul's house and the school.

   Make a mark on the paper at Paul's house and another mark at the school.

2. Put the strip of paper along the line scale, with the mark for Paul's house at 0.

   Read the number of metres at the mark for the school.

   This tells you that Paul's house is 150 m from the school.

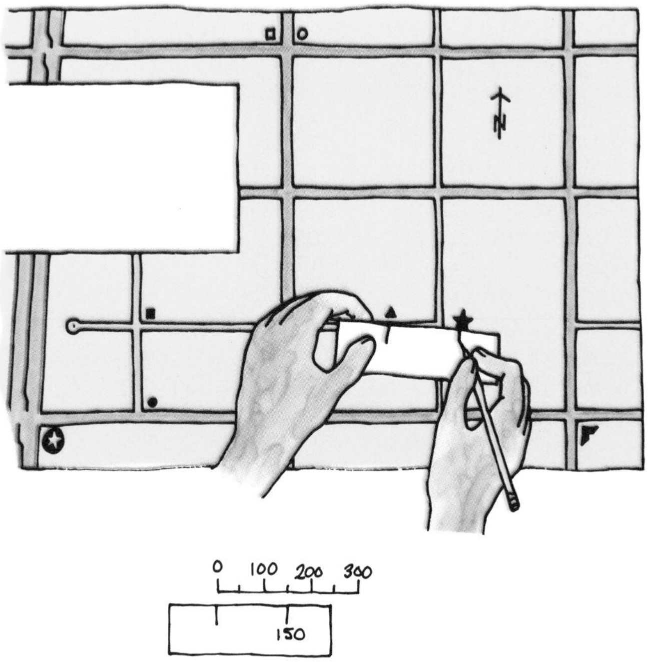

Find the real distance between Mary's house and the hockey rink. Use a fresh strip of paper, otherwise you may forget what each mark stands for. (You might end up measuring the distance between *Paul's* house and the hockey rink!)

- How far is it from Peter's house to the hockey rink?
- How far is the library from Donwood School?

Now you know how to use the line scale to find out real distances between places on a map. But all of the distances you have measured have been within the length of the line scale. How can you find out real distances between places that are farther apart than 300 m? You can see that the distance between Paul's house and the shopping centre is longer than the length of the line scale. How can you find the real distance between these two places? You can still use the line scale. Here's how to do it.

1. Place a strip of paper between Paul's house and the shopping centre. Make a mark on the paper for each place.

2. Put the mark for Paul's house at 0 and make a mark on the strip of paper where the line scale ends. Write down 300 m at this mark.

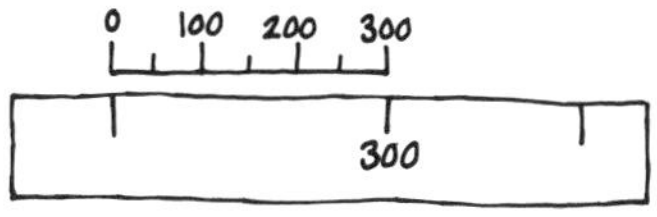

3. Now place your 300 m mark at 0. Read the number of metres at the mark for the shopping centre. Write down the number at the mark.

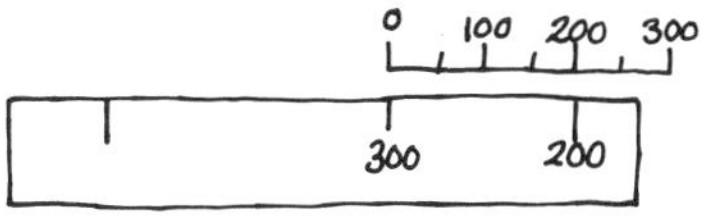

Add the two numbers you have written down. That is the distance between Paul's house and the shopping centre.

$$\begin{array}{r} 300\text{ m} \\ +\ 200\text{ m} \\ \hline 500\text{ m} \end{array}$$

- What is the distance between Peter's house and the library?
- How far is the library from the bank?
- What is the distance from the hockey rink to the library?

Sometimes places are very far apart. They may be even farther apart than twice the length of the line scale. You can see that the distance from the hockey rink at one end of Donwood Heights to the shopping centre at the other looks longer than 600 m. How can you use the line scale to find out the exact size of the Donwood Heights neighborhood? It's easy. You just keep repeating the steps you have learned.

1. Place the strip of paper across the whole Donwood Heights neighborhood.

 Make a mark at the hockey rink and another mark at the shopping centre.

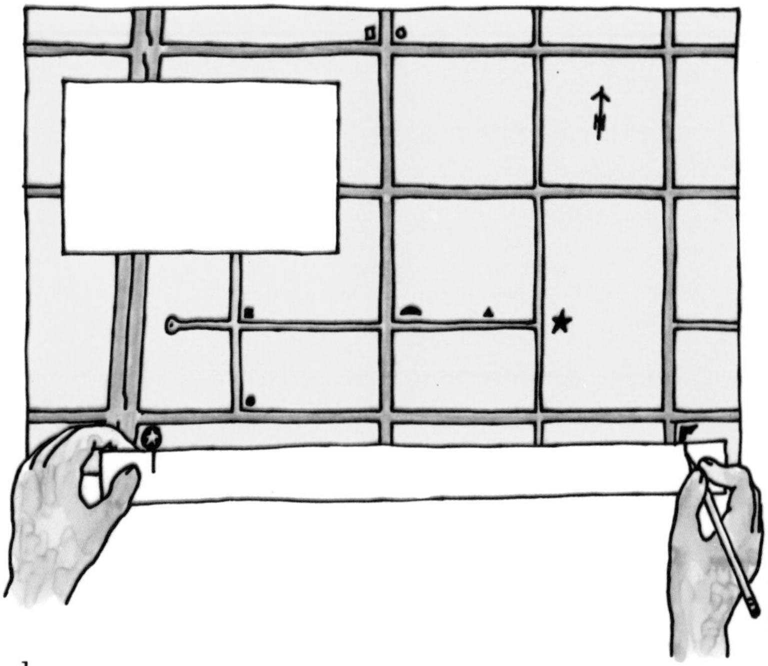

2. Place the mark for the hockey rink at 0 and make a mark at the end of the line scale. Write down 300 m at this mark.

3. Place your 300 m mark at 0 and make another mark at the end of the line scale. Write down 300 m at this mark.

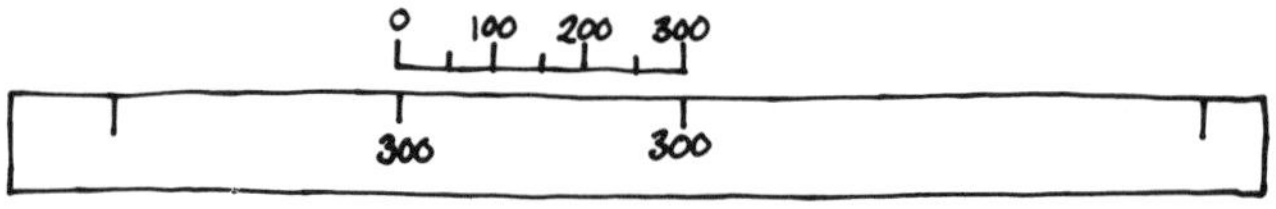

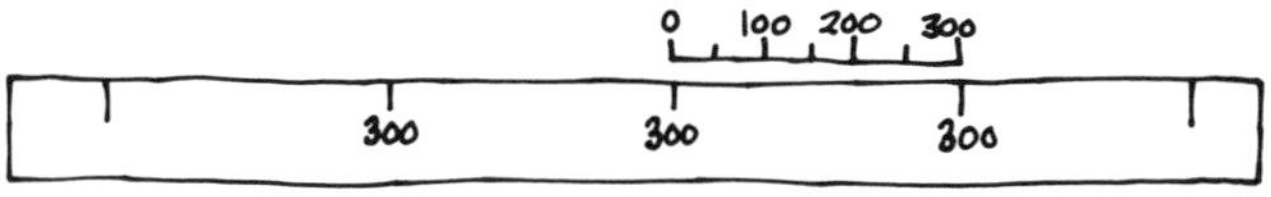

4. Keep doing this until the mark for the shopping centre comes within the length of the line scale. Write down the number at this mark.

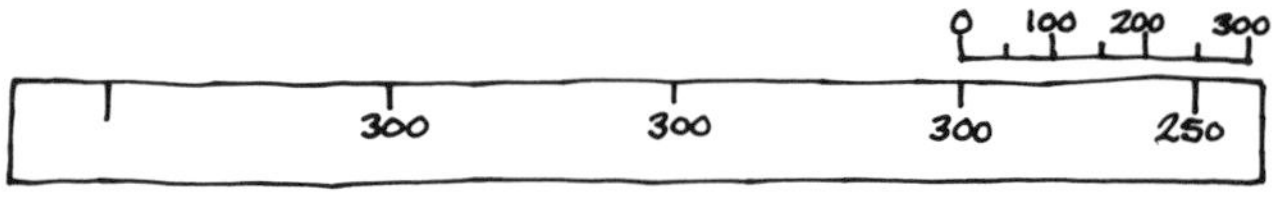

 Add all the numbers and you have the distance from one end of Donwood Heights to the other.

$$
\begin{array}{r}
300\text{ m}\\
300\text{ m}\\
300\text{ m}\\
+\ 250\text{ m}\\
\hline
1150\text{ m}
\end{array}
$$

You now know the real distance across Donwood Heights. Use the same method to find the distance from the north end of Donwood Heights to the south end. You will then know the size of the real neighborhood. It's a lot easier using a line scale to find the real size than trying to fit a piece of paper over the whole area and then tracing a map of the neighborhood!

- Measure the distance between Mary's house and the shopping centre.
- Measure the distance between Peter's house and the bank.

If your measurements of the distances weren't exactly the same as your classmates', don't worry about it. It's hard to line up one mark exactly with another mark. And when a large area is represented on a small map, a mark that doesn't line up exactly can mean a difference of several metres. Even so, you now have a fairly good idea of the real size of the neighborhood and of the real distance between places in Donwood Heights.

In fact, when you read a map to find out how far it is from one place to another, you don't usually need to know the absolutely exact distance. Most people read a road map to find out *about* how far it is to the place they're going. Then they can figure out about how long it will take them to get there. For most of our purposes in reading a map, *approximate* distances are good enough.

Maps can be drawn in almost any size. One map of an area can be twice as large as another map of the same area. Or it can be half as large. Obviously, the size of the *real* area doesn't shrink or expand. The difference in *map* sizes is due to the difference in the scale.

Courtesy Canada Post Office

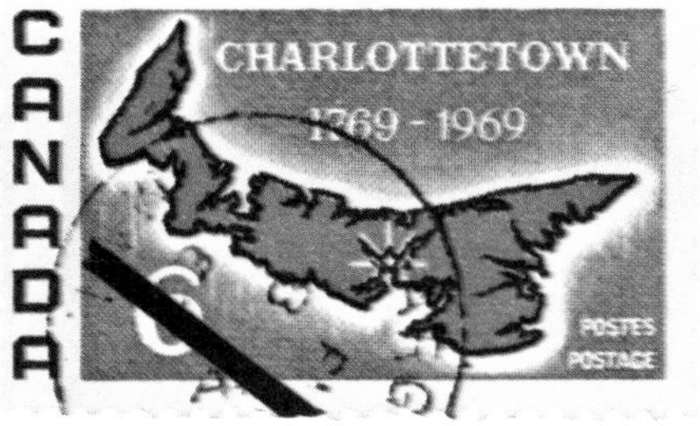

This map of Donwood Heights is smaller than the map on page 16.

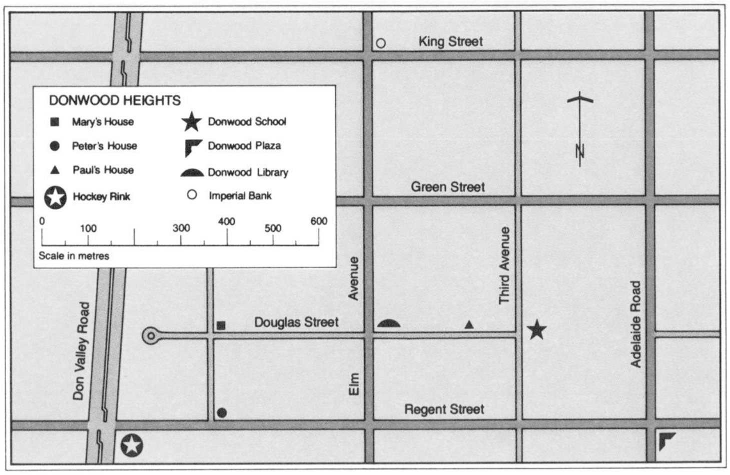

Look at the line scale on this map. Place a strip of paper along it and make a mark on the paper at each end. Now place the marked strip of paper along the line scale on the larger map on page 16. You can see that the length of the lines is the same on both maps.

But

How many metres does the length of the line represent on *this* map? How many metres does the length of the line represent on the map on page 16?

Donwood Heights is still the same size, so the reason this map is smaller than the one on page 16 is because it is drawn to a smaller scale.

Measure these distances on the smaller map. (*Remember to use the line scale that is marked on the smaller map.*)

- How far is it from the hockey rink to the shopping centre?
- What is the distance between Mary's house and the shopping centre?
- How far is it from Peter's house to the bank?

Compare these distances with those you found for the larger map. Are the real distances the same on both maps? You can see now that *real* size and distance do not change; *map* size and distance do.

REMEMBER

1. Scale is not the same on all maps.
2. To measure any distance on a map, you have to use the line scale for that particular map.

Here is a map of the capital cities of Canada. Use the line scale to answer these questions. If you have any problems, look back at the diagrams in the boxes that show how to use the line scale to measure distance.

1. How far is it from your provincial capital to Ottawa?
2. What is the distance between Winnipeg and Edmonton?
3. How far is it from Regina to Fredericton?
4. What is the distance between Yellowknife and Ottawa?
5. How far is it from Edmonton to Quebec City?
6. What is the distance from Victoria to St. John's?

Location

You have learned how to use a line scale to measure distances between places on a map. But before you can do this, you have to be able to *find* places. You can find some places because you know the province or country in which they're located. You can probably look at a map and locate Vancouver or the Great Lakes or the Rocky Mountains without too much difficulty.

But how can you find a place you don't know about? If you hear a news report about Arrandale, or Bellin, or Minnedosa, or some other unfamiliar place, how can you locate it? How can you read a map to find out where in the world it is located?

The *legend* helps you read what's represented on a map.
The *scale* helps you measure distance on a map.
Let's look at a globe map to see if there's something that helps you locate places on a map.

LATITUDE

Look at the globe in your classroom. First of all, find the North Pole and the South Pole. Halfway between the poles, find a circle going around the globe. This line is called the *equator*. Above and below the equator are other circles going around the globe, all the way to the North Pole and all the way to the South Pole.

These circles are called *parallels of latitude*.

Move your finger along one of the parallels of latitude until you come to a number on the line. The ° mark beside the number is the symbol for *degree*.

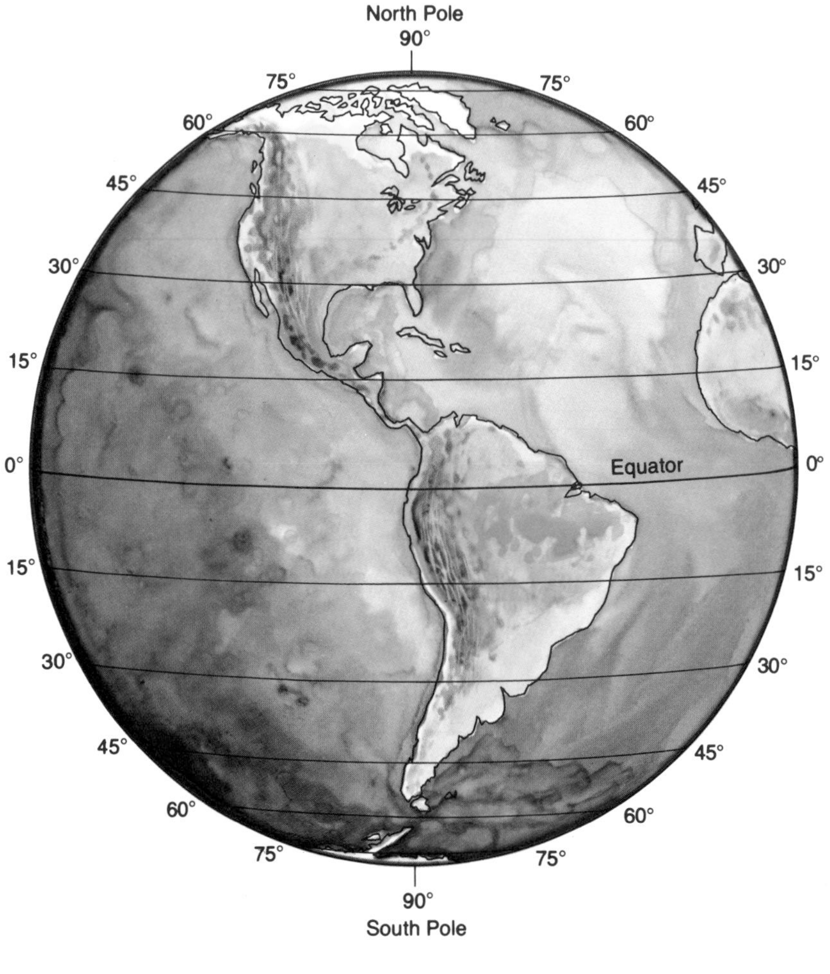

Degrees are the names of the units that measure distance between parallels of latitude. Find the number of degrees at each of the lines north and south of the equator. Notice that the numbers start from 0° at the equator and get larger as the parallels of latitude get farther away from the equator.

So you can see that parallels of latitude measure, in degrees, distance north and south from the equator.

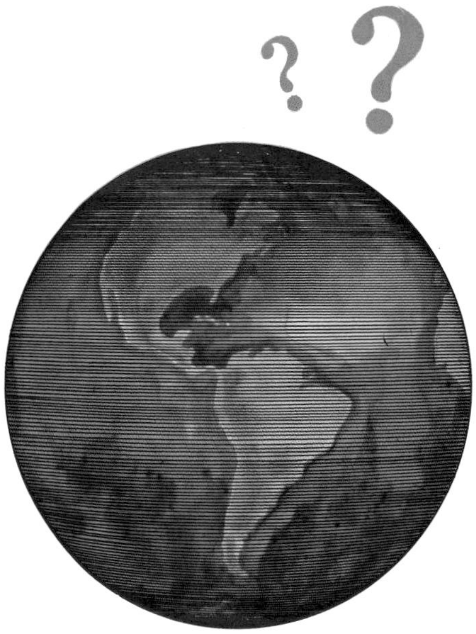

The parallel of latitude that is fifteen degrees *north* of the equator is 15°N. The parallel of latitude that is fifteen degrees *south* of the equator is 15°S.

The distance from the equator to each of the poles is ninety degrees. So there are ninety parallels of latitude north of the equator and ninety parallels of latitude south of the equator. The North Pole is at 90°N. The South Pole is at 90°S.

As you can see by looking at the globe in your classroom, only some of the lines of latitude are drawn. If they were all shown, there would be 180 circles going around the globe! Imagine trying to read a globe or flat map of the world with 180 lines drawn on it!

On some globes and flat maps of the world, every tenth parallel is drawn — 10°, 20°, 30°, and so on. On others, every fifteenth parallel is drawn — 15°, 30°, 45°, and so on. Look at the globe in your classroom to see which latitudes are marked.

Parallels of latitude help to locate places on a globe or map. The latitude of a place tells where that place is located north or south of the equator. If the latitude of a place is 45°N, you know it's located on the parallel of latitude that is forty-five degrees north of the equator.

Find 45°N on the globe in your classroom and move your finger along the line.

The latitude of Cornwall, Ontario, is 45°N, so Cornwall is *somewhere* on that line.

But

Where, exactly, on that parallel of latitude is Cornwall located? Is there any way of pinpointing a place so that you can locate it exactly?

Let's look at a globe to see if there's something that helps you find the *exact* location of a place.

LONGITUDE

On the globe in your classroom, find the circles that go from the North Pole to the South Pole. These lines are called *meridians of longitude*. If you move your finger down the meridian of longitude marked 0°, you will see that the line passes through Greenwich, England.

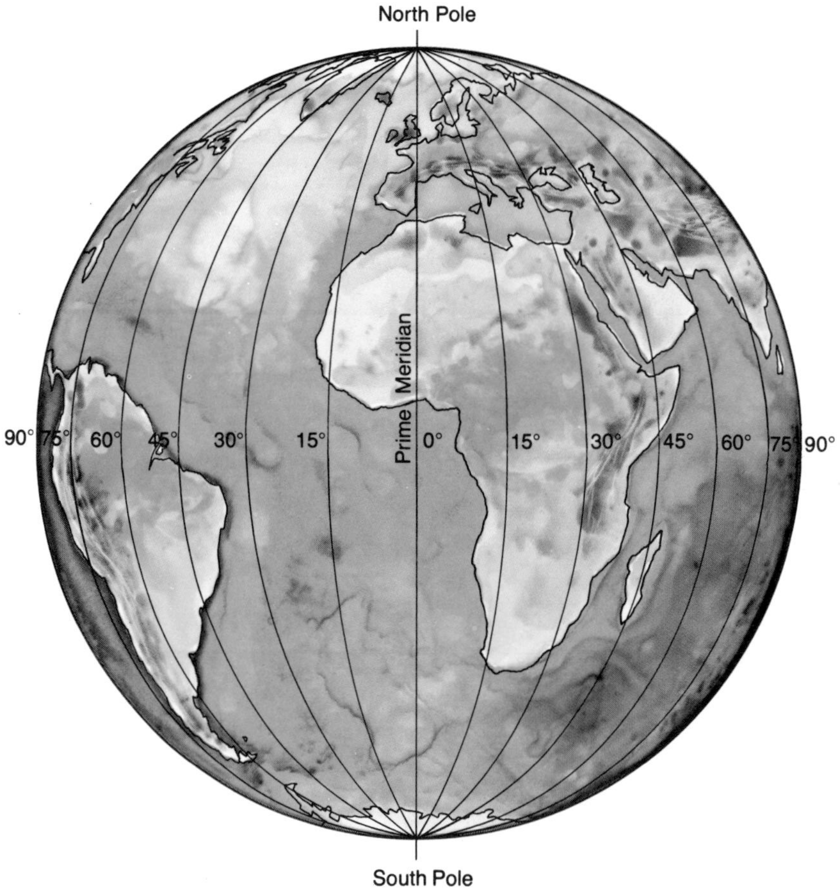

This line is called the *Prime Meridian*.

As you turn the globe around, you can see that meridians of longitude also are numbered in degrees. Meridians of longitude measure, in degrees, distance east and west from the Prime Meridian.

The lines of longitude are numbered from 0° to 180° *west* from the Prime Meridian and from 0° to 180° *east* from the Prime Meridian. Again, only certain meridians of longitude are shown. Imagine what a globe would look like if *all* the parallels of latitude and *all* the meridians of longitude were marked—180 + 360 = 540 lines!

The meridian of longitude that is fifteen degrees *west* of the Prime Meridian is 15°W. Any place that is fifteen degrees west of the Prime Meridian is on that line of longitude. The meridian of longitude that is fifteen degrees *east* of the Prime Meridian is 15°E. Any place that is fifteen degrees east of the Prime Meridian is on that line of longitude.

Meridians of longitude *also* help to locate places on a globe or map. The longitude of a place tells where that place is located east or west of the Prime Meridian. If the longitude of a place is 75°W, you know it's located on the meridian of longitude that is seventy-five degrees west of the Prime Meridian.

The longitude of Cornwall, Ontario, is 75°W, so Cornwall is somewhere on that meridian of longitude. Find 75°W on the globe in your classroom.

The latitude of Cornwall, as you remember, is 45°N, so Cornwall is somewhere on that parallel of latitude. Find 45°N on the globe.

Now, move one finger down the 75°W line of longitude and another finger along the 45°N line of latitude. The point where these two lines of longitude and latitude meet is where Cornwall is located. The location of Cornwall, Ontario, is 45°N, 75°W.

Latitude + longitude = *location*.

When you know the latitude and longitude of a place, you can locate that place on any globe or map of the world. Using latitude and longitude, you can find where a place is located even if its name isn't shown on a map. And even if a place is not located exactly on marked lines of latitude and longitude, you can still find its *approximate* location. For example, if the latitude of a city is 45°N, you know that it is located about halfway between 40°N and 50°N. Or if the longitude of a city is 65°W, you know that it is located one-third of the distance between 60°W and 75°W.

Here are the latitudes and longitudes of Arrandale, Bellin, and Minnedosa. Now you know how to locate them, even though they aren't marked on a globe. Find their location on your globe. What country are they in?

Arrandale: 55°N, 130°W
Bellin: 60°N, 70°W
Minnedosa: 50°N, 100°W

If you want to locate some other places on the globe, you can play a game called "Vacation Destination." This is a game for two, three, or four players. Here's how it's played.

One of the players is "the traveller." The traveller finds a place on the globe while the other players keep their eyes closed. The traveller writes down the location of the place — the latitude and longitude — on a piece of paper. The other players can then open their eyes. Then the traveller says:

I have an inclination
To take a vacation.
This is the location
Of my destination.

The traveller then tells the other players the latitude and longitude of the place. The other players see how quickly they can find it on the globe. The player who names the place first becomes the next traveller.

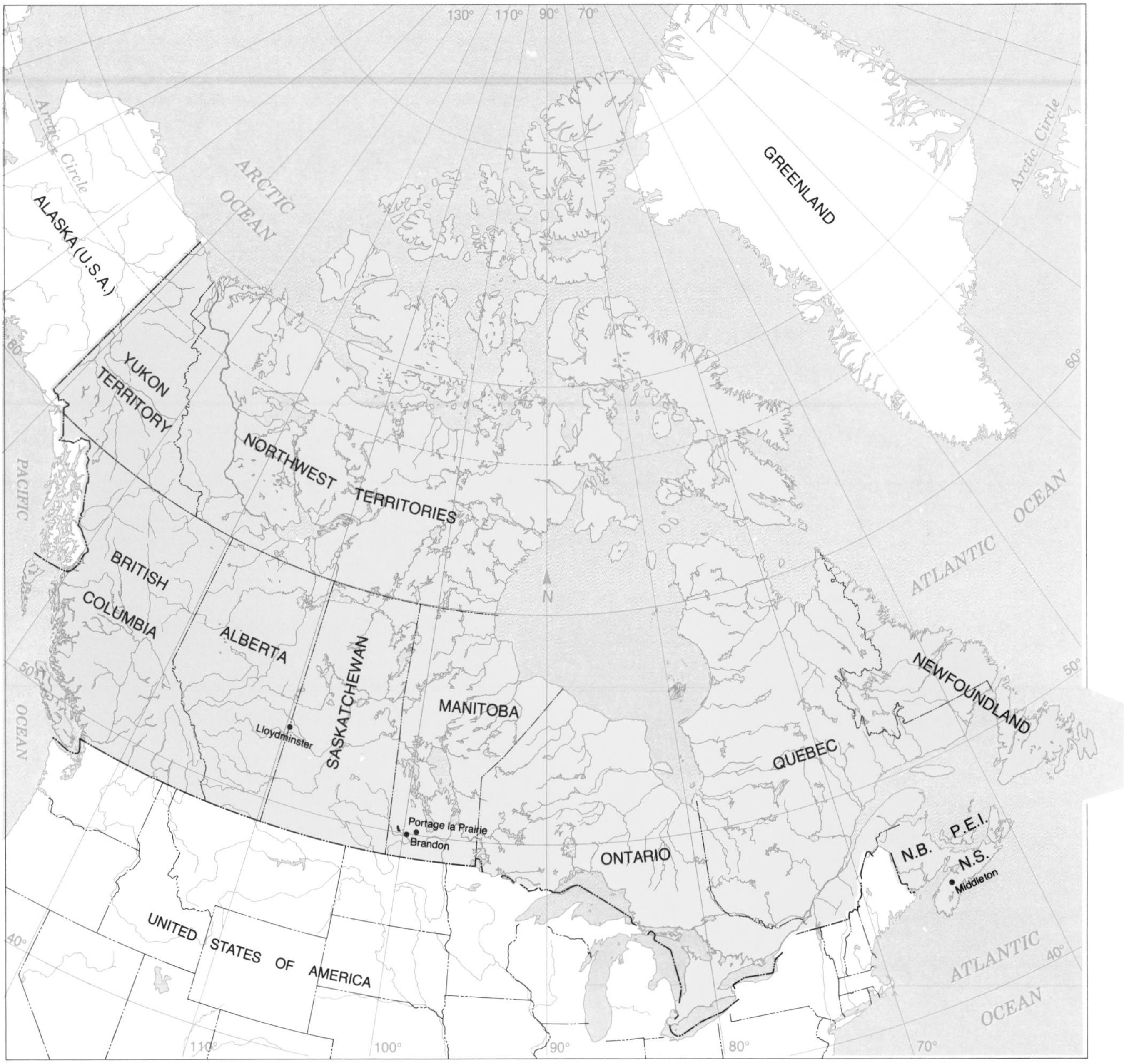

Use the lines of latitude and longitude shown on this map of Canada to answer these questions.

1. What is the latitude of Portage la Prairie?
2. What is the longitude of the western boundary of Saskatchewan?
3. What city is located on this meridian of longitude?
4. What is the location of Brandon, Manitoba?
5. What city is located at 45°N, 65°W?
6. Between what latitudes is most of mainland Canada located?
7. Between what longitudes is most of mainland Canada located?
8. What parallel of latitude forms most of the border between Canada and the United States?

REMEMBER *REMEMBER* *REMEMBER* *REMEMBER*

Reading a Map = Symbols + Direction + Scale + Location

REMEMBER: SYMBOLS

1. Symbols do not always look like the things they represent.
2. Map symbols do not always represent the same things.
3. Check the legend of a map to find out what the symbols on that map represent.

REMEMBER: DIRECTION

1. Direction on a map is indicated by a symbol for north.
2. Once you know the direction of north, you know where south, east, and west are, too.
3. Check the north marker to know the direction of one place from another.

REMEMBER: SCALE

1. The scale tells you the real size and distance that are represented on a map.
2. The scale is not the same on all maps.
3. Check the scale of a map before you measure any distances on that map.

REMEMBER: LOCATION

1. Parallels of latitude measure degrees of distance north and south from the equator.
2. Meridians of longitude measure degrees of distance east and west from the Prime Meridian.
3. The location of a place is the point where two lines of latitude and longitude meet.

CANADIANS...

.AND WHERE THEY LIVE

Scale in kilometres

■ Most Canadians	■ Few Canadians
■ Many Canadians	■ Very Few Canadians

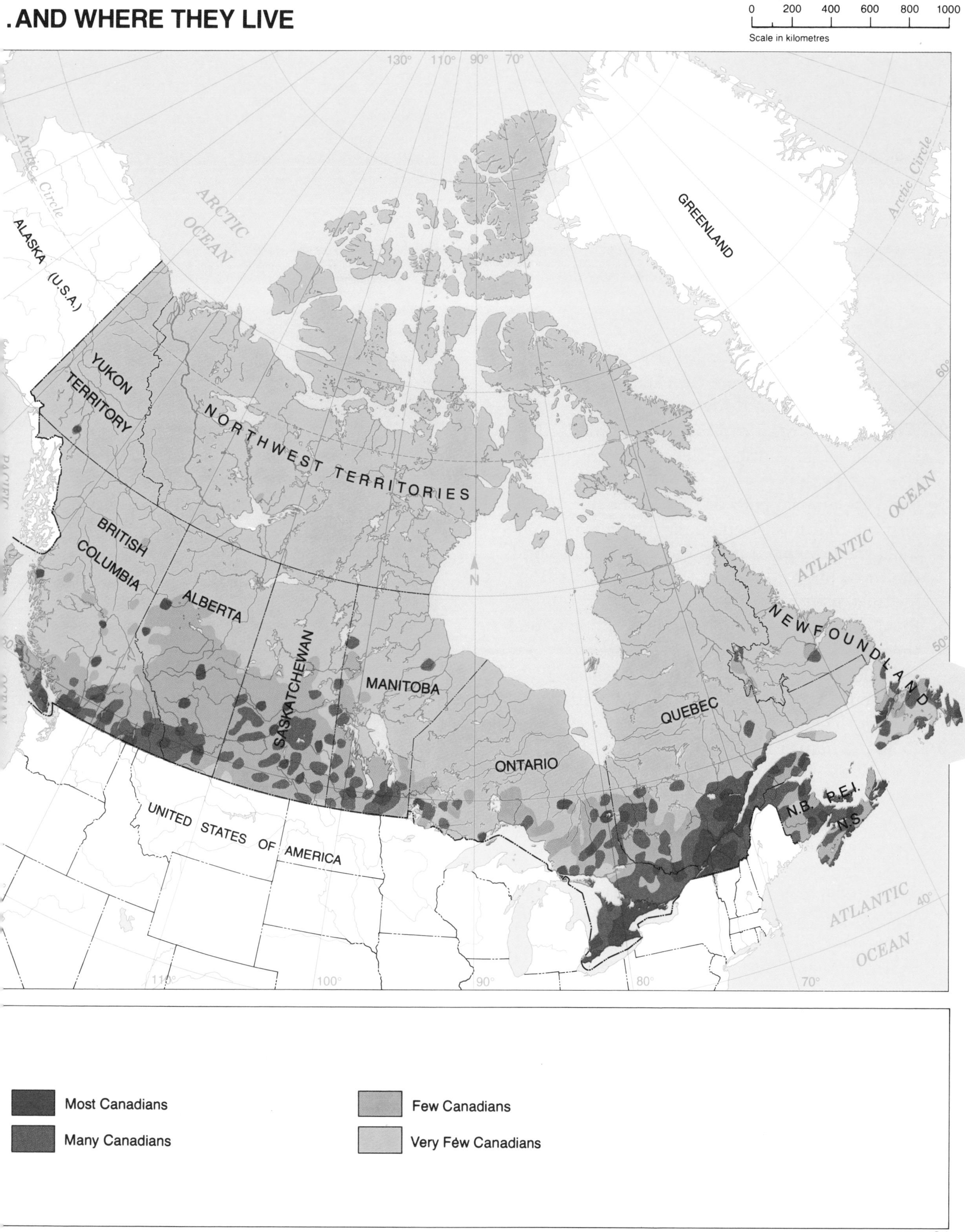

PEOPLE AND PLACES

Most Canadians live in towns and cities. In fact, over 50 per cent of Canadians live in places that have more than 100 000 people! As you read the maps in this section and answer the questions below, you will find out the size of places in Canada, where most large towns and cities are located, and why most Canadians live where they do.

1. What is the smallest capital city in Canada? In what direction is it from the capital of Alberta? How far away from Edmonton is it?
2. What is the largest capital city in Canada? In what direction is it from the capital of Quebec? How far away is it from the city of Quebec?
3. Read the map on page 31. Name the parallel of latitude that most Canadians live south of.
4. Read the provincial maps in this section to find the three largest cities in Canada. What is the latitude of each?
5. Read each provincial map in this section to find the cities with populations of more than 100 000. South of what latitude are most of these cities located? Does this agree with your answer to Question 3?
6. Read the map of British Columbia in this section. Where do most of the people live? Why do you think they live there? Read the maps of British Columbia in the sections on The Look of the Land and Using Land and Water to find some of the reasons.
7. Read the map of Newfoundland in this section. Where do most of the people live? Why do you think they live there? Find the maps in the atlas that will help you answer this question.
8. Where do most of the people in your province or territory live? Find the maps that will tell you some reasons why most of the people live there.
9. Look again at the map on page 31. Now, read the maps of Canada in the sections on Climate, Using Land and Water, and The Look of the Land. Find some reasons why most Canadians live where they do.

anada *People and Places*

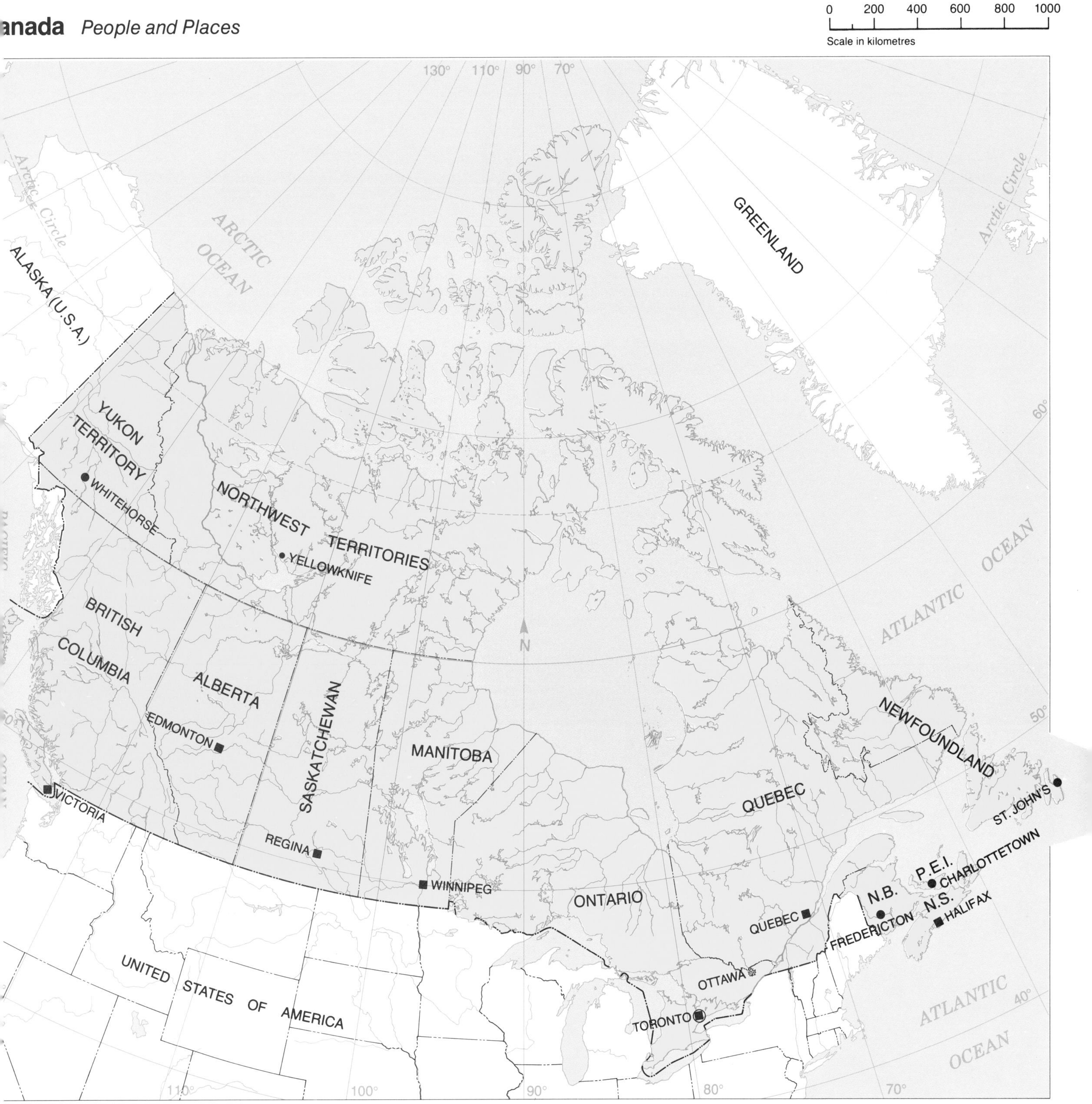
0 200 400 600 800 1000
Scale in kilometres
ARCTIC OCEAN
GREENLAND
Arctic Circle
ALASKA (U.S.A.)
YUKON TERRITORY
WHITEHORSE
NORTHWEST TERRITORIES
YELLOWKNIFE
BRITISH COLUMBIA
ALBERTA
EDMONTON
VICTORIA
SASKATCHEWAN
REGINA
MANITOBA
WINNIPEG
ONTARIO
TORONTO
OTTAWA
QUEBEC
QUEBEC
NEWFOUNDLAND
ST. JOHN'S
P.E.I.
CHARLOTTETOWN
N.B.
FREDERICTON
N.S.
HALIFAX
ATLANTIC OCEAN
ATLANTIC OCEAN
UNITED STATES OF AMERICA
N
130° 110° 90° 70°
60° 50° 40°
110° 100° 90° 80° 70°

Population of Capital Cities:

•	5 000-10 000 People
●	10 000 -100 000 People
■	Over 100 000 People
◙	Over 1 000 000 People
✱	National Capital: OTTAWA (population over 100 000)

Newfoundland *People and Places*

0 100
Scale in kilometres

1
2
3
4
5
6
A
B
C
D
60°
58°
56°
54°
52°
50°
48°
LABRADOR
QUEBEC
Belle Isle
Strait of Belle Isle
Cape Bauld
St. Anthony
Port Saunders
White Bay
N
Baie Verte
Notre Dame Bay
Fogo Island
Twillingate
Springdale
Gulf of St. Lawrence
Deer Lake
Botwood
Lewisporte
Wesleyville
Corner Brook
Windsor
Bishops Falls
Grand Falls
Gander
Bonavista Bay
Bonavista
ATLANTIC OCEAN
Stephenville
St. George's Bay
ISLAND OF NEWFOUNDLAND
Clarenville
Conception Bay
Cape Ray
Channel-Port aux Basques
Burgeo
Carbonear
Wabana
ST. JOHN'S
Harbour Breton
Bay Roberts
Cabot Strait
Fortune Bay
Marystown
Argentia
Placentia Bay
St. Pierre and Miquelon (France)
Grand Bank
Burin
Cape Race
70°
65°
55°
Hebron
Nain
ATLANTIC OCEAN
Hopedale
Schefferville
LABRADOR
Labrador City
Goose Bay
Happy Valley
Battle Harbour
QUE.
Gulf of St. Lawrence
NEWFOUNDLAND
P.E.I.
N.S.
0 100 200

•	Population under 5 000
•	Population 5 000-10 000
●	Population 10 000-100 000

Provincial Capital:
ST. JOHN'S

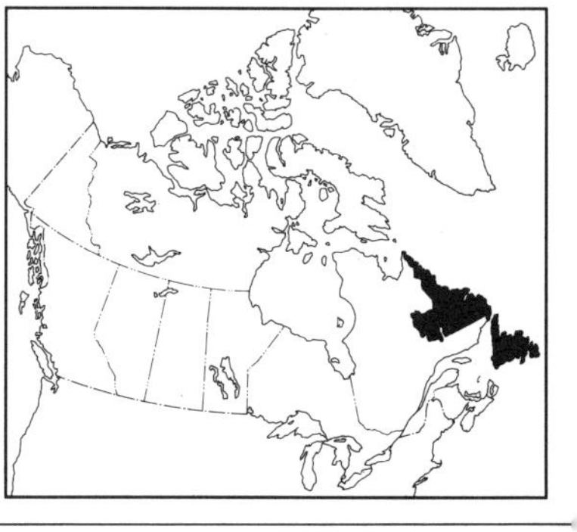

0 50 100 150
Scale in kilometres

Gulf of St. Lawrence
NEWFOUNDLAND
Cabot Strait
Cape North
N
CAPE
BRETON
ISLAND
Victoria
Sydney Mines
Inverness
Baddeck
Sydney
Port Hood
Inverness
Cape Breton
NEW BRUNSWICK
PRINCE EDWARD ISLAND
Northumberland Strait
Amherst
Cumberland
Chignecto Bay
Pictou
Antigonish
Antigonish
Strait of Canso
Richmond
Arichat
Stellarton
Colchester
Pictou
Guysborough
Truro
Minas Basin
Hants
Guysborough
Kentville
Windsor
Kings
Halifax
Bay of Fundy
Annapolis
Royal
Annapolis
Digby
Lunenburg
HALIFAX
Digby
Lunenburg
Queens
ATLANTIC
Liverpool
Yarmouth
Shelburne
Yarmouth
Shelburne
OCEAN
Sable Island
Cape Sable
66° 65° 64° 63° 62° 61° 60°
47° 46° 45° 44° 43°
1 2 3 4 5 6 7 8
A B C D E

Population under 5 000	Population 10 000-100 000
Population 5 000-10 000	Population over 100 000

Provincial Capital:
HALIFAX

County boundaries, names of counties and county seats are shown in RED

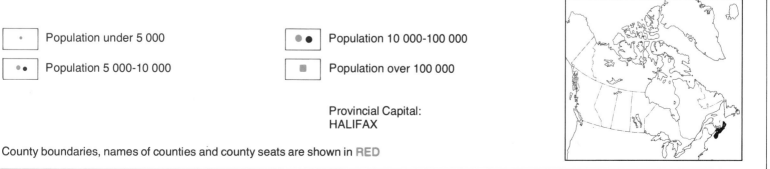

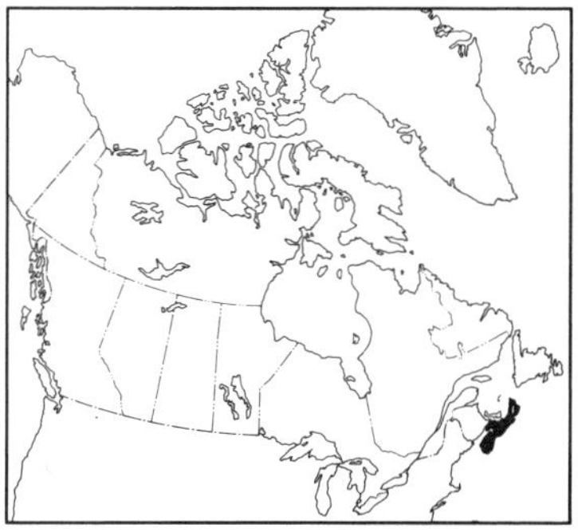

Prince Edward Island *People and Places*

0 20 40 60

Scale in kilometres

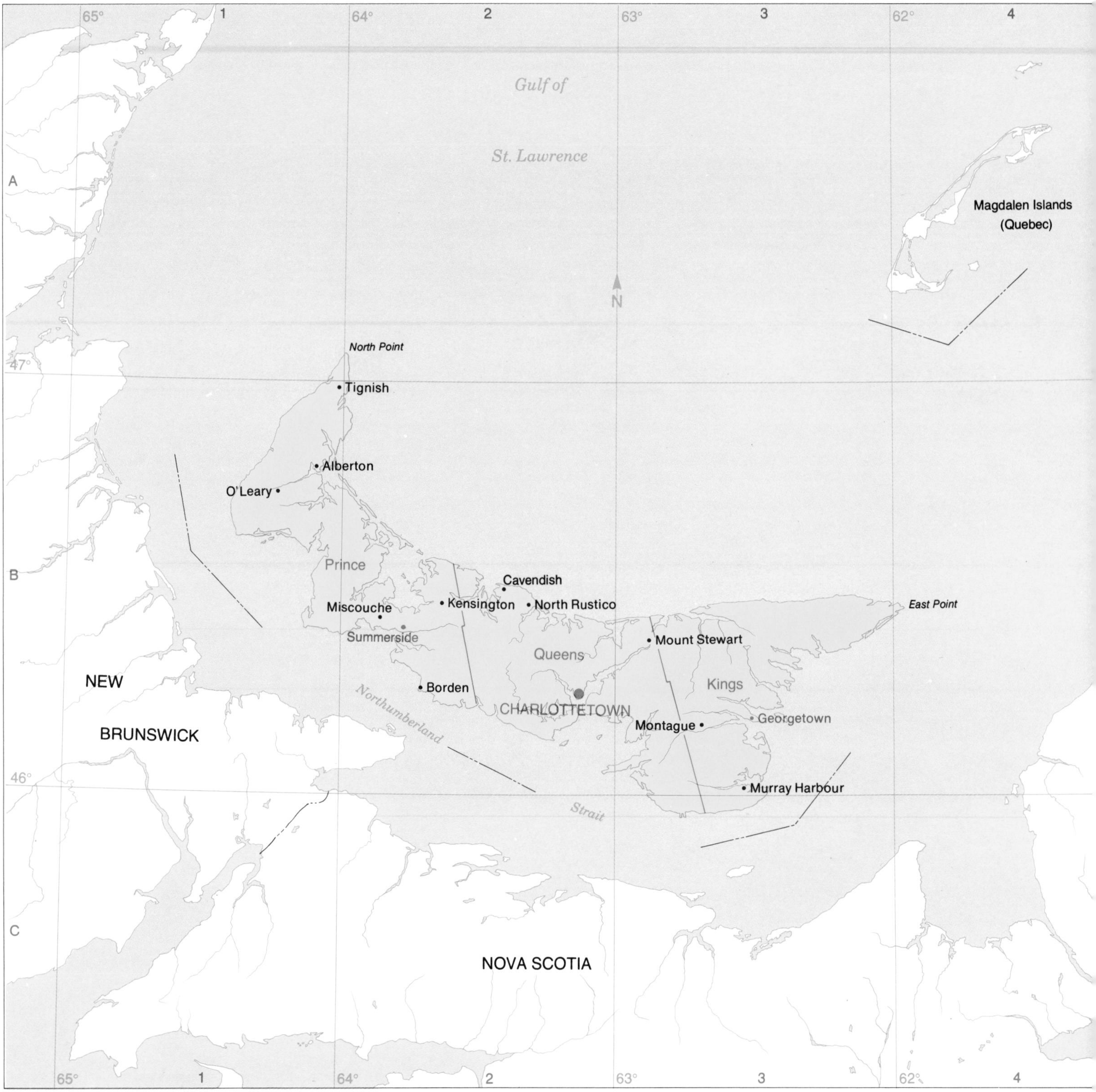

Gulf of
St. Lawrence
Magdalen Islands
(Quebec)
N
North Point
Tignish
Alberton
O'Leary
Prince
Cavendish
Miscouche
Kensington
North Rustico
Summerside
East Point
Mount Stewart
Queens
Kings
Borden
CHARLOTTETOWN
Georgetown
Montague
Murray Harbour
Northumberland
Strait
NEW
BRUNSWICK
NOVA SCOTIA
65°
64°
63°
62°
47°
46°
1
2
3
4
A
B
C

- Population under 5 000
- Population 5 000-10 000
- Population 10 000-100 000

Provincial Capital:
CHARLOTTETOWN

County boundaries, names of counties and county seats are shown in RED

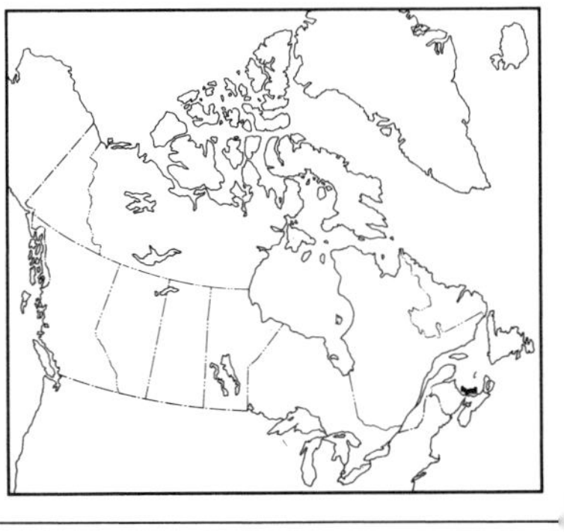

New Brunswick *People and Places*

QUEBEC

Scale in kilometres
0 50 100

Campbellton
• Dalhousie

Chaleur Bay

Restigouche

Caraquet •

Gulf of

Madawaska

Bathurst •

St. Lawrence

Gloucester

• Edmundston
• St. Basile

Victoria

Newcastle •

• Chatham

UNITED STATES

• Grand Falls

Northumberland

PRINCE

EDWARD

ISLAND

OF AMERICA

• Perth-Andover

Richibucto •

Northumberland

Carleton

Kent

Strait

Woodstock •

York

Sunbury

Westmorland

Cape
Tormentine •

• Minto

Moncton • • Dieppe

Nashwaaksis •

FREDERICTON • • Marysville

Queens

• Dorchester
• Hopewell Cape

Oromocto • • Burton

Albert

Gagetown •

Kings

Chignecto Bay

• Sussex

St. John

• Hampton

Charlotte

Saint John

• St. Stephen

St. Andrews •

Bay of Fundy

NOVA SCOTIA

Grand Manan
Island

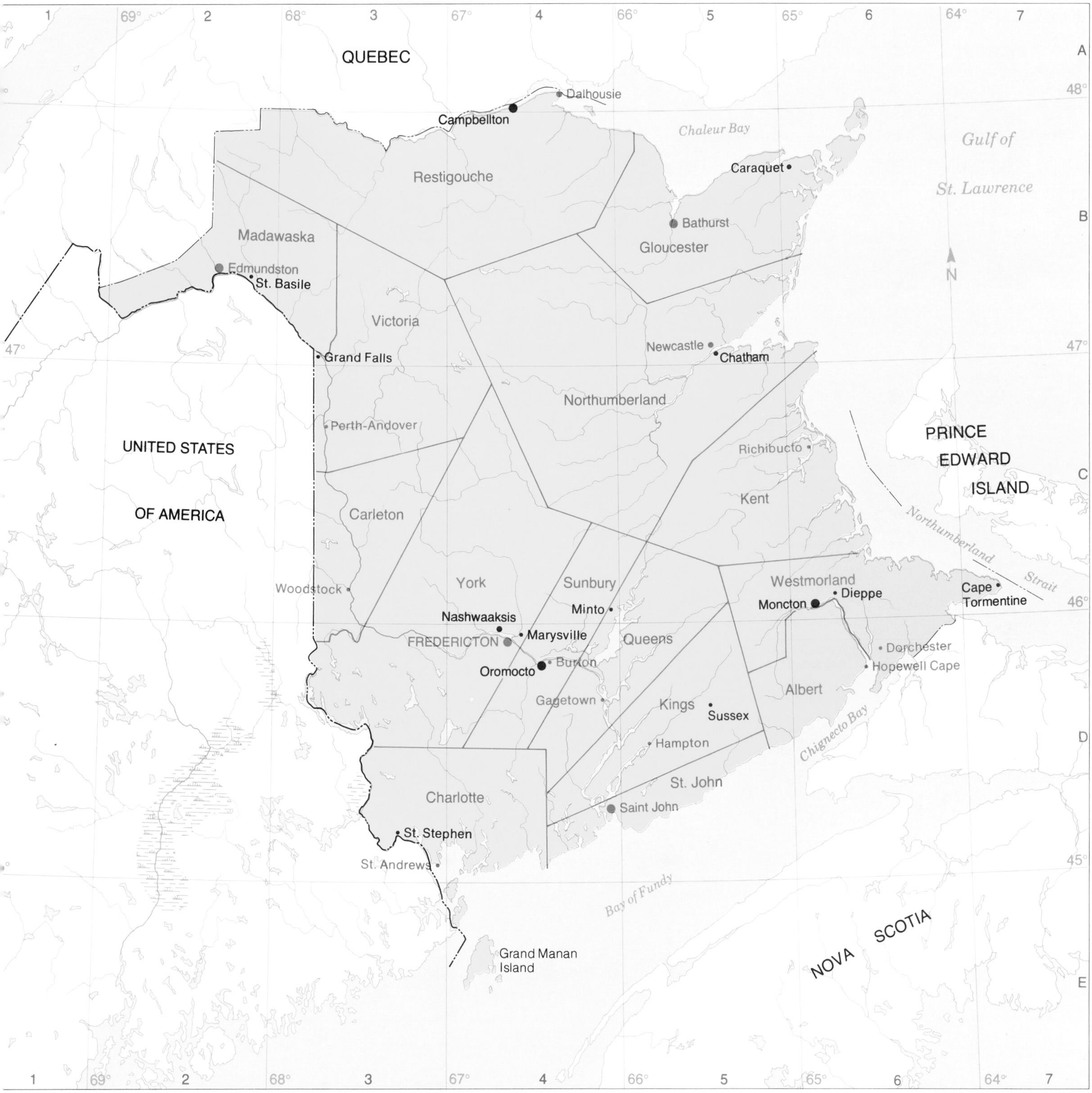

•• Population under 5 000

•• Population 5 000-10 000

•• Population 10 000-100 000

Provincial Capital:
FREDERICTON

County boundaries, names of counties and county seats are shown in RED

0 100 200 300 400
Scale in kilometres
A
B
C
D
E
1
2
3
4
5
6
7
8
85°
80°
75°
70°
65°
60°
55°
50°
45°
Ivujivik
Povungnituk
Inoucdjouac
HUDSON
BAY
Belcher Islands
(N.W.T.)
Poste de la Baleine
Great Whale R.
James
Bay
Fort George
Eastmain
Fort Rupert
Caniapiscau River
Schefferville
ATLANTIC
OCEAN
Churchill River
NEWFOUNDLAND
N
ONTARIO
Chibougamau
La Sarre
Amos
Noranda
Rouyn
Val d'Or
Sept Îles
Anticosti Island
Baie Comeau
St. Lawrence River
Gaspé
Matane
Rimouski
Percé
Gulf of
St. Lawrence
New Richmond
Roberval
Alma
Arvida
Chicoutimi
La Tuque
Rivière du Loup
Magdalen
Islands
La Pocatière
Shawinigan
QUEBEC
Lévis
Trois Rivières
Thetford Mines
Maniwaki
Ottawa River
U.S.A.
NEW
BRUNSWICK
P.E.I.
NOVA SCOTIA
Joliette
St. Jérôme
Drummondville
Hull
Montreal
Lac Megantic
Valleyfield
Sherbrooke
Granby

- Population under 5 000
- Population 5 000-10 000
- Population 10 000-100 000
- Population over 100 000
- Population over 1 000 000

Provincial Capital:
QUEBEC

outhern Quebec *People and Places*

0 100 200
Scale in kilometres

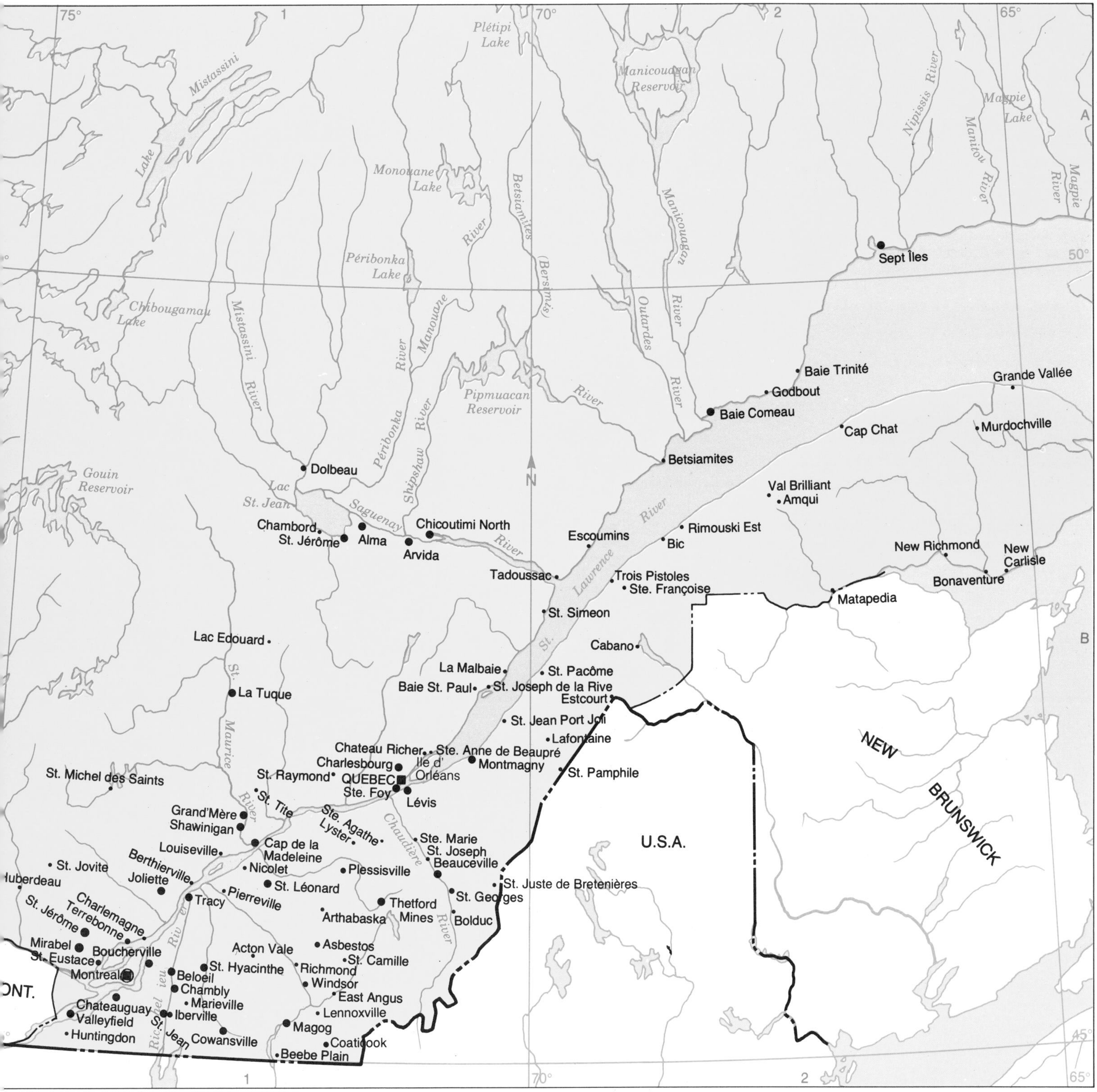

75°
70°
65°
50°
45°
1
2
A
B
N
Mistassini
Lake
Plétipi Lake
Manicouagan Reservoir
Magpie Lake
Nipissis River
Manitou River
Magpie River
Monouane Lake
Betsiamites (Bersimis) River
Manicouagan River
Péribonka Lake
Chibougamau Lake
Mistassini River
Manouane River
Outardes River
Pipmuacan Reservoir
Péribonka River
Shipshaw River
Gouin Reservoir
Lac St. Jean
Saguenay River
St. Lawrence River
St. Maurice River
Chaudière River
Richelieu River
Sept Îles
Baie Trinité
Godbout
Baie Comeau
Grande Vallée
Cap Chat
Murdochville
Betsiamites
Dolbeau
Val Brilliant
Amqui
Rimouski Est
Bic
Escoumins
Chambord
St. Jérôme
Alma
Chicoutimi North
Arvida
New Richmond
New Carlisle
Bonaventure
Tadoussac
Trois Pistoles
Ste. Françoise
Matapedia
St. Simeon
Lac Edouard
Cabano
La Malbaie
St. Pacôme
Baie St. Paul
St. Joseph de la Rive
Estcourt
La Tuque
St. Jean Port Joli
Lafontaine
Chateau Richer
Ste. Anne de Beaupré
Charlesbourg
Ile d' Orléans
Montmagny
St. Pamphile
St. Michel des Saints
St. Raymond
QUEBEC
Ste. Foy
Lévis
St. Tite
Grand'Mère
Shawinigan
Ste. Agathe
Lyster
Ste. Marie
St. Joseph
Beauceville
Louiseville
Cap de la Madeleine
Nicolet
Plessisville
St. Jovite
Berthierville
Joliette
St. Léonard
St. Juste de Bretenières
Huberdeau
Pierreville
Tracy
Thetford Mines
St. Georges
Charlemagne
Terrebonne
St. Jérôme
Arthabaska
Bolduc
Asbestos
Mirabel
St. Eustace
Boucherville
Acton Vale
St. Camille
Montreal
St. Hyacinthe
Richmond
Windsor
Beloeil
Chambly
East Angus
Marieville
Chateauguay
Valleyfield
Iberville
Lennoxville
St. Jean
Huntingdon
Cowansville
Magog
Coaticook
Beebe Plain
U.S.A.
NEW BRUNSWICK
ONT.

Population under 5 000

Population 5 000-10 000

Population 10 000-100 000

Population over 100 000

Population over 1 000 000

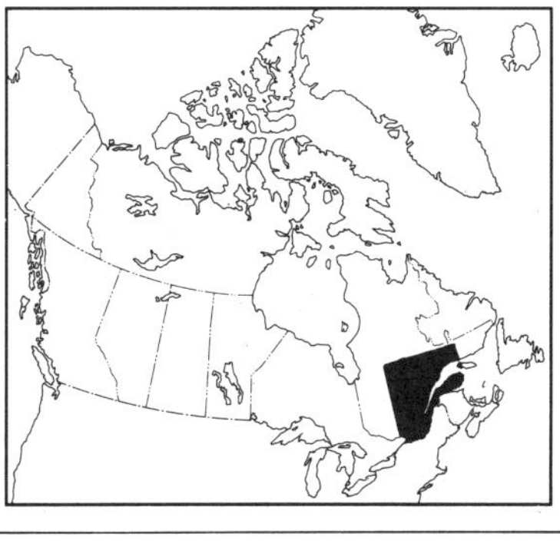

Ontario *People and Places*

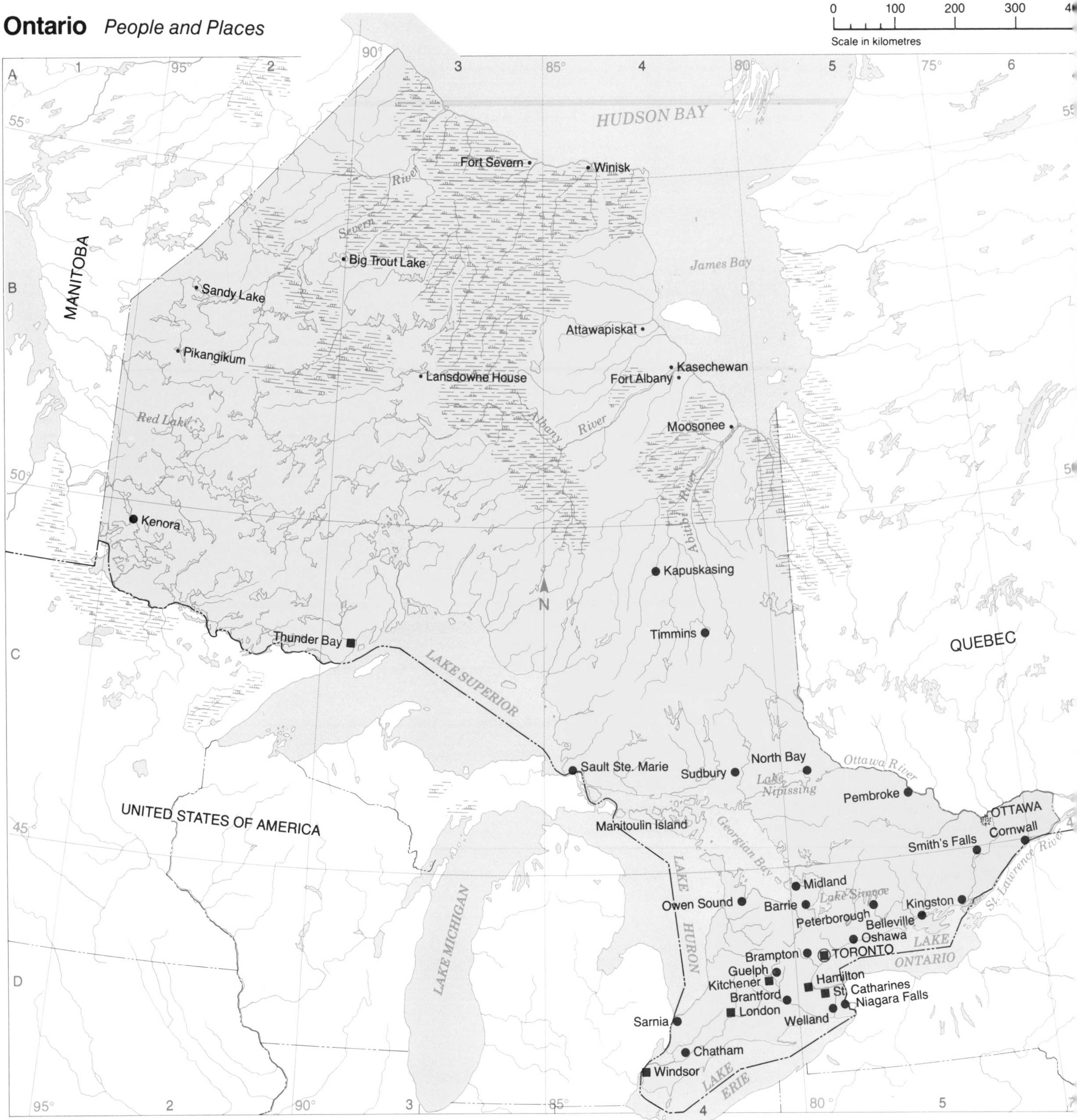
0 100 200 300
Scale in kilometres
HUDSON BAY
James Bay
MANITOBA
QUEBEC
UNITED STATES OF AMERICA
Fort Severn
Winisk
Severn River
Big Trout Lake
Sandy Lake
Pikangikum
Lansdowne House
Attawapiskat
Kasechewan
Fort Albany
Albany River
Moosonee
Red Lake
Kenora
Abitibi River
Kapuskasing
Timmins
Thunder Bay
LAKE SUPERIOR
Sault Ste. Marie
Sudbury
North Bay
Lake Nipissing
Ottawa River
Pembroke
OTTAWA
Cornwall
Smith's Falls
Manitoulin Island
Georgian Bay
LAKE HURON
LAKE MICHIGAN
Midland
Lake Simcoe
Owen Sound
Barrie
Peterborough
Kingston
Belleville
Oshawa
Brampton
TORONTO
LAKE ONTARIO
St. Lawrence River
Guelph
Kitchener
Hamilton
St. Catharines
Niagara Falls
Brantford
London
Welland
Sarnia
Chatham
Windsor
LAKE ERIE
N

Population under 5 000

Population 10 000-100 000

Population over 100 000

Population over 1 000 000

National Capital:
OTTAWA (population over 100 000)

Provincial Capital:
TORONTO

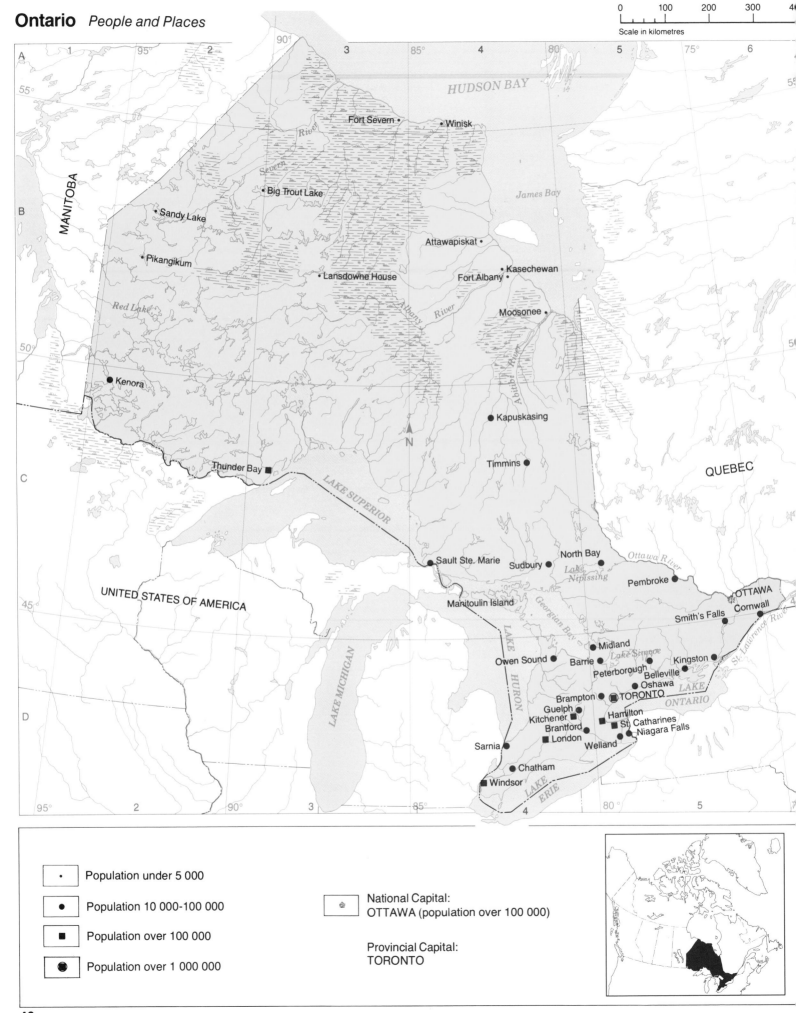

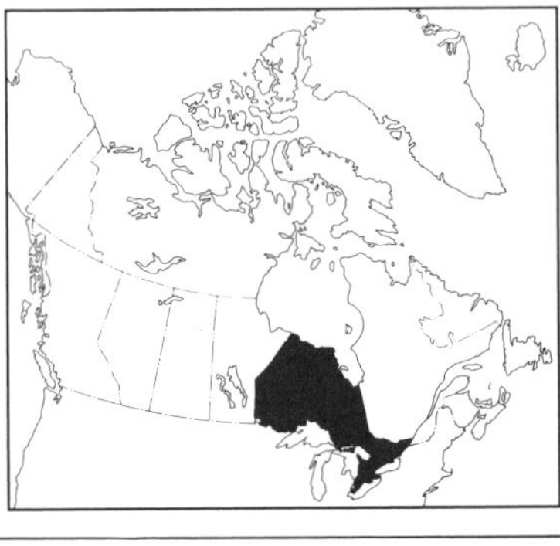

Southern Ontario *People and Places*

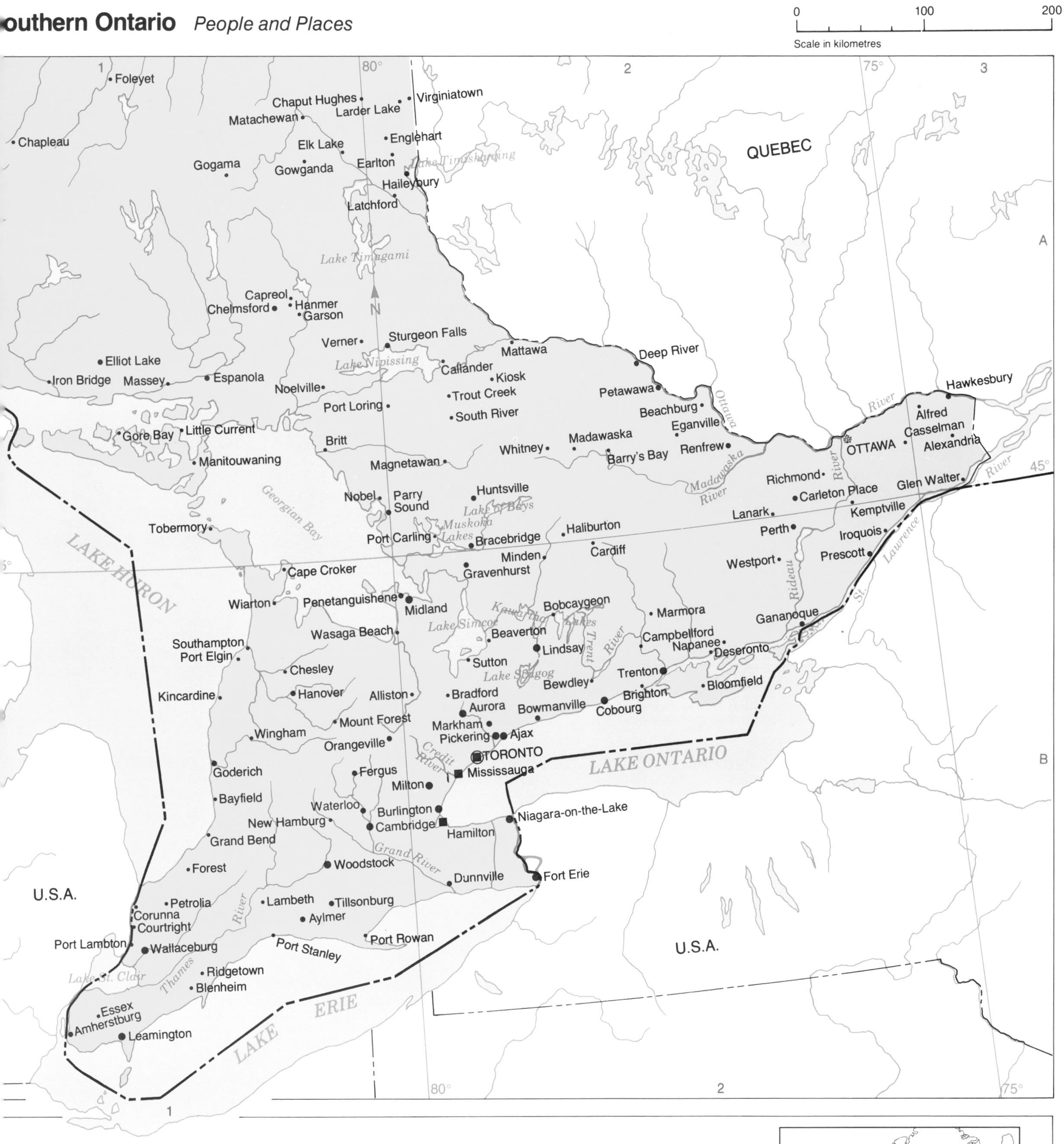
0
100
200
Scale in kilometres
80°
75°
1
2
3
A
B
Foleyet
Chapleau
Chaput Hughes
Larder Lake
Virginiatown
Matachewan
Englehart
Elk Lake
Gogama
Gowganda
Earlton
Lake Timiskaming
QUEBEC
Haileybury
Latchford
Lake Temagami
N
Capreol
Chelmsford
Hanmer
Garson
Verner
Sturgeon Falls
Mattawa
Deep River
Elliot Lake
Lake Nipissing
Callander
Kiosk
Iron Bridge
Massey
Espanola
Noelville
Trout Creek
Petawawa
Hawkesbury
Port Loring
South River
Beachburg
Ottawa
River
Alfred
Eganville
Casselman
Gore Bay
Little Current
Britt
Madawaska
Whitney
Renfrew
OTTAWA
Alexandria
Manitouwaning
Barry's Bay
Magnetawan
Madawaska River
Richmond
River
Glen Walter
River
45°
Georgian Bay
Nobel
Parry Sound
Huntsville
Carleton Place
Lake of Bays
Lanark
Kemptville
Muskoka Lakes
Tobermory
LAKE HURON
Port Carling
Bracebridge
Haliburton
Perth
Iroquois
Minden
Cardiff
Prescott
Westport
Rideau
St. Lawrence
Cape Croker
Gravenhurst
Wiarton
Penetanguishene
Midland
Kawartha Lakes
Bobcaygeon
Marmora
Gananoque
Lake Simcoe
Wasaga Beach
Beaverton
Trent
River
Campbellford
Southampton
Lindsay
Napanee
Deseronto
Port Elgin
Sutton
Chesley
Lake Scugog
Bewdley
Trenton
Kincardine
Hanover
Alliston
Bradford
Brighton
Bloomfield
Aurora
Bowmanville
Cobourg
Mount Forest
Markham
Wingham
Pickering
Ajax
Orangeville
Credit River
TORONTO
LAKE ONTARIO
Goderich
Fergus
Mississauga
Milton
Bayfield
Waterloo
Burlington
Niagara-on-the-Lake
New Hamburg
Cambridge
Hamilton
Grand Bend
Grand River
Forest
Woodstock
Dunnville
Fort Erie
U.S.A.
Petrolia
Lambeth
Tillsonburg
Corunna
River
Aylmer
Courtright
Port Lambton
Wallaceburg
Port Stanley
Port Rowan
U.S.A.
Lake St. Clair
Thames
Ridgetown
Blenheim
Essex
Amherstburg
Leamington
LAKE ERIE

•	Population under 5 000
•	Population 5 000-10 000
●	Population 10 000-100 000
■	Population over 100 000
◉	Population over 1 000 000

Manitoba *People and Places*

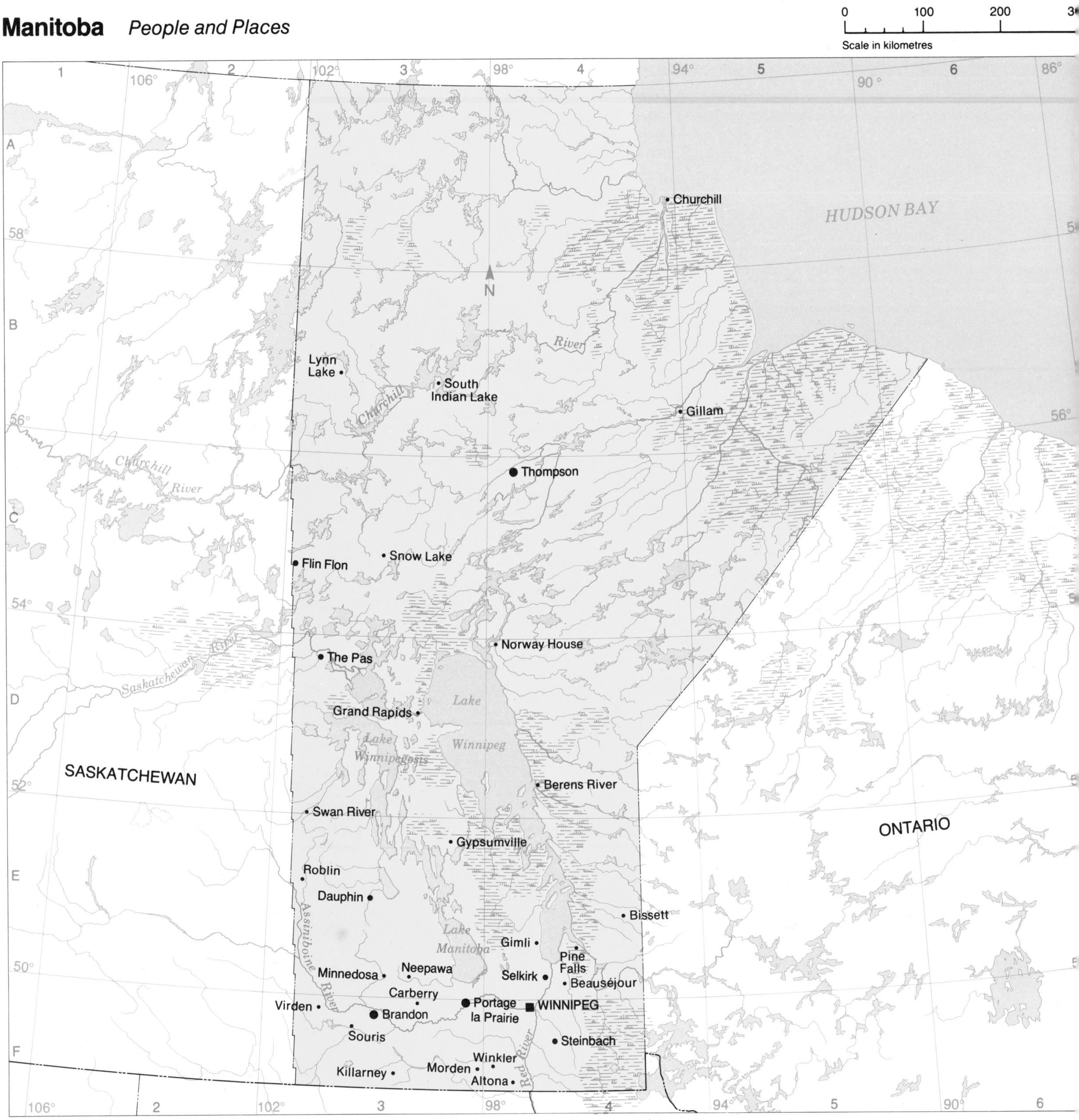

0
100
200
Scale in kilometres
1
2
3
4
5
6
106°
102°
98°
94°
90°
86°
A
B
C
D
E
F
58°
56°
54°
52°
50°
N
Churchill
HUDSON BAY
River
Lynn Lake
South Indian Lake
Churchill
Gillam
Churchill River
Thompson
Flin Flon
Snow Lake
Norway House
The Pas
Saskatchewan River
Grand Rapids
Lake Winnipeg
Lake Winnipegosis
SASKATCHEWAN
Berens River
Swan River
Gypsumville
ONTARIO
Roblin
Dauphin
Bissett
Assiniboine River
Lake Manitoba
Gimli
Pine Falls
Minnedosa
Neepawa
Selkirk
Beauséjour
Carberry
Virden
Brandon
Portage la Prairie
WINNIPEG
Souris
Steinbach
Red River
Winkler
Killarney
Morden
Altona

- Population under 5 000
- Population 5 000-10 000
- Population 10 000-100 000
- Population over 100 000

Provincial Capital:
WINNIPEG

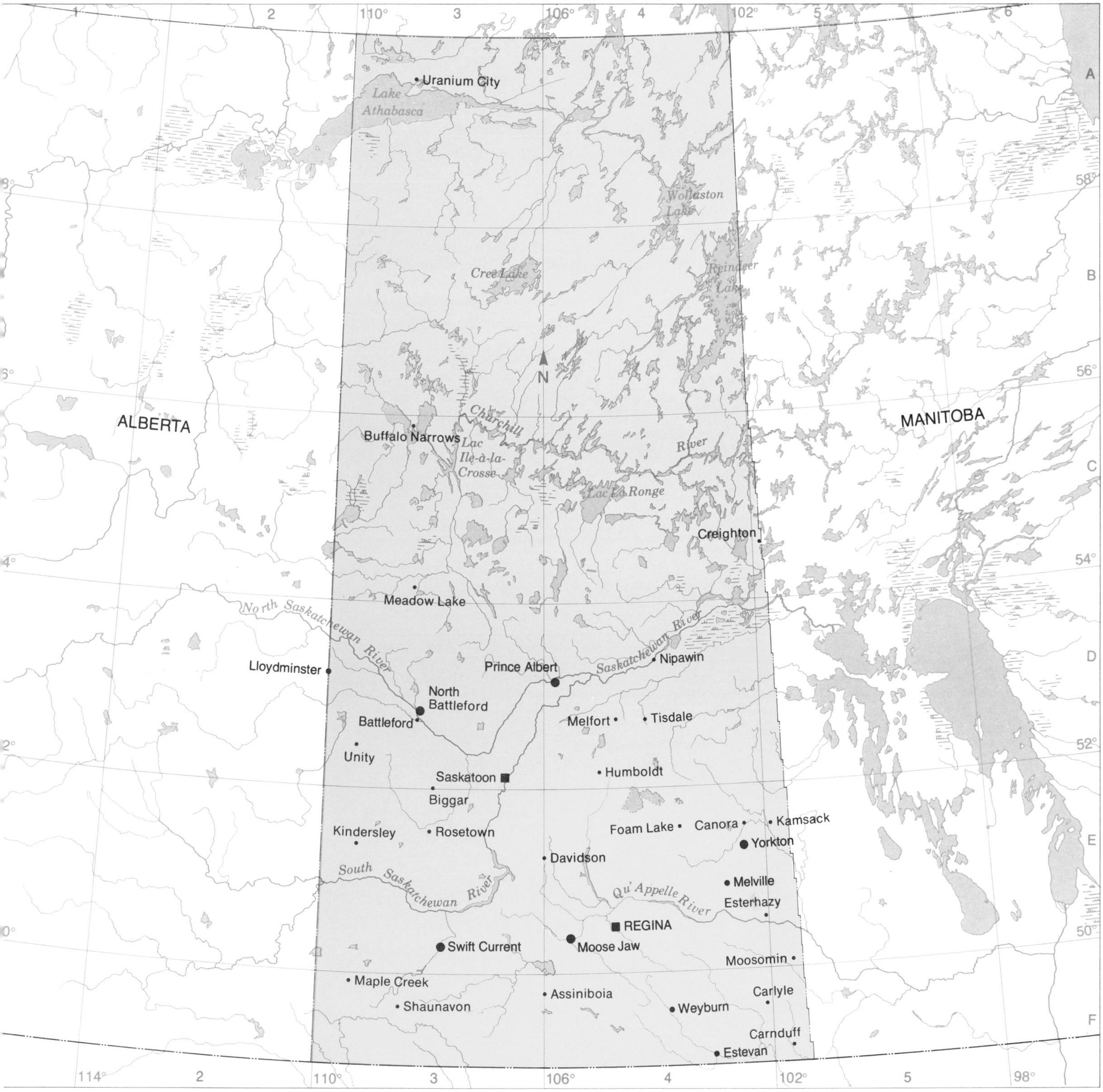

0 100 200 300
Scale in kilometres
1 2 3 4 5 6
110° 106° 102°
A B C D E F
58° 56° 54° 52° 50°
114° 110° 106° 102° 98°
Uranium City
Lake Athabasca
Wollaston Lake
Reindeer Lake
Cree Lake
N
ALBERTA
MANITOBA
Churchill River
Buffalo Narrows
Lac Île-à-la-Crosse
Lac La Ronge
Creighton
Meadow Lake
North Saskatchewan River
Saskatchewan River
Lloydminster
Prince Albert
Nipawin
North Battleford
Battleford
Melfort
Tisdale
Unity
Saskatoon
Humboldt
Biggar
Kindersley
Rosetown
Foam Lake
Canora
Kamsack
Yorkton
Davidson
South Saskatchewan River
Qu'Appelle River
Melville
Esterhazy
REGINA
Swift Current
Moose Jaw
Moosomin
Maple Creek
Shaunavon
Assiniboia
Weyburn
Carlyle
Carnduff
Estevan

Population under 5 000

Population 5 000-10 000

Population 10 000-100 000

Population over 100 000

Provincial Capital:
REGINA

Alberta *People and Places*

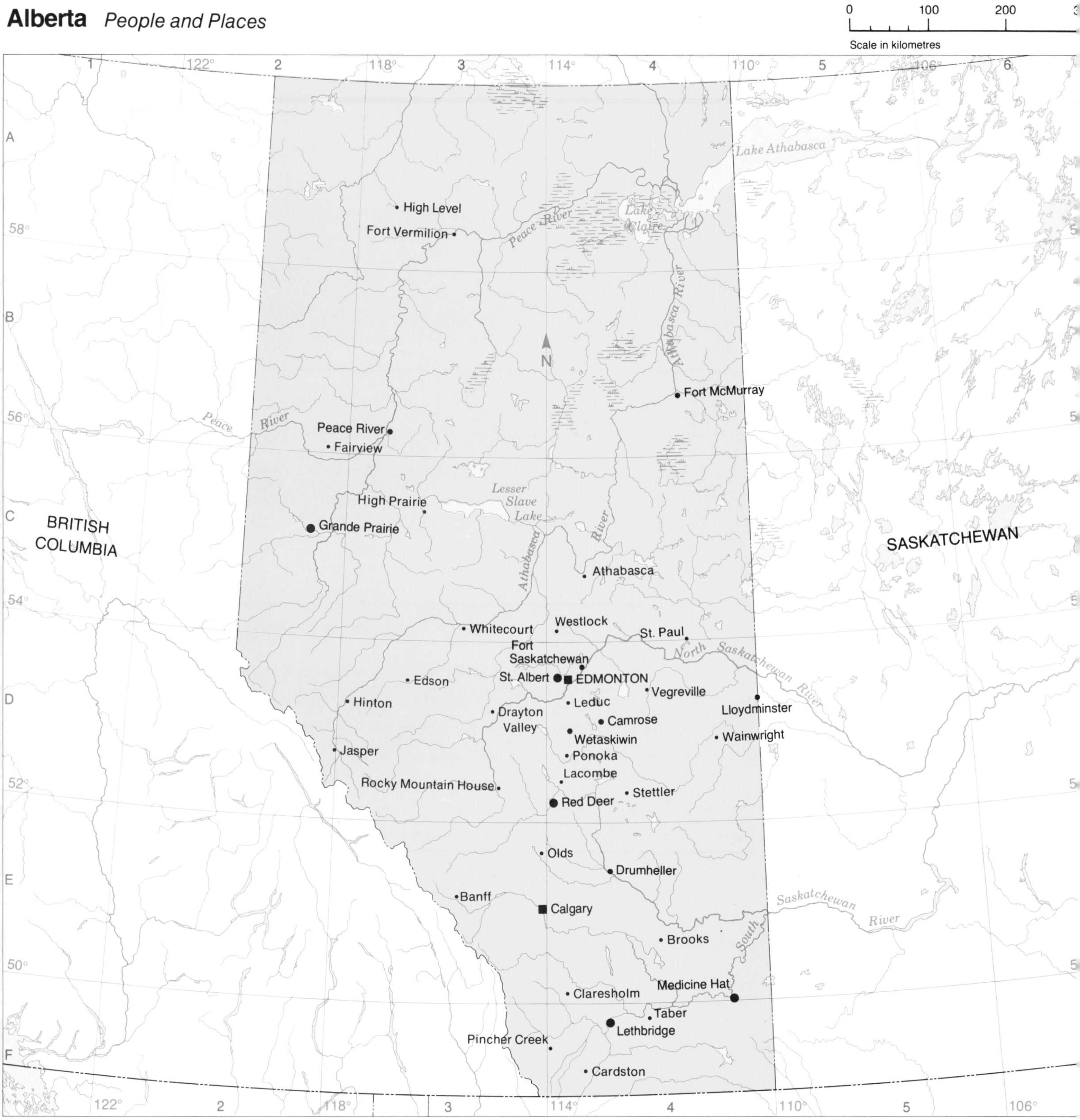

0
100
200
Scale in kilometres
BRITISH COLUMBIA
SASKATCHEWAN
Lake Athabasca
Lake Claire
Peace River
Athabasca River
Lesser Slave Lake
North Saskatchewan River
South Saskatchewan River
High Level
Fort Vermilion
Fort McMurray
Peace River
Fairview
High Prairie
Grande Prairie
Athabasca
Whitecourt
Westlock
St. Paul
Fort Saskatchewan
St. Albert
EDMONTON
Edson
Hinton
Vegreville
Leduc
Lloydminster
Drayton Valley
Camrose
Wetaskiwin
Wainwright
Jasper
Ponoka
Lacombe
Rocky Mountain House
Stettler
Red Deer
Olds
Drumheller
Banff
Calgary
Brooks
Medicine Hat
Claresholm
Taber
Lethbridge
Pincher Creek
Cardston

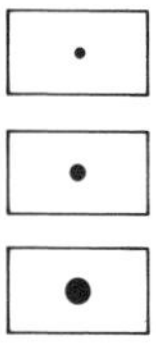

- Population under 5 000
- Population 5 000-10 000
- Population 10 000-100 000
- Population over 100 000

Provincial Capital:
EDMONTON

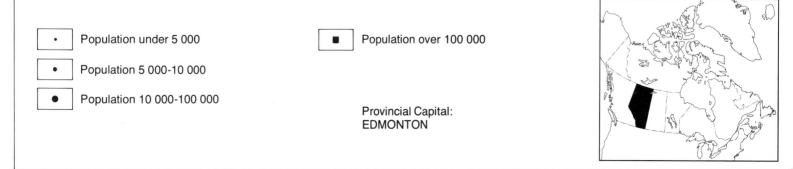

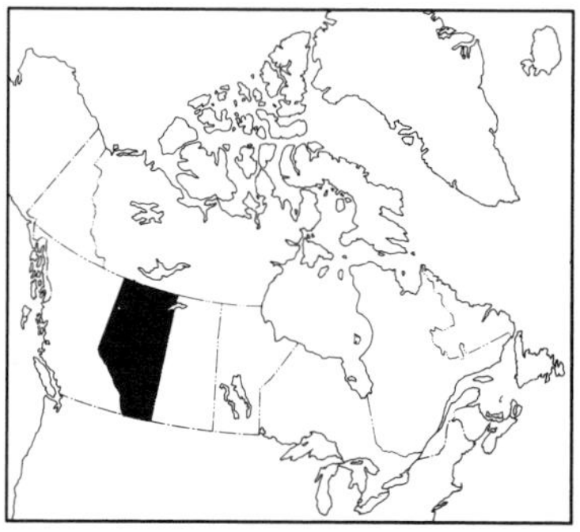

British Columbia *People and Places*

·	Population under 5 000
•	Population 5 000-10 000
●	Population 10 000-100 000
■	Population over 100 000
◙	Population over 1 000 000

Provincial Capital:
VICTORIA

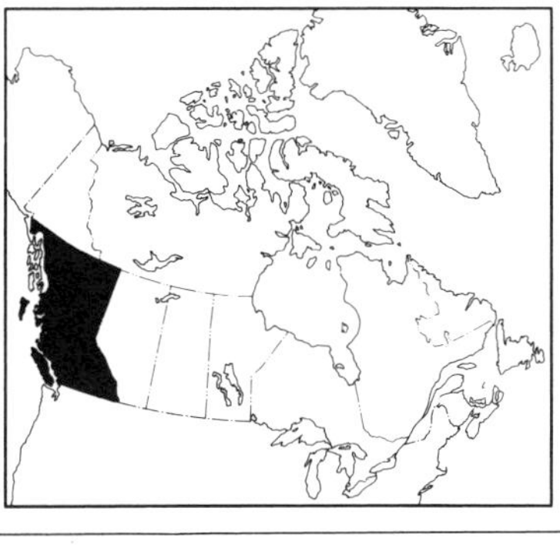

THE LOOK OF THE LAND

The maps in this section show what the land looks like. Such maps are called *physical* maps. They show lakes, rivers, high lands, low lands, bays, capes, islands, peninsulas, and so on. These are called *physical features*. As you read the maps in this section, you will find out the physical features of the provinces and territories.

1. What part of Canada has the most red? What does the red represent?
2. What color represents the lowest land? Around what bays and along what rivers are the main bands of low lands located?
3. What provinces have no coastline?
4. Which province or territory has the longest coastline?
5. What are the main mountain chains in British Columbia and Alberta?
6. What are the main mountain regions in Quebec and Newfoundland?
7. What is the *altitude* (height above sea level) of most of the land in Saskatchewan? In British Columbia? In New Brunswick?
8. List some of the physical features of your province or territory.
9. What are the two largest rivers in Canada? What is the approximate length of each? In what general direction does each flow?
10. The most important lake system in North America is the Great Lakes. Find these five lakes and name them.
11. Which of the following statements are true and which are false?
    - The longest river in Canada is the Mackenzie.
    - All rivers flow from north to south.
    - Rivers flow from high land to low land.
    - More rivers flow into Hudson Bay than into the Atlantic or Pacific oceans.
12. Explorers and fur traders travelled across most of Canada by water. Trace a route, mainly by water, that goes from the Gulf of St. Lawrence all the way to the northwest corner of Canada. Name the lakes and rivers along the route you traced. Use the maps of the provinces and territories to find the names.

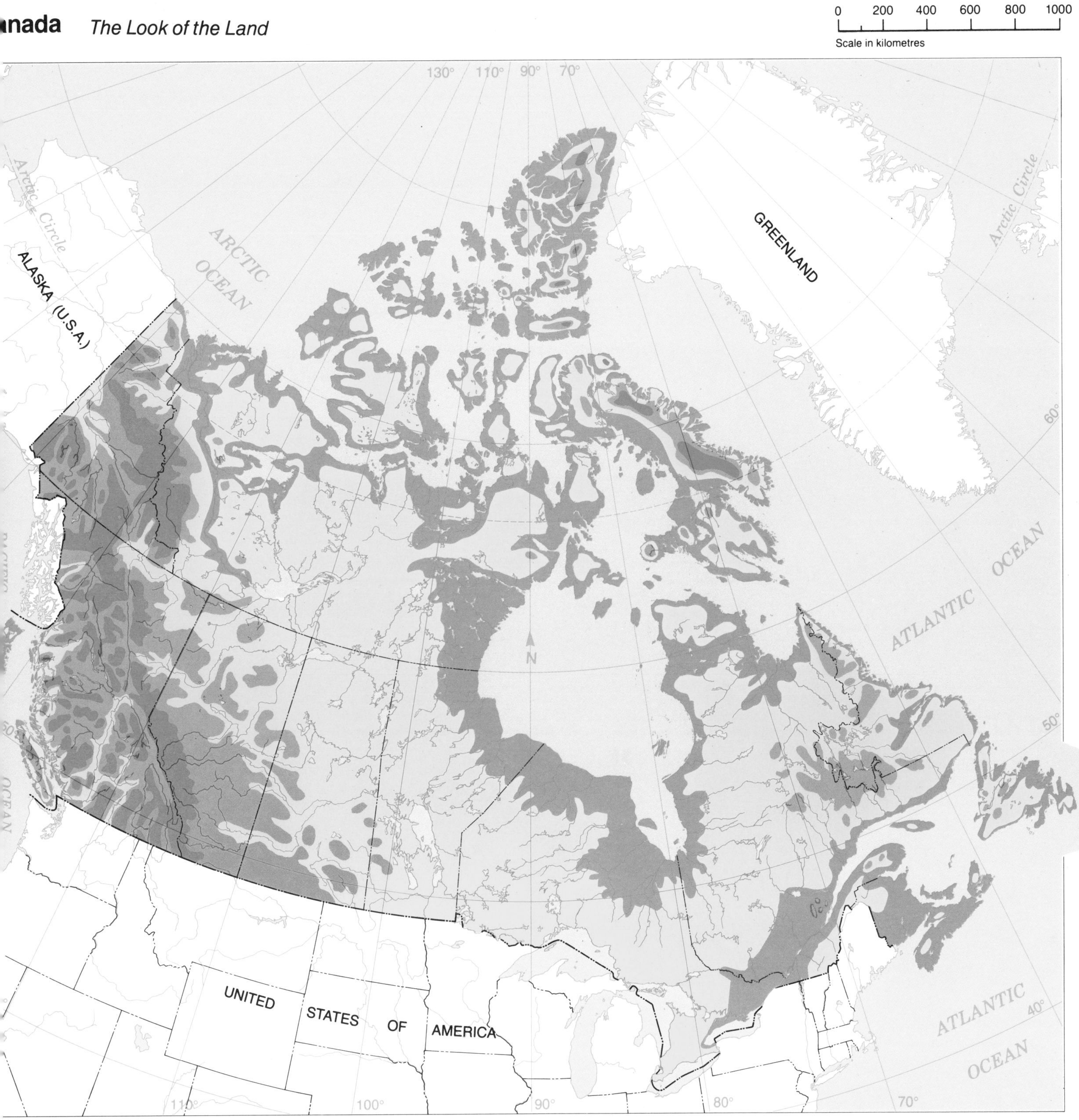
0 200 400 600 800 1000
Scale in kilometres
130° 110° 90° 70°
ARCTIC OCEAN
Arctic Circle
ALASKA (U.S.A.)
GREENLAND
60°
OCEAN
ATLANTIC
N
50°
UNITED STATES OF AMERICA
ATLANTIC
OCEAN
40°
110° 100° 90° 80° 70°

Land between 0 m (sea level*) and 200 m

Land between 200 m and 600 m

Land between 600 m and 1800 m

Land over 1800 m

*This term is explained in the Glossary.

Atlantic Canada *The Look of the Land*

70°
1
68°
2
66°
3
64°
4
62°
B
C
D
E
48°
46°
44°
QUEBEC
QUEBEC
St. Lawrence River
Restigouche River
Chaleur Bay
Miscou Island
Gulf of St. Lawrence
N
Mount Carleton 820 m
Nepisiguit River
UNITED STATES OF AMERICA
NEW BRUNSWICK
Miramichi River
North Cape
West Point
Saint John River
Grand Lake
Northumberland Strait
PRINCE EDWARD ISLAND
142 m
East Point
533
St. Croix River
Chignecto Bay
Cape Bear
CAPE BRETON ISLAND
Bras d'Or Lake
Bay of Fundy
Minas Basin
Grand Manan Island
Annapolis River
Strait of Canso
Isle Madame
Digby Neck
NOVA SCOTIA
St. Mary's River
Shubenacadie River
Chedabucto Bay
Cape Canso
Lake Rossignol
Medway River
Mahone Bay
Cape Sambro
68°
2
66°
3
64°
4
62°
5
60°
Cape Sable

▲ Highest Point of Land in Each Province

Relief*

*This term is explained in the Glossary.

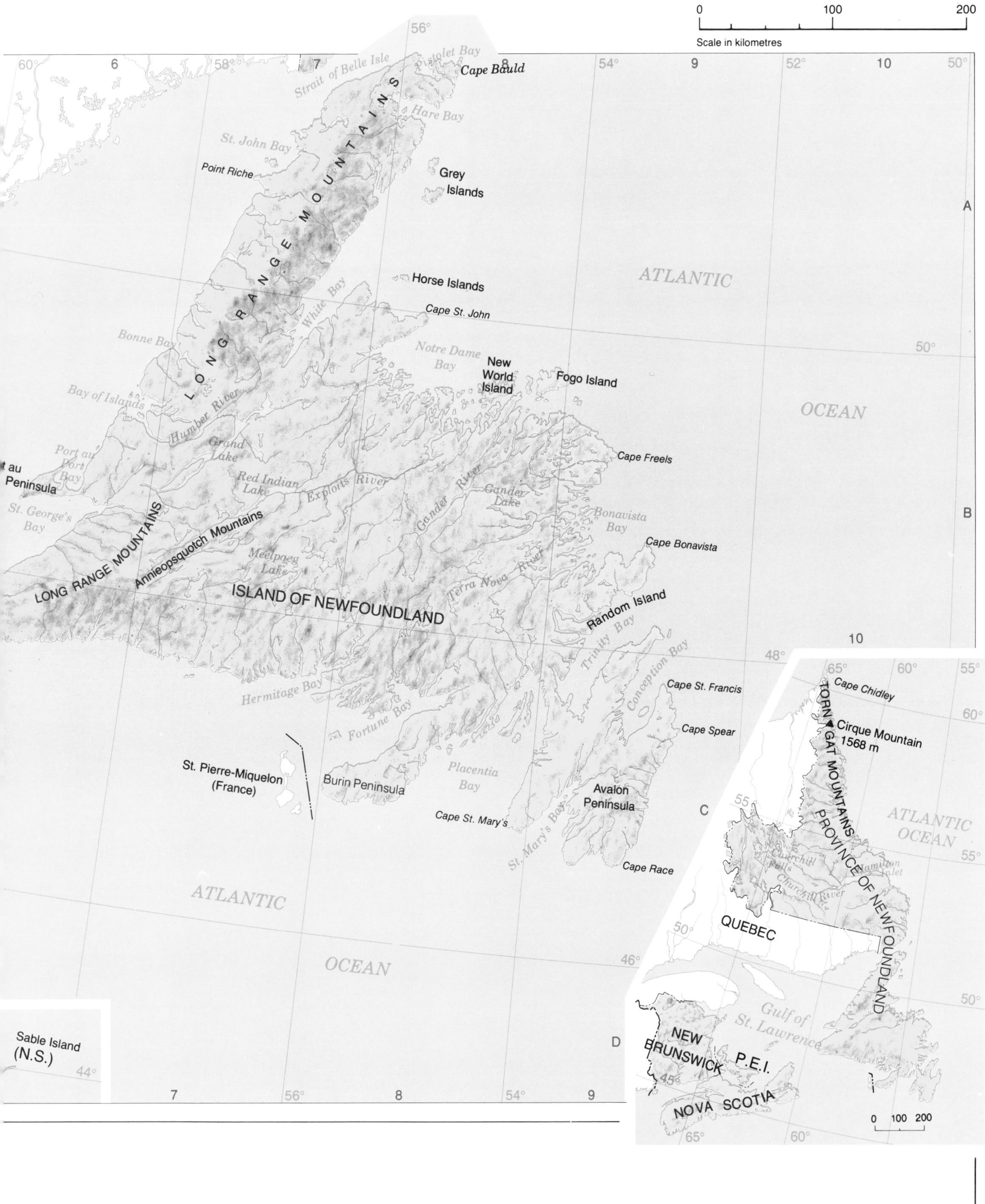
0 100 200
Scale in kilometres
Strait of Belle Isle
Pistolet Bay
Cape Bauld
Hare Bay
St. John Bay
Point Riche
Grey Islands
LONG RANGE MOUNTAINS
Horse Islands
White Bay
Cape St. John
ATLANTIC
Bonne Bay
Notre Dame Bay
New World Island
Fogo Island
Bay of Islands
Humber River
OCEAN
Grand Lake
Port au Port Bay
Port au Port Peninsula
Red Indian Lake
Exploits River
Gander River
Gander Lake
Cape Freels
St. George's Bay
Bonavista Bay
Annieopsquotch Mountains
Cape Bonavista
Meelpaeg Lake
Terra Nova River
ISLAND OF NEWFOUNDLAND
Random Island
Trinity Bay
Conception Bay
Hermitage Bay
Cape St. Francis
Fortune Bay
Cape Spear
St. Pierre-Miquelon (France)
Burin Peninsula
Placentia Bay
Avalon Peninsula
Cape St. Mary's
St. Mary's Bay
Cape Race
ATLANTIC
OCEAN
Sable Island (N.S.)
Cape Chidley
TORNGAT MOUNTAINS
Cirque Mountain 1568 m
ATLANTIC OCEAN
PROVINCE OF NEWFOUNDLAND
Churchill Falls
Churchill River
Hamilton Inlet
QUEBEC
Gulf of St. Lawrence
NEW BRUNSWICK
P.E.I.
NOVA SCOTIA
0 100 200

Quebec *The Look of the Land*

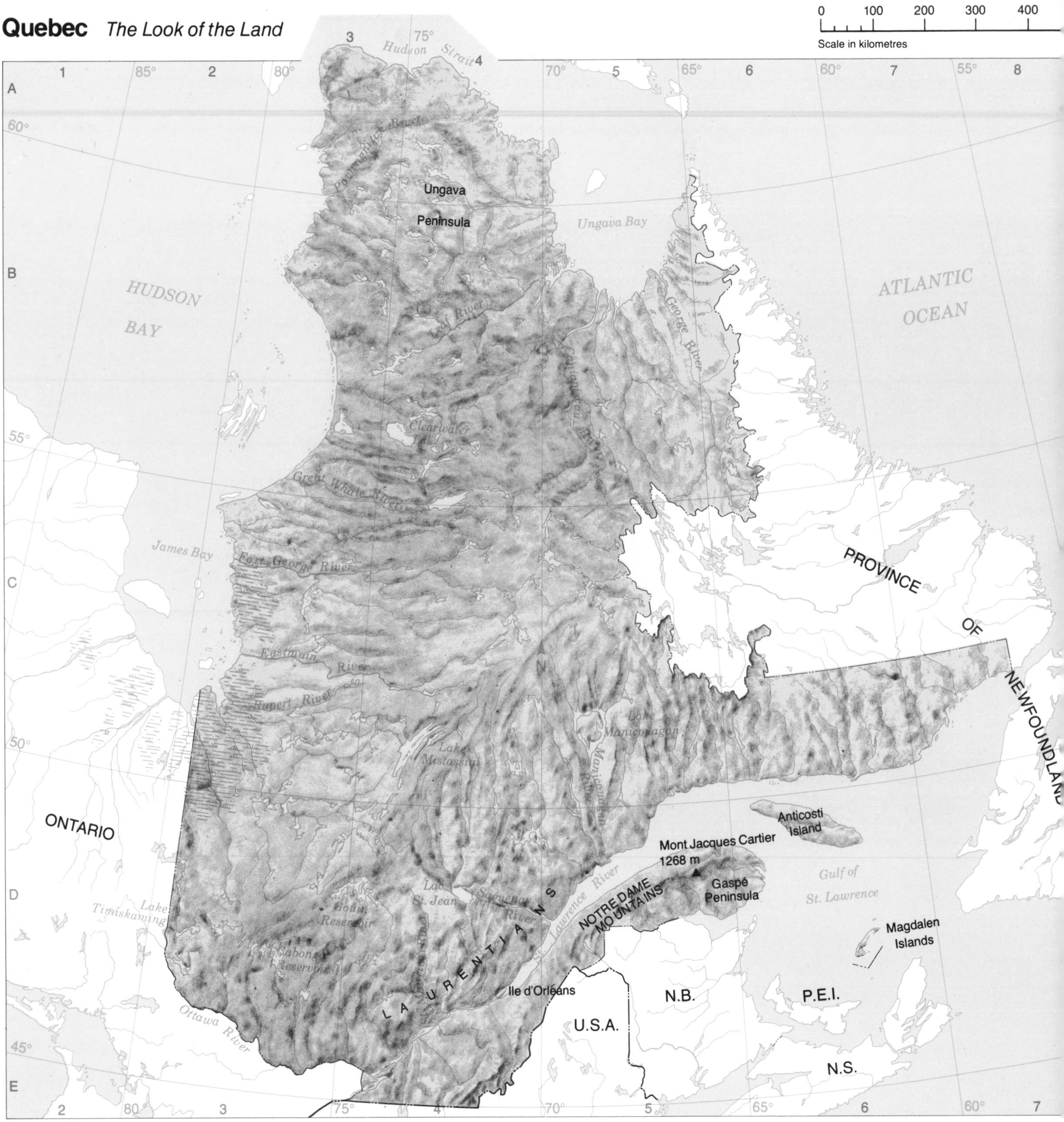

0 100 200 300 400
Scale in kilometres
Hudson Strait
Ungava Peninsula
Povungnituk River
Ungava Bay
HUDSON BAY
ATLANTIC OCEAN
Leaf River
George River
Caniapiscau River
Clearwater Lake
Great Whale River
James Bay
Fort George River
Eastmain River
Rupert River
Lake Mistassini
Lake Manicouagan
Manicouagan River
PROVINCE OF NEWFOUNDLAND
ONTARIO
Anticosti Island
Mont Jacques Cartier 1268 m
Gaspé Peninsula
Gulf of St. Lawrence
Magdalen Islands
NOTRE DAME MOUNTAINS
St. Lawrence River
Saguenay River
Lac St. Jean
Gouin Reservoir
Lake Timiskaming
Baskatong Reservoir
LAURENTIANS
Ile d'Orléans
Ottawa River
U.S.A.
N.B.
P.E.I.
N.S.
60°
55°
50°
45°
85°
80°
75°
70°
65°
60°
55°
A
B
C
D
E
1
2
3
4
5
6
7
8

▲ Highest Point of Land

Relief*

Marsh*

*These terms are explained in the Glossary.

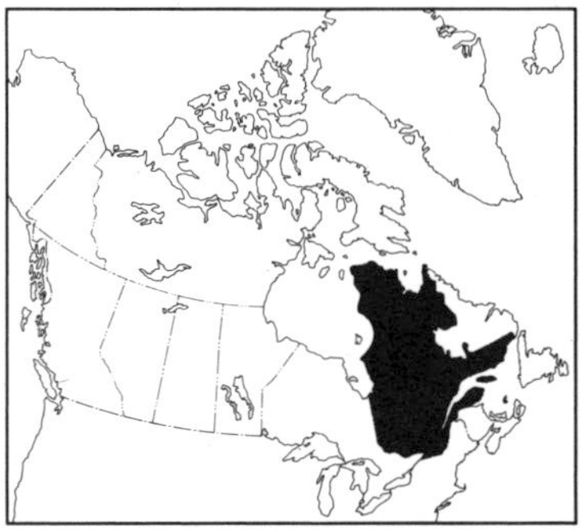

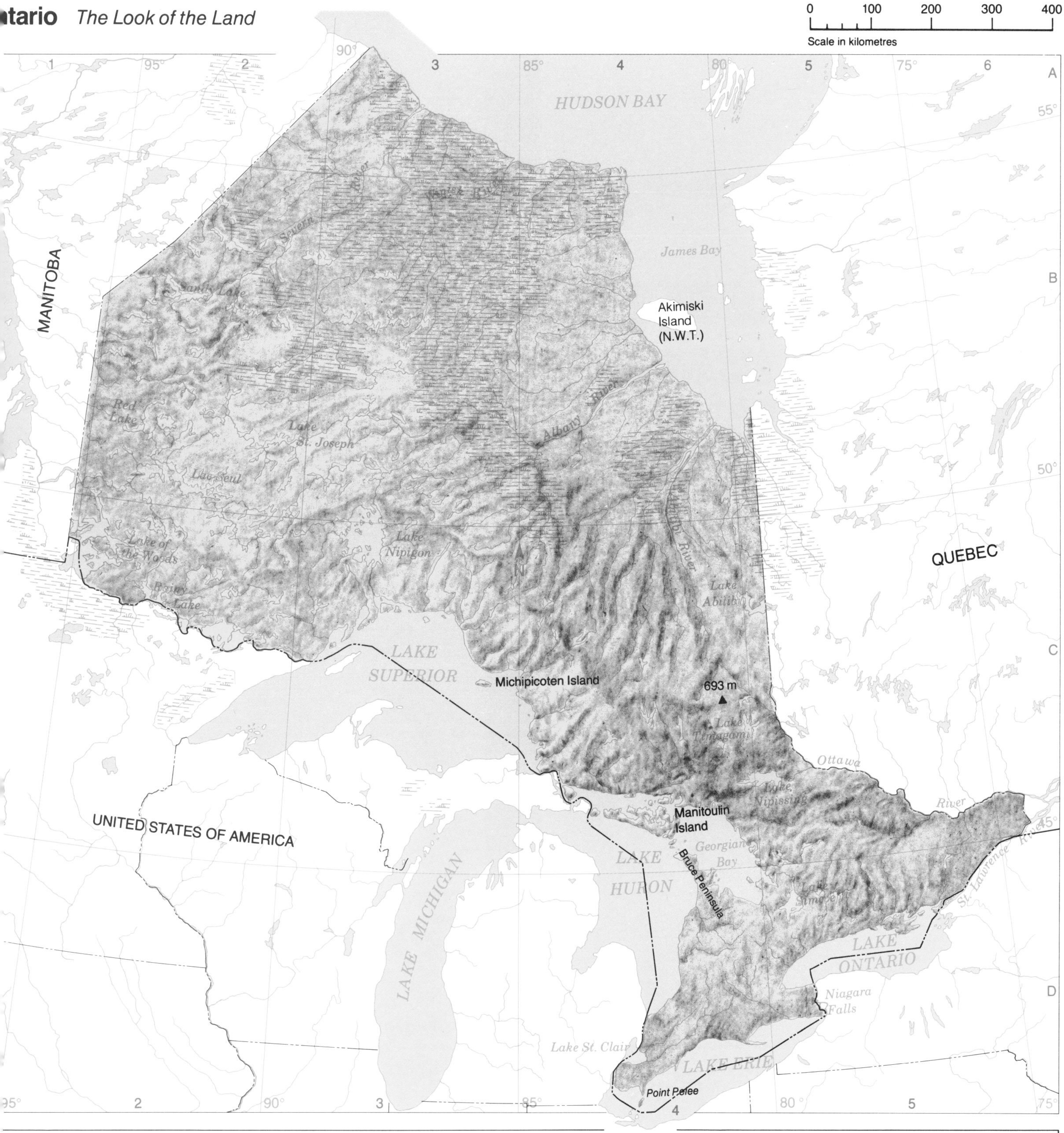

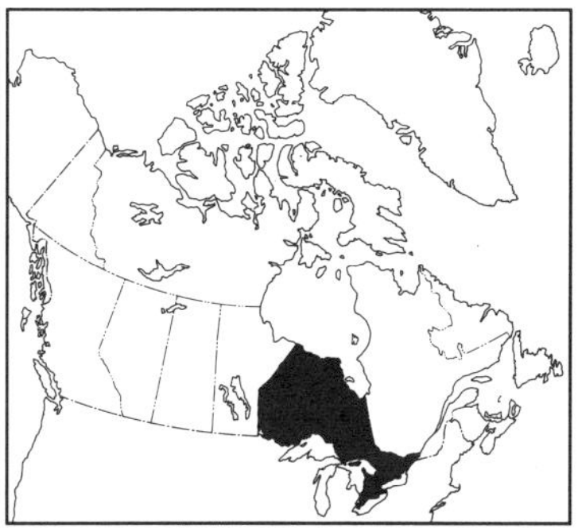

▲ Highest Point of Land

Relief*

Marsh*

*These terms are explained in the Glossary.

Manitoba *The Look of the Land*

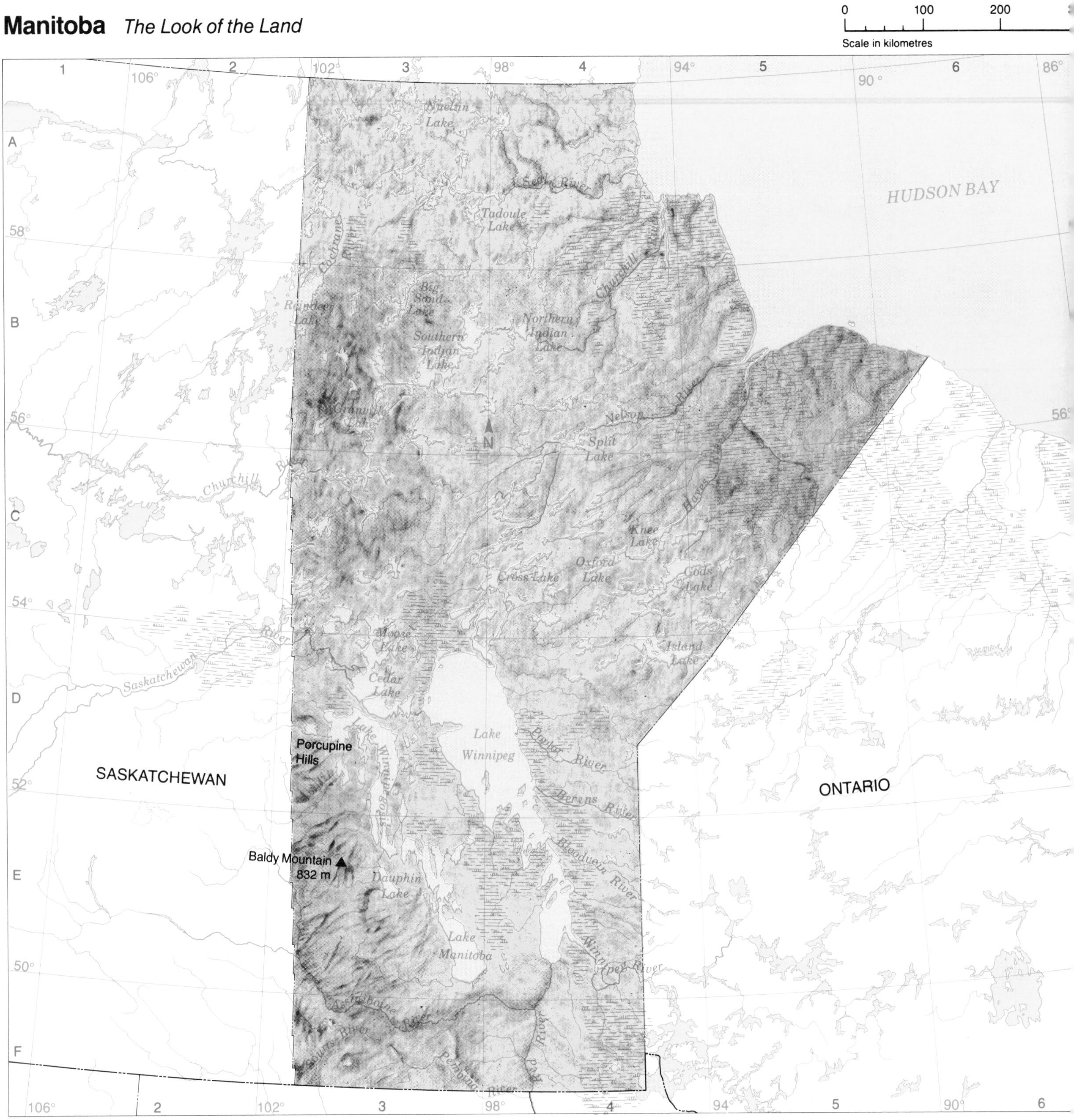

0
100
200
Scale in kilometres
1
2
3
4
5
6
A
B
C
D
E
F
106°
102°
98°
94°
90°
86°
58°
56°
54°
52°
50°
HUDSON BAY
Nueltin Lake
Seal River
Tadoule Lake
Cochrane River
Churchill River
Big Sand Lake
Reindeer Lake
Southern Indian Lake
Northern Indian Lake
Granville Lake
Nelson River
Split Lake
N
Churchill River
Hayes River
Knee Lake
Oxford Lake
Cross Lake
Gods Lake
Island Lake
Moose Lake
Saskatchewan River
Cedar Lake
Lake Winnipeg
Poplar River
Porcupine Hills
Lake Winnipegosis
SASKATCHEWAN
ONTARIO
Berens River
Baldy Mountain 832 m
Bloodvein River
Dauphin Lake
Lake Manitoba
Winnipeg River
Assiniboine River
Souris River
Pembina River
Red River

▲	Highest Point of Land
	Relief*
	Marsh*

*These terms are explained in the Glossary.

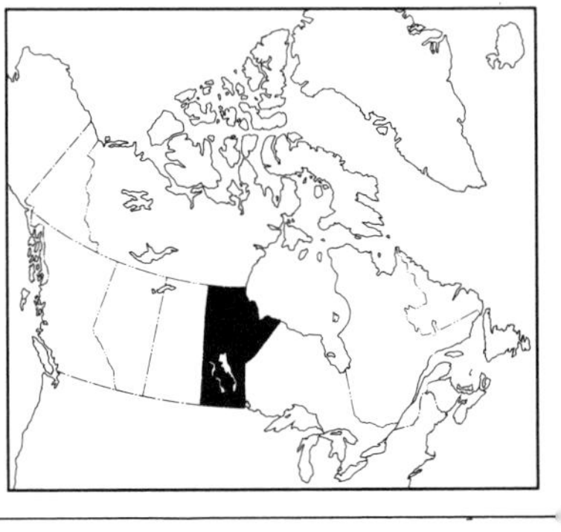

skatchewan *The Look of the Land*

0 100 200 300
Scale in kilometres

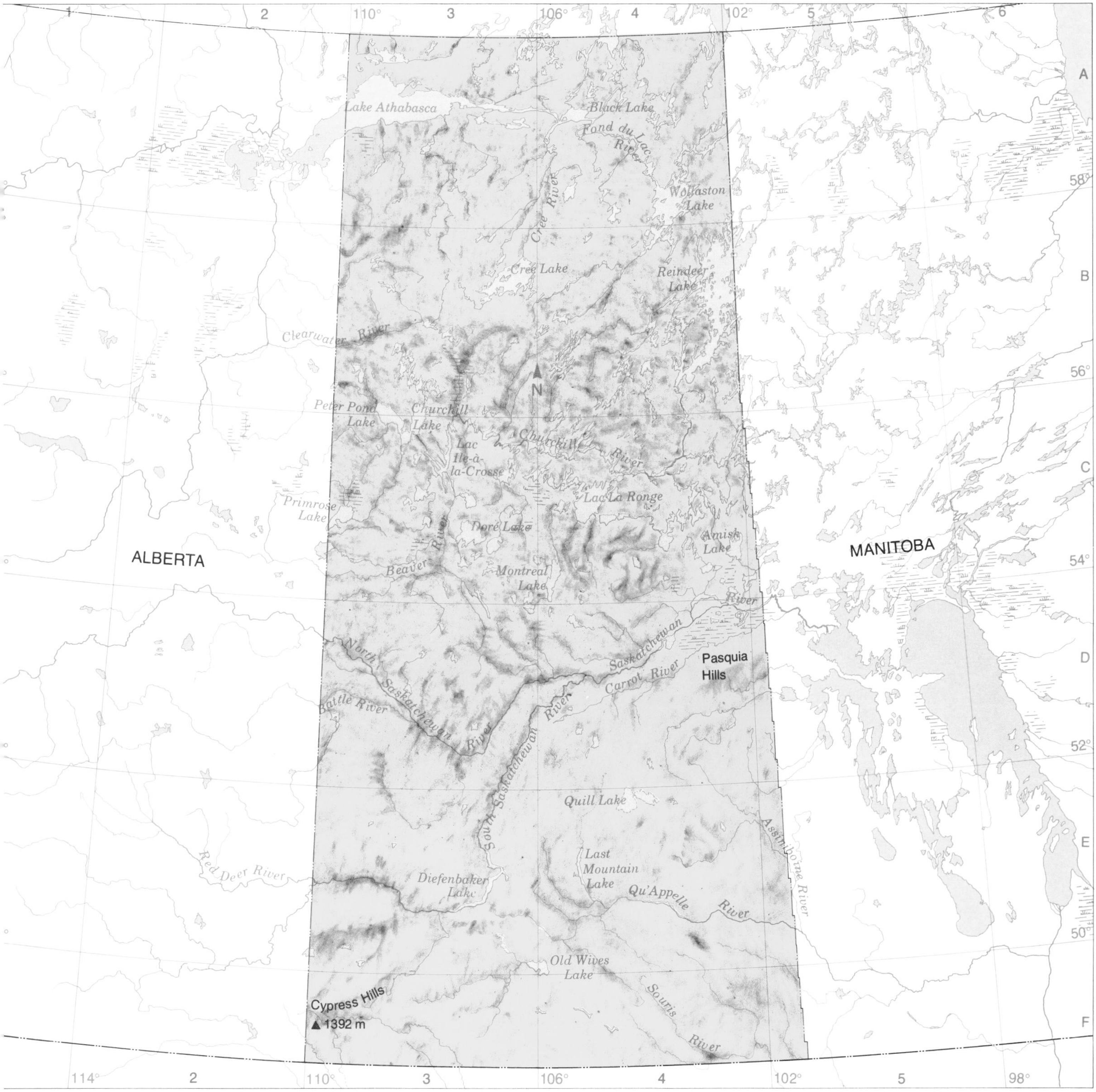

1
2
3
4
5
6
110°
106°
102°
114°
98°
58°
56°
54°
52°
50°
A
B
C
D
E
F
Lake Athabasca
Black Lake
Fond du Lac River
Wollaston Lake
Cree River
Cree Lake
Reindeer Lake
Clearwater River
N
Peter Pond Lake
Churchill Lake
Lac Ile-à-la-Crosse
Churchill River
Lac La Ronge
Primrose Lake
Doré Lake
Amisk Lake
ALBERTA
MANITOBA
Beaver River
Montreal Lake
River
Saskatchewan
North Saskatchewan River
Battle River
Pasquia Hills
Carrot River
South Saskatchewan River
Quill Lake
Assiniboine River
Red Deer River
Diefenbaker Lake
Last Mountain Lake
Qu'Appelle River
Old Wives Lake
Souris River
Cypress Hills
▲ 1392 m

▲ Highest Point of Land

Relief*

Marsh*

*These terms are explained in the Glossary.

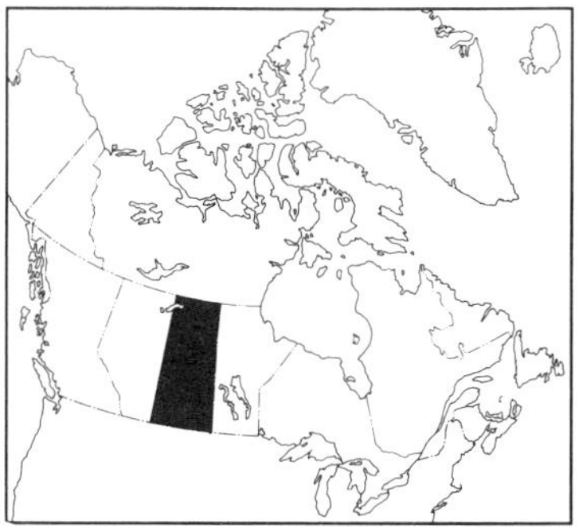

Alberta *The Look of the Land*

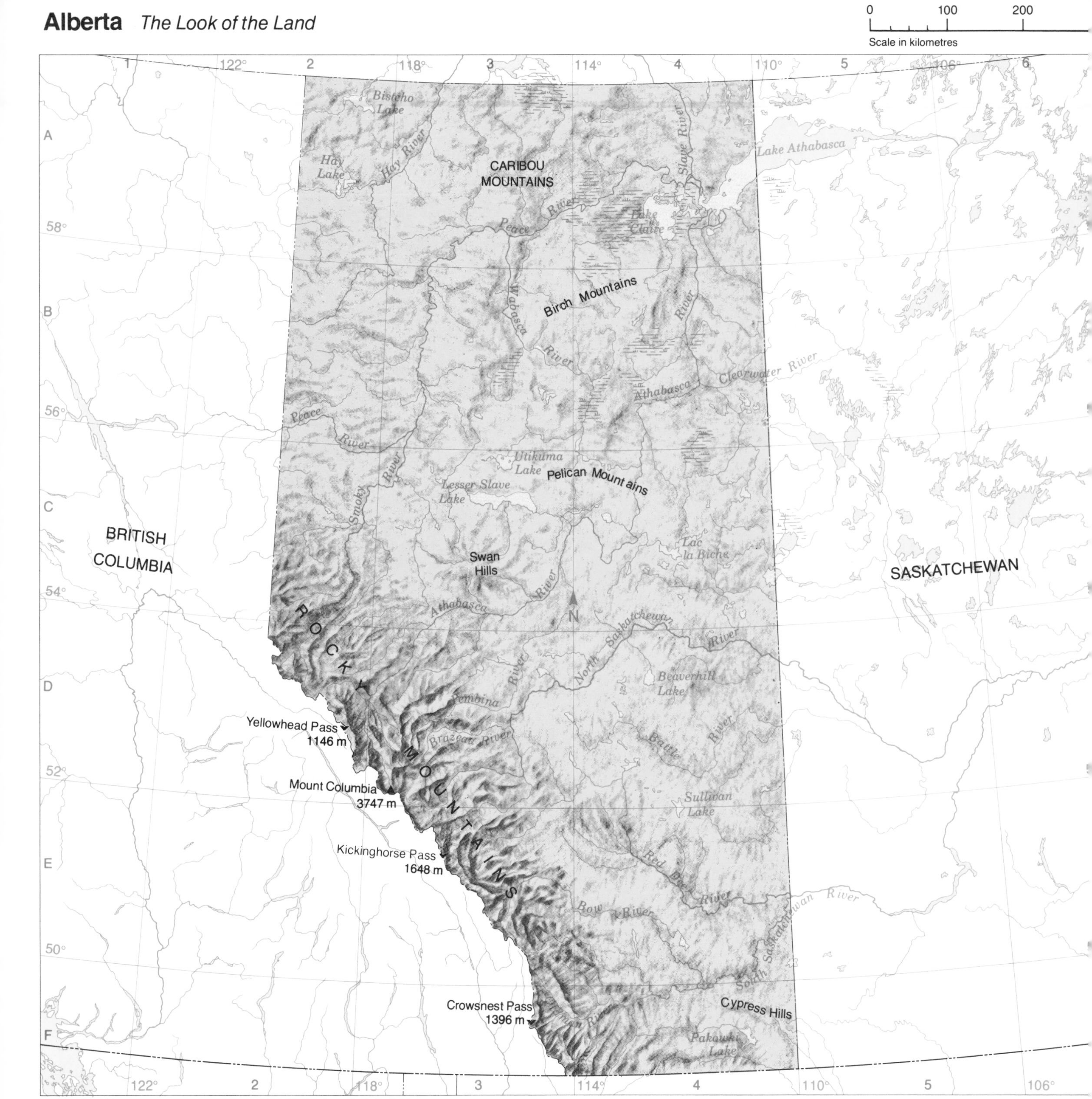

0 100 200
Scale in kilometres
122°
118°
114°
110°
106°
1
2
3
4
5
6
A
B
C
D
E
F
58°
56°
54°
52°
50°
Bistcho Lake
Hay Lake
Hay River
CARIBOU MOUNTAINS
Slave River
Lake Athabasca
Peace River
Lake Claire
Birch Mountains
Wabasca River
River
Clearwater River
Athabasca
Peace River
Smoky River
Utikuma Lake
Pelican Mountains
Lesser Slave Lake
BRITISH COLUMBIA
Swan Hills
Lac la Biche
SASKATCHEWAN
River
Athabasca
N
ROCKY MOUNTAINS
North Saskatchewan River
Pembina River
Beaverhill Lake
Yellowhead Pass 1146 m
Brazeau River
Battle River
Mount Columbia 3747 m
Sullivan Lake
Kickinghorse Pass 1648 m
Red Deer River
Bow River
South Saskatchewan River
Crowsnest Pass 1396 m
Cypress Hills
Pakowki Lake

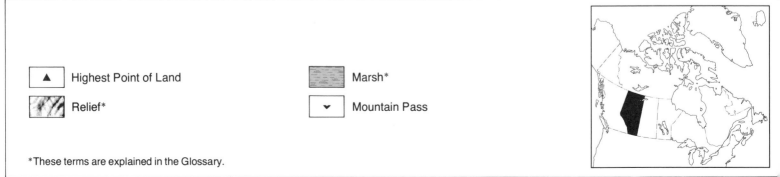

 Highest Point of Land

 Relief*

 Marsh*

 Mountain Pass

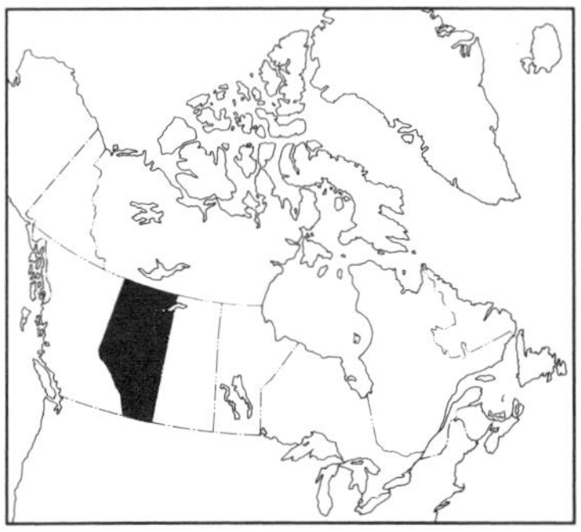

*These terms are explained in the Glossary.

0 100 200 300
Scale in kilometres

▲ Highest Point of Land	Relief*

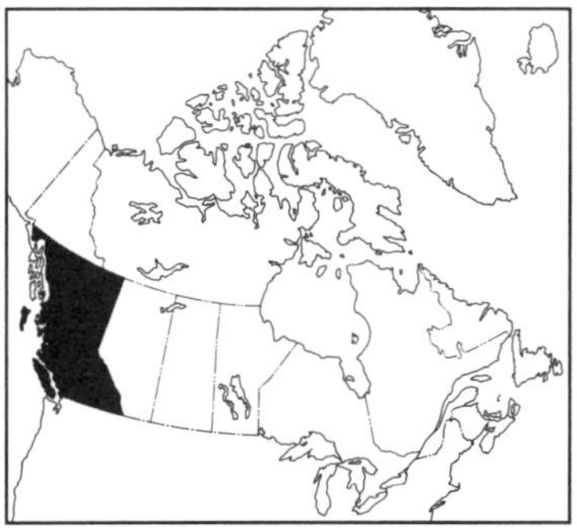

*This term is explained in the Glossary.

150°
B
1
140°
2
130°
3
120°
4
110°
C
D
E
65°
60°
ARCTIC
OCEAN
BEAUFORT SEA
Melville Island
Viscount Melville Sound
Banks Island
Sachs Harbour
ALASKA (U.S.A.)
Arctic Circle
Yukon
River
DISTRICT
Amundsen Gulf
Tuktoyaktuk
Old Crow
Aklavik
Inuvik
Fort McPherson
Arctic Red River
Holman
Victoria Island
Paulatuk
Cambridge Bay
YUKON
Clinton Creek
Colville Lake
Coppermine
Coronation Gulf
Fort Good Hope
Dawson
Elsa
Mayo
MACKENZIE
NORTH
Baychimo
Great Bear Lake
Norman Wells
Port Radium
Bathurst Inlet
Beaver Creek
TERRITORY
Pelly Crossing
Fort Franklin
Fort Norman
Coppermine River
Contwoyto Lake
ST. ELIAS
Carmacks
Destruction Bay
Mount Logan 6054 m
Faro
Pelly River
Ross River
DISTRICT OF MACKENZ
MOUNTAINS
Wrigley
WHITEHORSE
Carcross
Teslin
Tungsten
Lac La Martre
Rae-Edzo
Fort Simpson
Jean Marie River
YELLOWKNIFE
Reliance
Snowdrift
Watson Lake
Nahanni Butte
Fort Providence
Great Slave Lake
Fort Resolution
Hay River
Fort Liard
Trout Lake
Pine Point
BRITISH COLUMBIA
ALBERTA
Fort Smith
Hay River
Slave River
2
130°
3
120°
4
110°

Marsh*

Relief*

Highest Point of Land in Each Territory

*These terms are explained in the Glossary.

0 100 200 300 400 500
Scale in kilometres
Grise Fiord
Devon Island
Cornwallis Island
Resolute
Lancaster Sound
Baffin Bay
GREENLAND
Pond Inlet
Arctic Bay
Somerset Island
Clyde River
Davis Strait
Arctic Circle
FRANKLIN
Wales
Bellot Strait
Baffin Island
Broughton Island
Cape Dyer
Penny Ice Cap 2042 m
Pangnirtung
Boothia Peninsula
Gulf of Boothia
Igloolik
Hall Beach
Spence Bay
Pelly Bay
Gjoa Haven
TERRITORIES
Foxe Basin
Frobisher Bay
Repulse Bay
Cape Dorset
Lake Harbour
Back River
DISTRICT
Hudson Strait
Southampton Island
Coral Harbour
Port Burwell
Ungava Bay
Baker Lake
Chesterfield Inlet
OF
Rankin Inlet
Yathkyed Lake
Whale Cove
KEEWATIN
QUEBEC
HUDSON BAY
Eskimo Point
Nueltin Lake

Population under 5 000

Population 5 000-10 000

Population 10 000-100 000

Capital of Northwest Territories:
YELLOWKNIFE

Capital of Yukon Territory:
WHITEHORSE

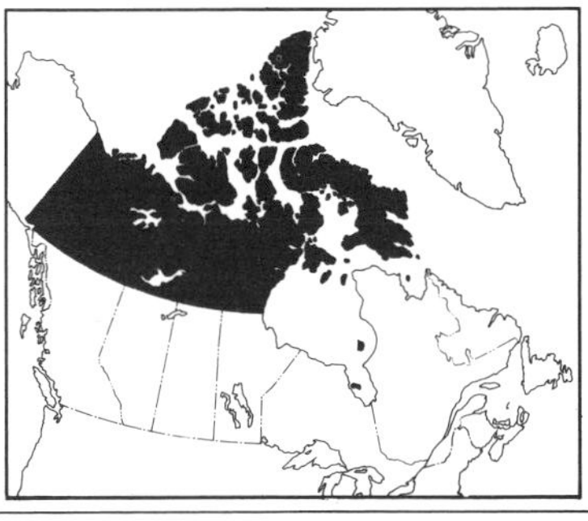

CLIMATE

Weather changes from day to day. One day will be sunny, another will be rainy. One day may be hot and sticky, and the next day, the temperature may drop ten degrees.

Climate is what the weather *usually* is during a certain period of the year. If a place is usually hot and rainy in July, then the July climate for that place is hot and wet. If January is usually sunny with only a slight snowfall, then the January climate for the place is cold and dry.

In some years, July may be hot and dry or cool and wet. January may be cold and wet with lots of snow. *But*, usually, over a long period of many, many years, the July climate of that place is hot and wet, and the January climate is cold and dry.

The rainfall marked on the map on page 59 includes any kind of precipitation that falls from the sky — rain, snow, sleet, hail, or freezing rain. People who study climate measure the amount of any form of precipitation as if it were rain. These scientists use a special way of measuring that tells them how much snow, sleet, or hail it takes to make one millimetre of rainfall.

1. What parts of Canada have the heaviest rainfall?
2. What part of Canada has the lightest rainfall?
3. How hot is July in most of Canada?
4. What place in Canada has the kind of climate you like best?
5. What part of Canada is coldest in January? How cold is it there?
6. If you didn't like cold winters, where would you choose to live in Canada?
7. Choose a phrase in the right-hand column that best describes the winter climate of a place in the left-hand column.

Southern Ontario	wet and cool
British Columbia coast	dry and cool
Southern Manitoba	dry and cold
Newfoundland	wet and warm
Baffin Island	wet and cold
Northern Saskatchewan	dry and warm

8. What phrase would you use to describe the summer climate of these same places?

anada: Annual Rainfall

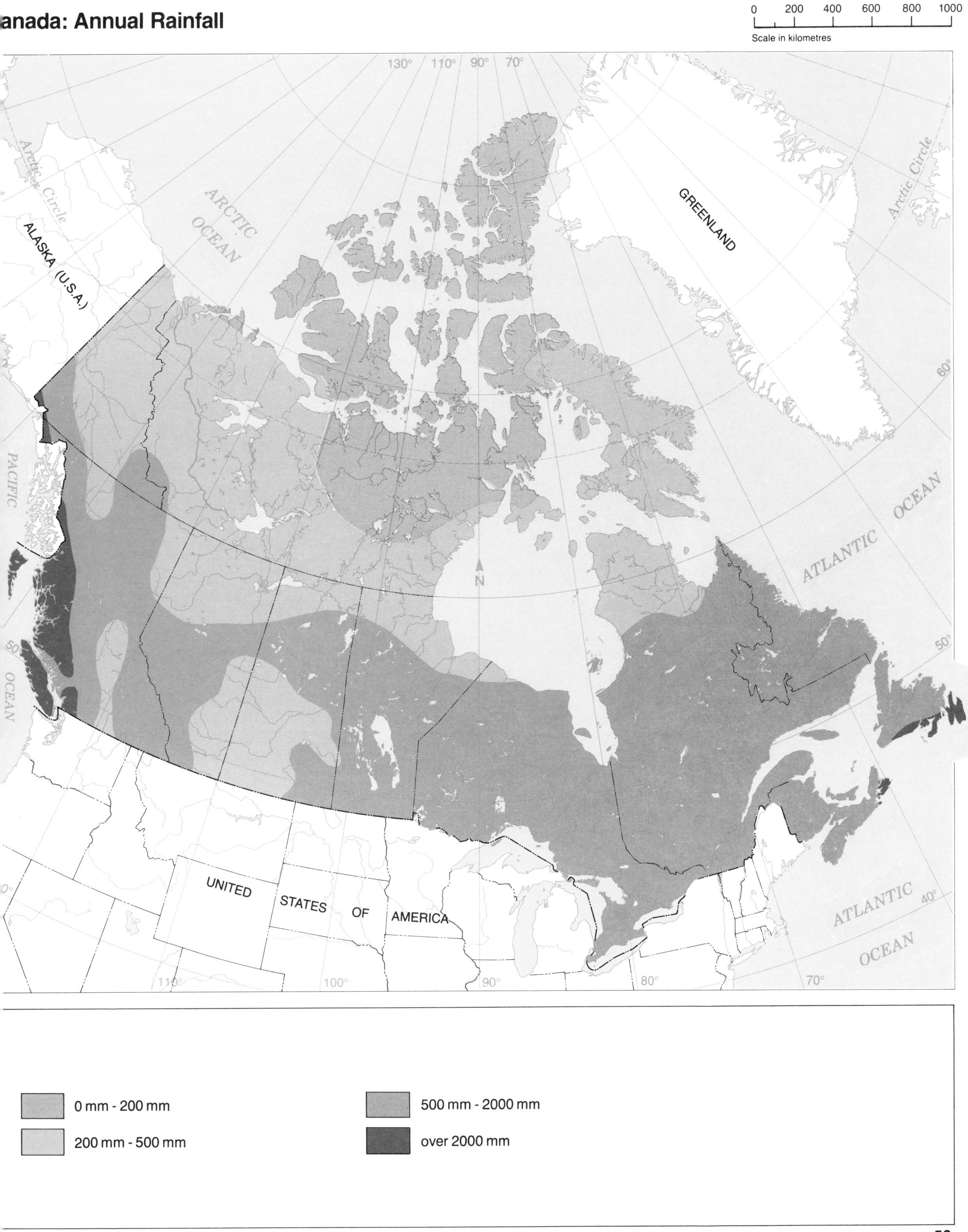
0 200 400 600 800 1000
Scale in kilometres
130° 110° 90° 70°
Arctic Circle
ARCTIC OCEAN
ALASKA (U.S.A.)
GREENLAND
Arctic Circle
60°
PACIFIC OCEAN
50°
N
ATLANTIC OCEAN
50°
UNITED STATES OF AMERICA
ATLANTIC OCEAN
40°
110° 100° 90° 80° 70°
0 mm - 200 mm
200 mm - 500 mm
500 mm - 2000 mm
over 2000 mm

Canada: Temperature in January

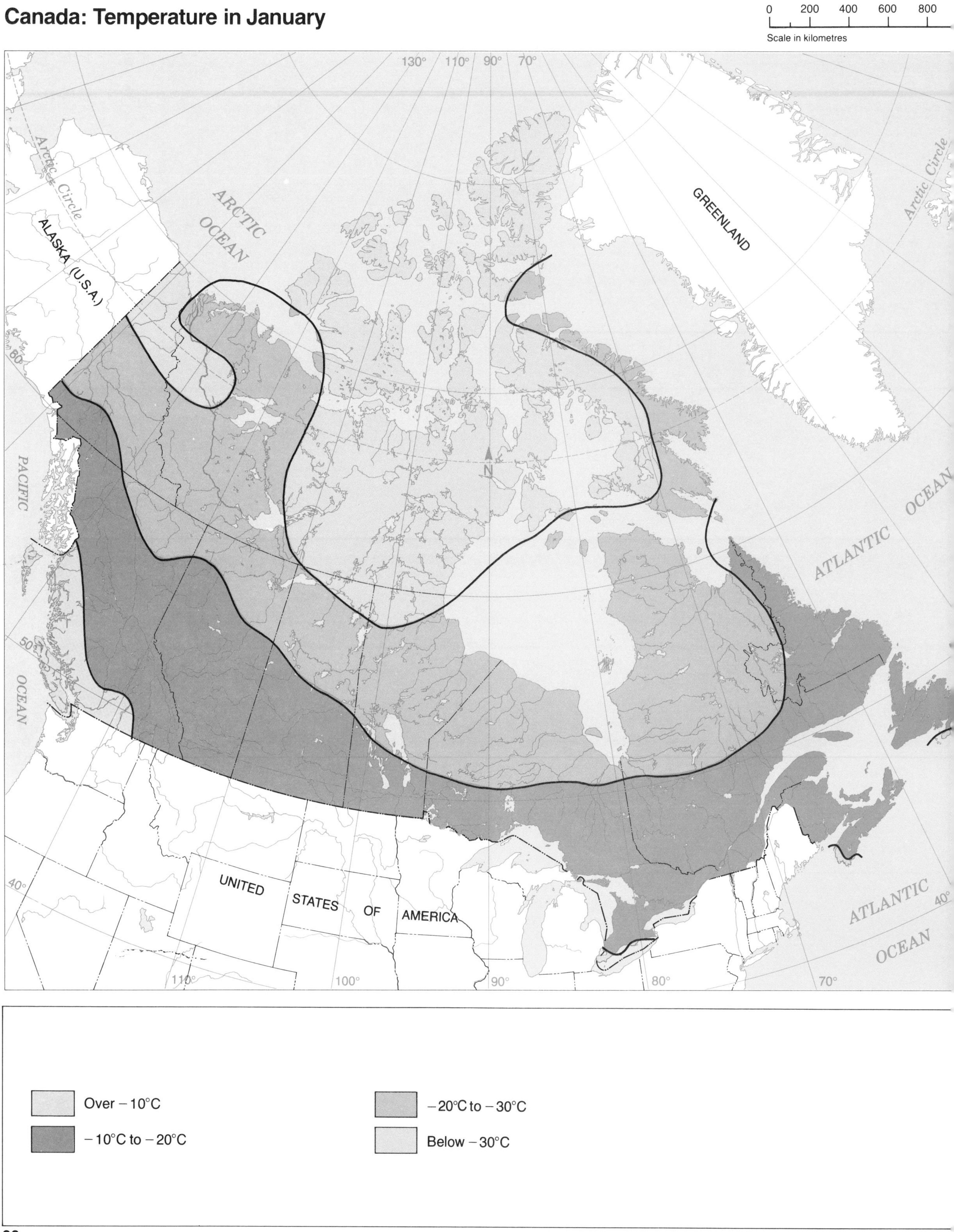

anada: Temperature in July

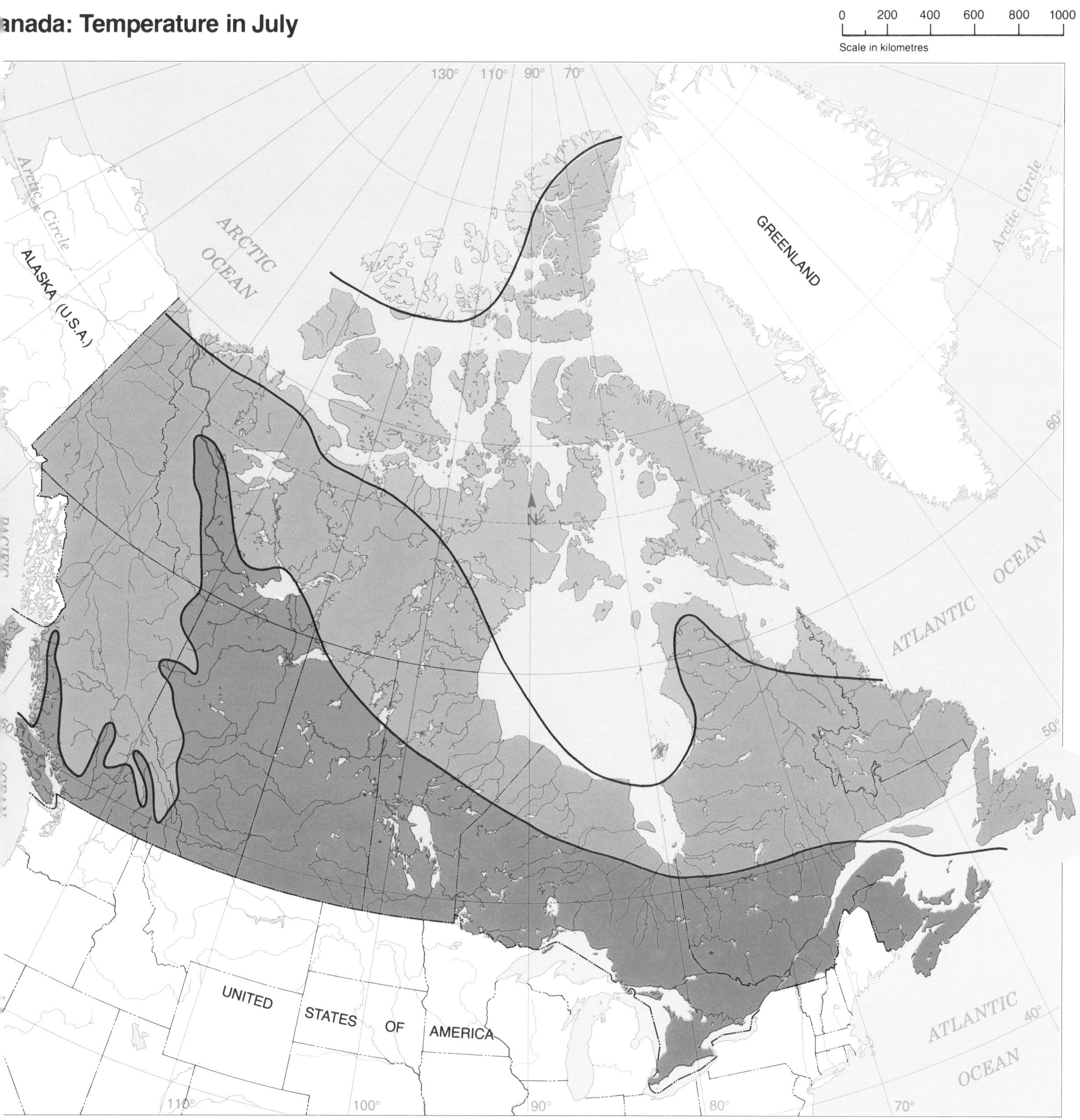

Below 5°C

5°C to 10°C

10°C to 15°C

over 15°C

USING LAND AND WATER

FISH, FURS, FARMS AND FORESTS

We get so many things from the land and the water that they could not all be shown in one series of maps. So, we have divided this section into three parts to show the different ways we use land and water.

The maps in this part show "crops" that we harvest from the land and the water. These crops provide the basic things that people need in order to live— food, clothing, and shelter.

1. What are the three main land regions in Canada? Which region is the largest?
2. Describe each of the following kinds of farming. Use the *Glossary* to help you with any terms you don't understand.
   dairy farming — mixed farming
   grain farming — livestock
   fruit farming
3. For each province, name the kinds of farming that are carried on.
4. In what province is *all* the land suitable for farmland?
5. In what province is only a little of the land suitable for farming?
6. In what province is there more grain farming than any other kind of farming?
7. In what provinces can people earn a living from fishing?
8. Which coast has no lobster fishing? In what provinces is there lobster fishing?
9. What kinds of activities are carried on in regions that are mainly forest?
10. What "crops" do we get from forested regions? What do we use these crops for?
11. List the "crops" that are harvested in your province. Which crops do you think are most important? If you know of any crops that are not shown on the map of your province, add them to your list.
12. What "crops" are harvested near the place you live in?

Treeless Regions*

Mainly Forested Land

Mainly Farmland

*This term is explained in the Glossary.

Newfoundland *Fish, Furs, Farms, and Forests*

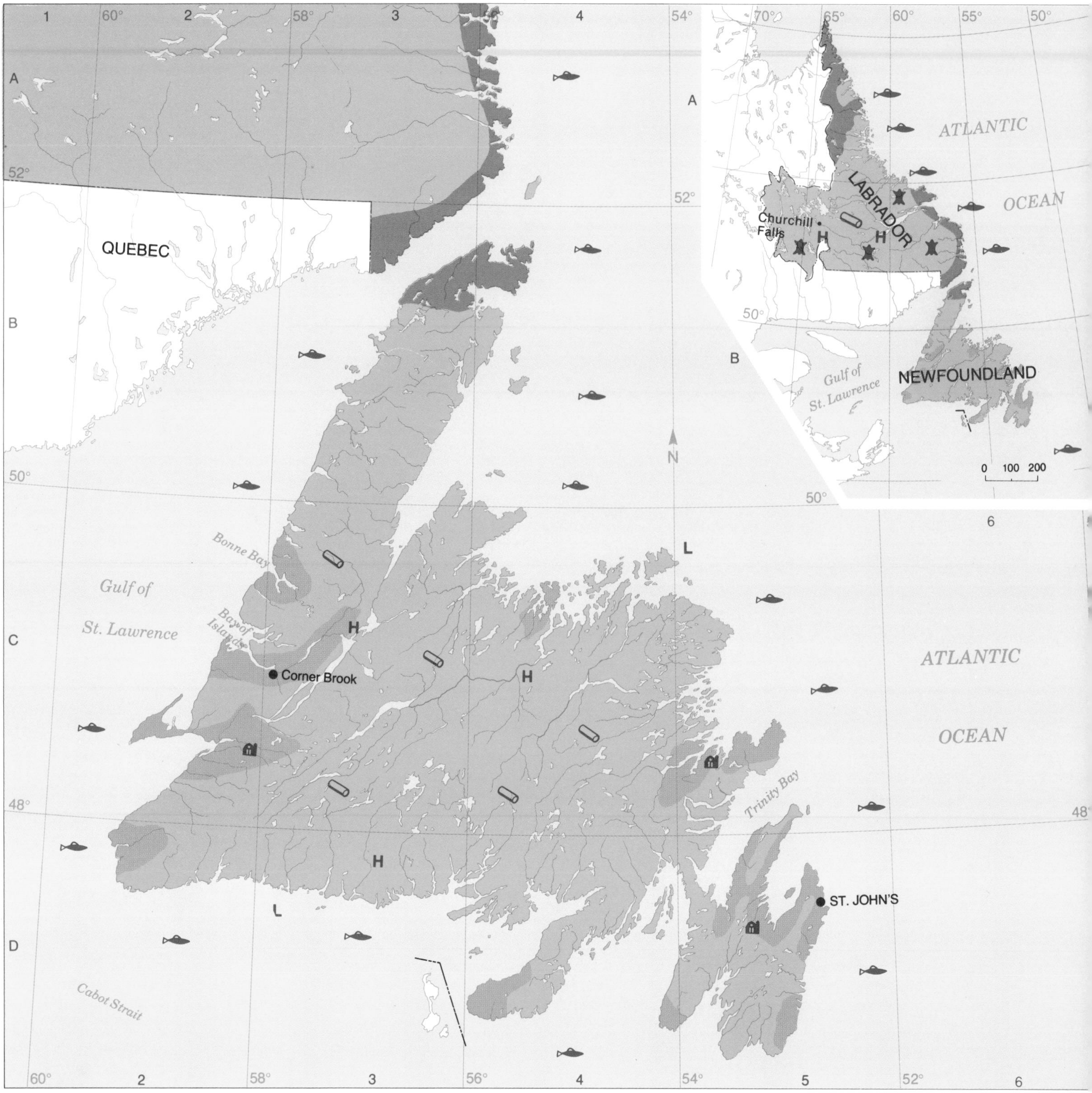

Scale in kilometres
0 — 100

Tundra*	
Mainly Forested Land	
Mainly Farmland	
Mixed Farming*	

Fishing*	
L	Lobster Fishing
Trapping	
Logging and Lumbering*	
H	Hydro-electric Power Plants*

*These terms are explained in the Glossary.

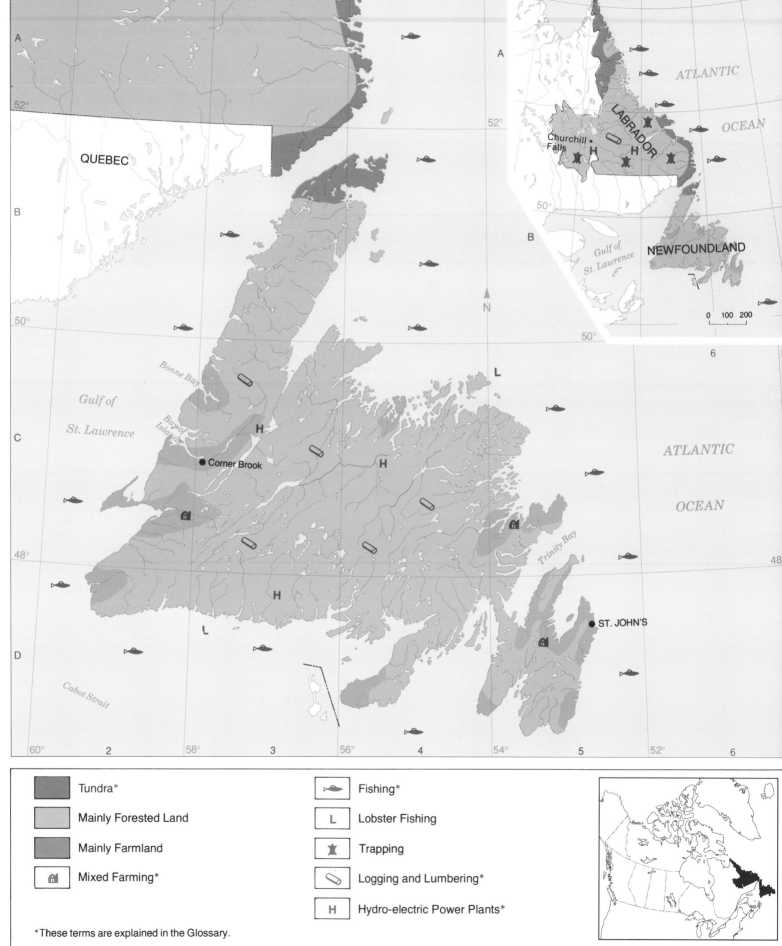

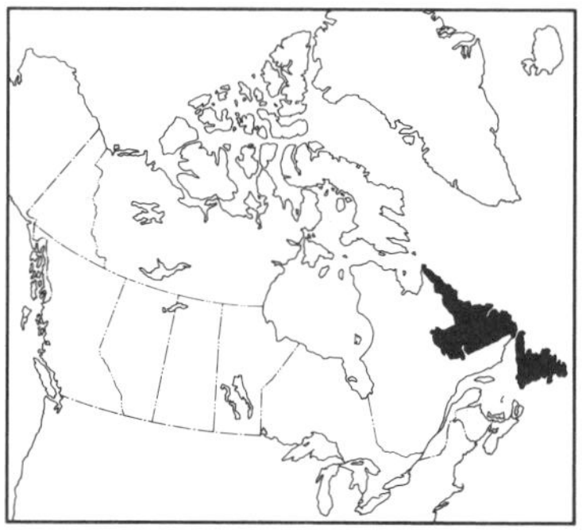

va Scotia *Fish, Furs, Farms, and Forests*

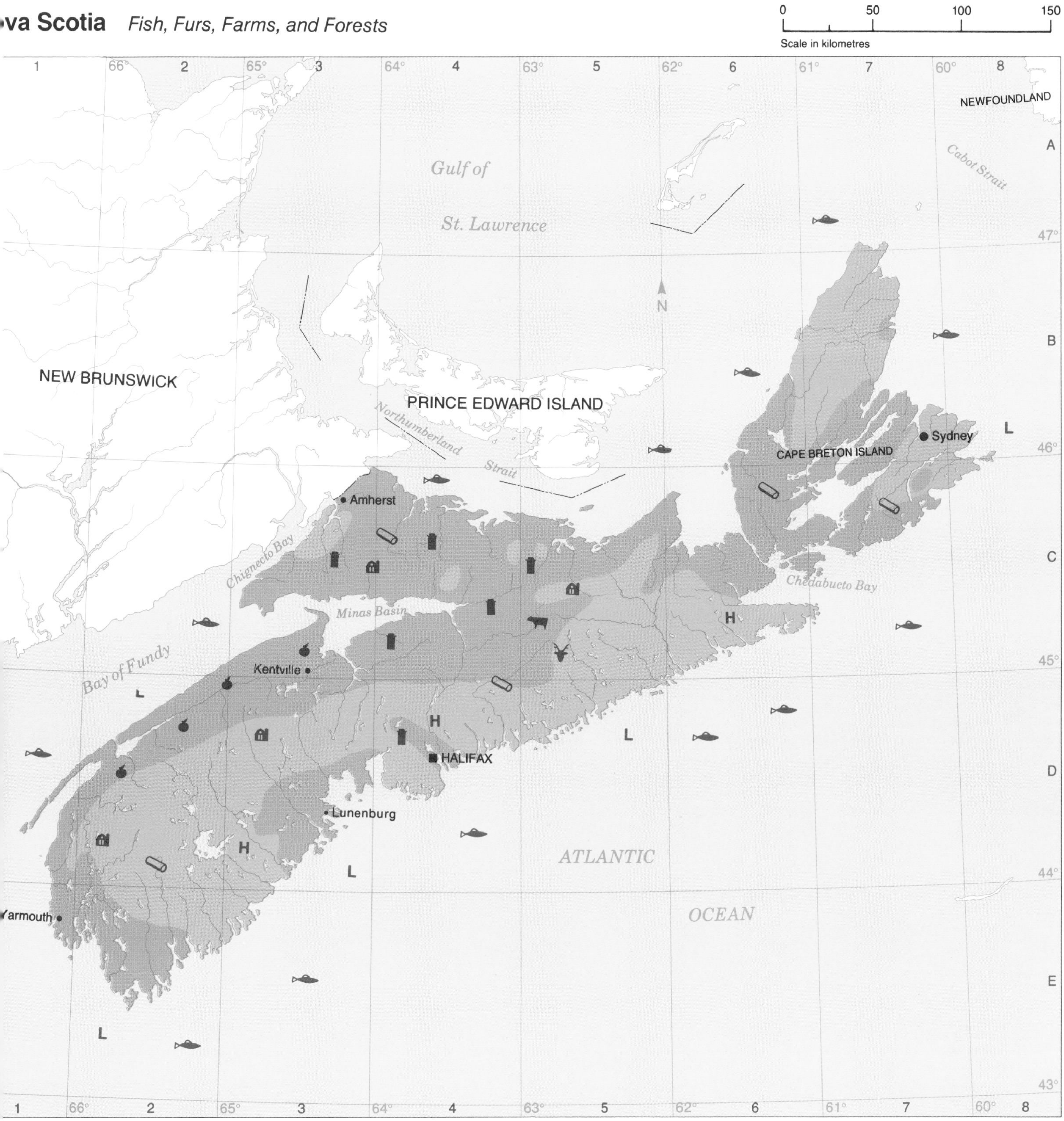

Mainly Forested Land

Mainly Farmland

Fishing*

L Lobster Fishing

Hunting

Logging and Lumbering*

Dairy Farming*

Fruit Farming*

Livestock*

Mixed Farming*

H Hydro-electric Power Plants*

*These terms are explained in the Glossary.

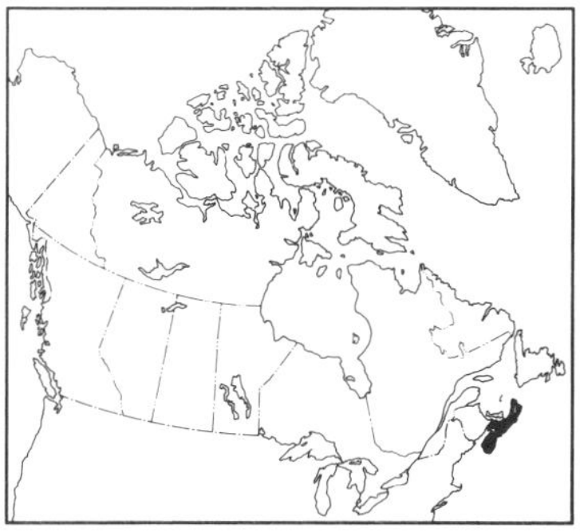

Prince Edward Island *Fish, Furs, Farms, and Forests*

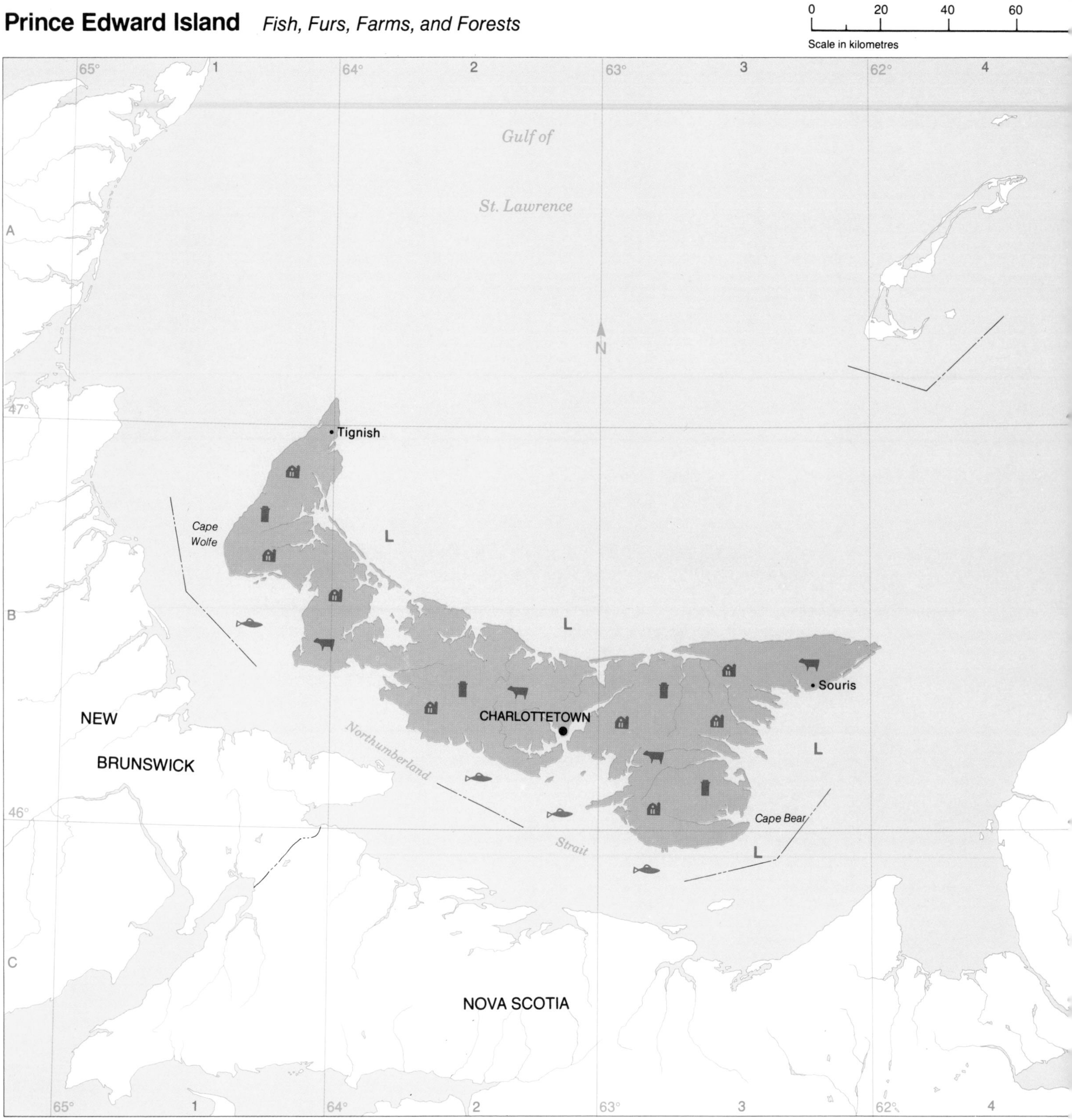

ew Brunswick *Fish, Furs, Farms, and Forests*

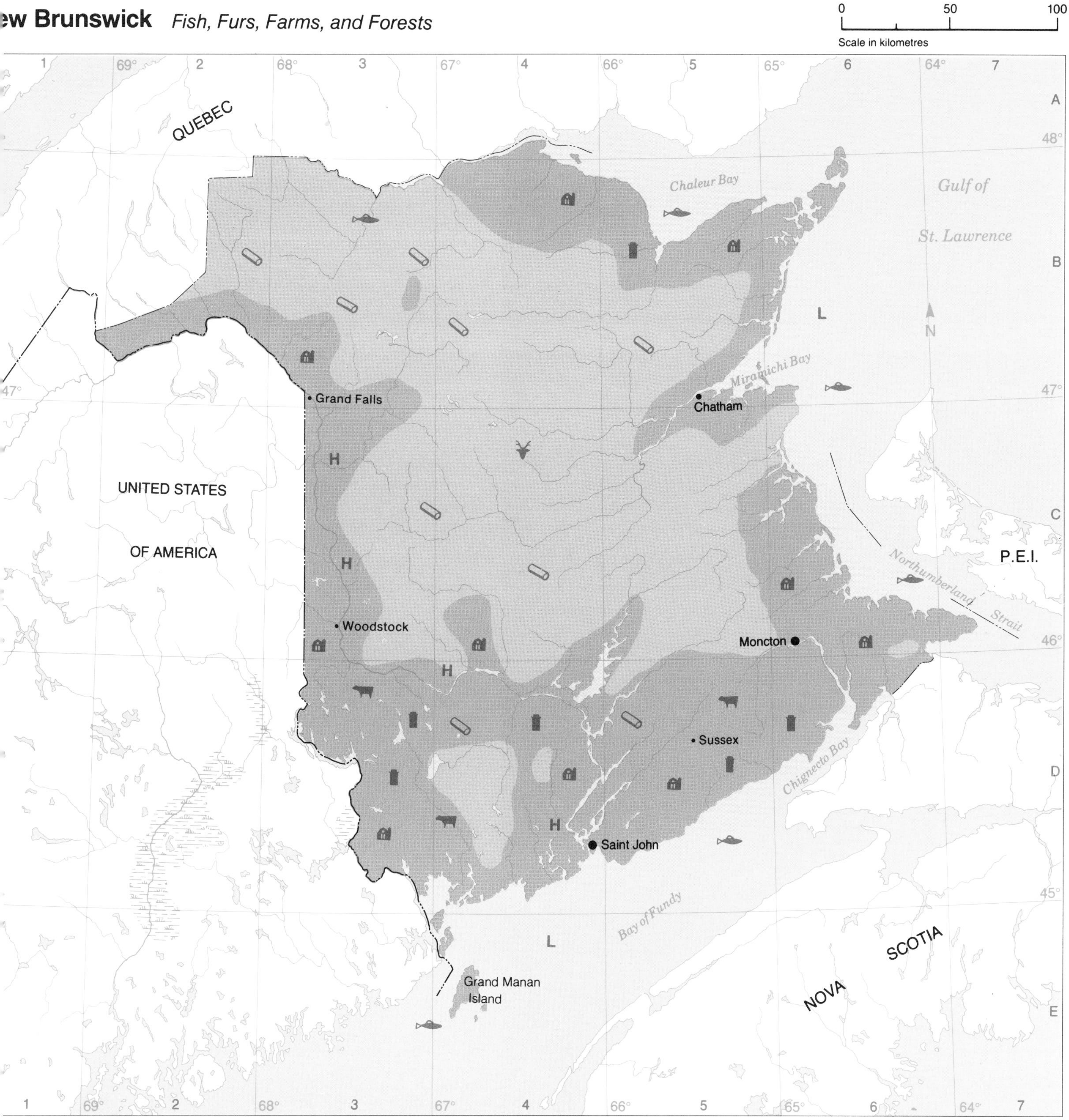

Mainly Forested Land

Mainly Farmland

Fishing*

Lobster Fishing

Hunting

Dairy Farming*

Livestock*

Mixed Farming*

Logging and Lumbering*

Hydro-electric Power Plants*

*These terms are explained in the Glossary.

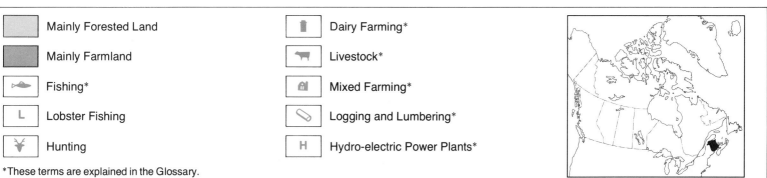

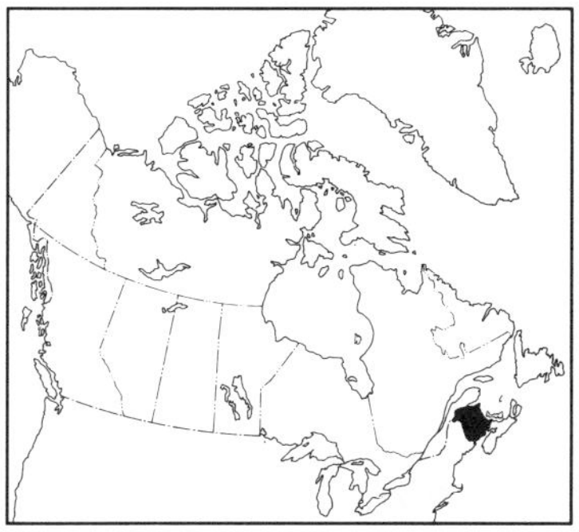

Quebec *Fish, Furs, Farms, and Forests*

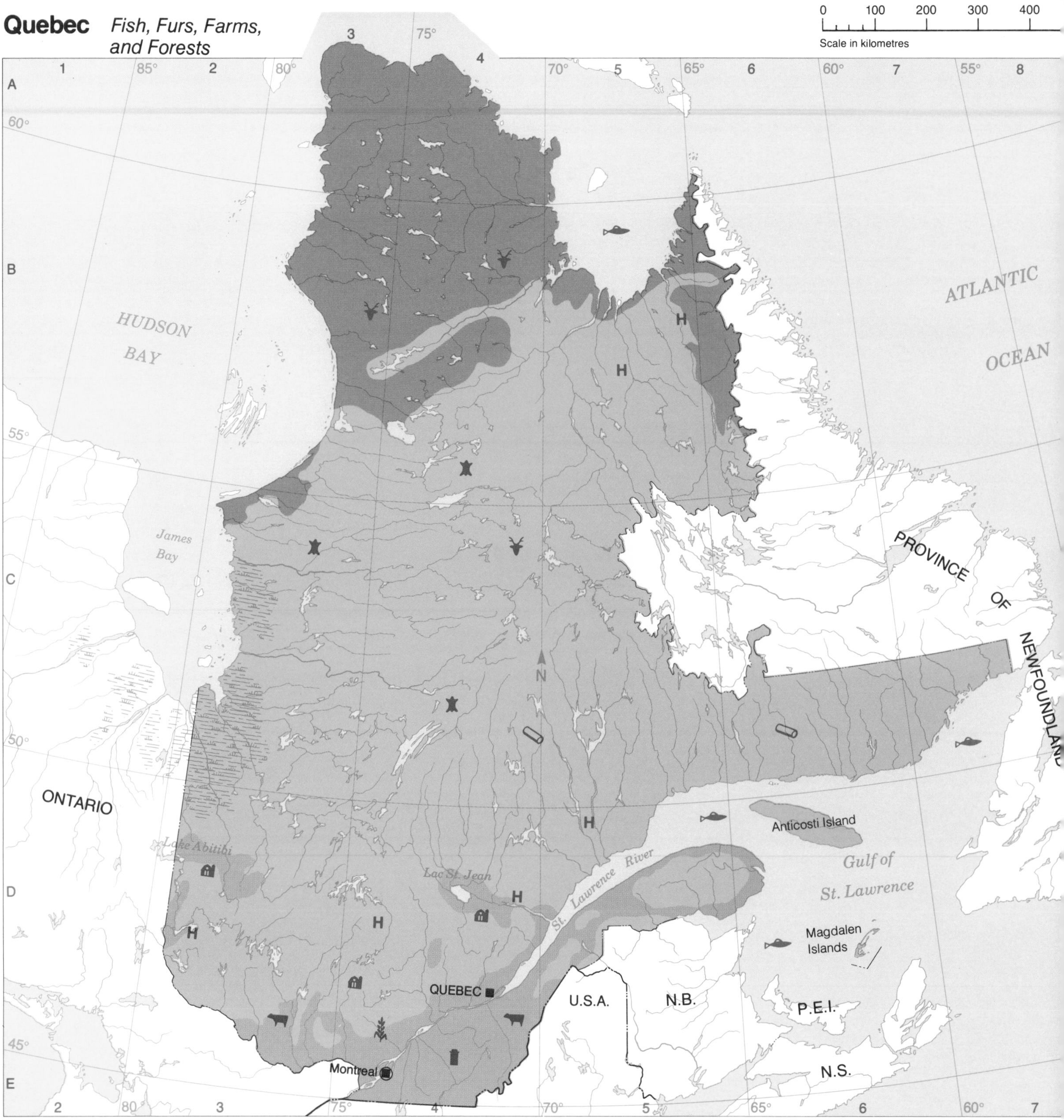
0 100 200 300 400
Scale in kilometres
A
B
C
D
E
1
2
3
4
5
6
7
8
85°
80°
75°
70°
65°
60°
55°
60°
55°
50°
45°
HUDSON BAY
James Bay
ATLANTIC OCEAN
PROVINCE OF NEWFOUNDLAND
ONTARIO
Lake Abitibi
Lac St. Jean
St. Lawrence River
Anticosti Island
Gulf of St. Lawrence
Magdalen Islands
QUEBEC
Montreal
U.S.A.
N.B.
P.E.I.
N.S.
N
H

Tundra*
Mainly Forested Land
Mainly Farmland
Dairy Farming*
Mixed Farming*
Grain Farming*
Livestock*
Logging and Lumbering*
Fishing*
Hydro-electric Power Plants*
Hunting
Trapping

*These terms are explained in the Glossary.

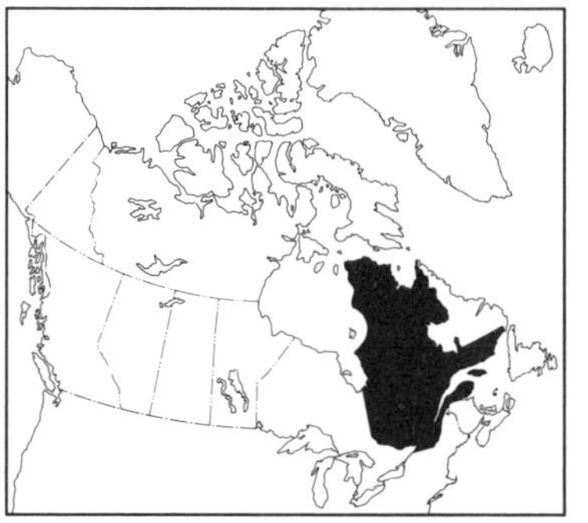

Ontario *Fish, Furs, Farms, and Forests*

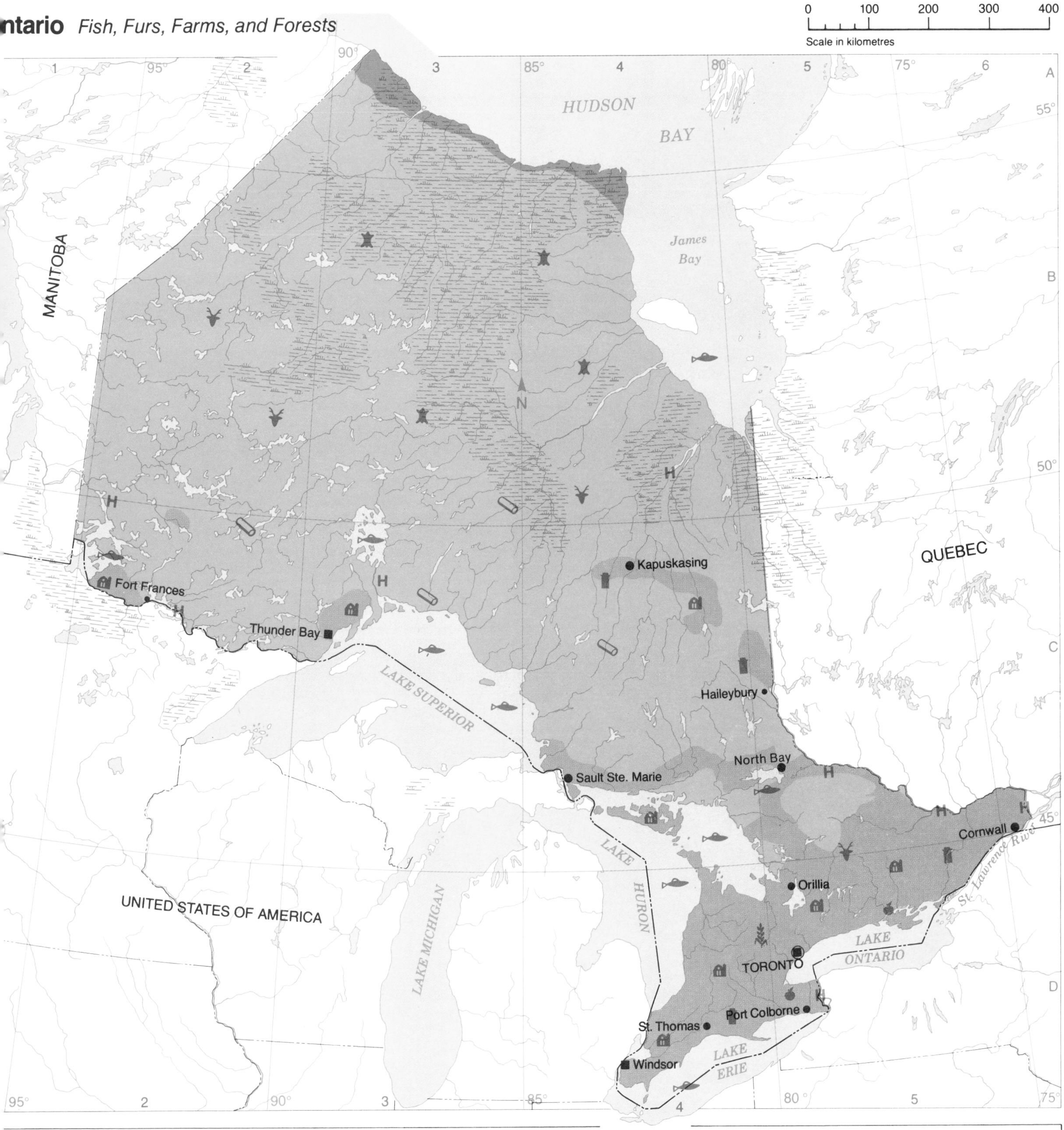

0 100 200 300 400
Scale in kilometres
HUDSON
BAY
James
Bay
MANITOBA
QUEBEC
UNITED STATES OF AMERICA
Kapuskasing
Fort Frances
Thunder Bay
LAKE SUPERIOR
Haileybury
North Bay
Sault Ste. Marie
Cornwall
St. Lawrence River
LAKE
HURON
Orillia
LAKE MICHIGAN
TORONTO
LAKE
ONTARIO
Port Colborne
St. Thomas
Windsor
LAKE
ERIE
55°
50°
45°
95°
90°
85°
80°
75°
A
B
C
D
1
2
3
4
5
6
N
H

Tundra*

Mainly Forested Land

Mainly Farmland

Marsh*

Mixed Farming*

Dairy Farming*

Fruit Farming*

Grain Farming*

Hunting

Fishing*

Trapping

Logging and Lumbering*

Hydro-electric Power Plants*

*These terms are explained in the Glossary.

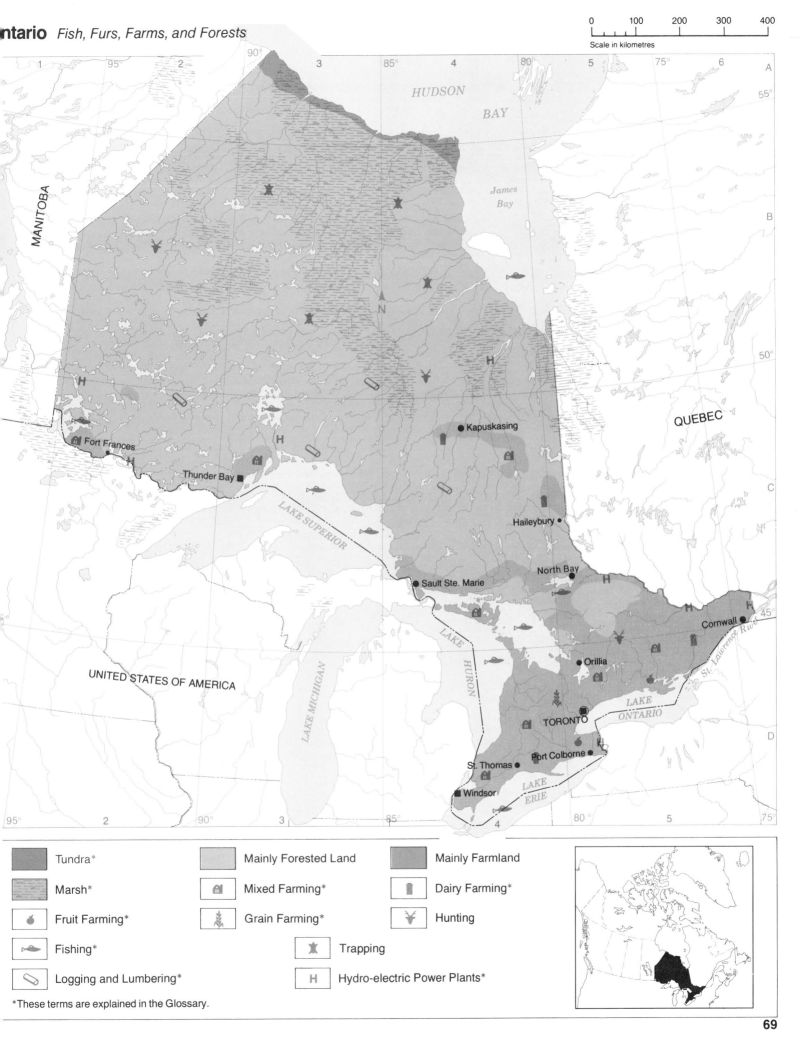

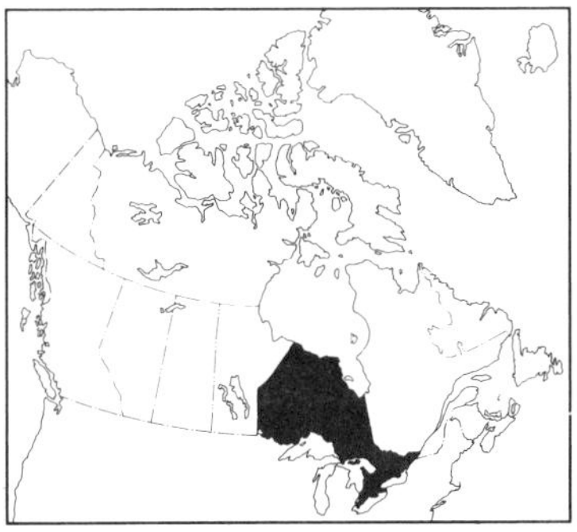

Manitoba *Fish, Furs, Farms, and Forests*

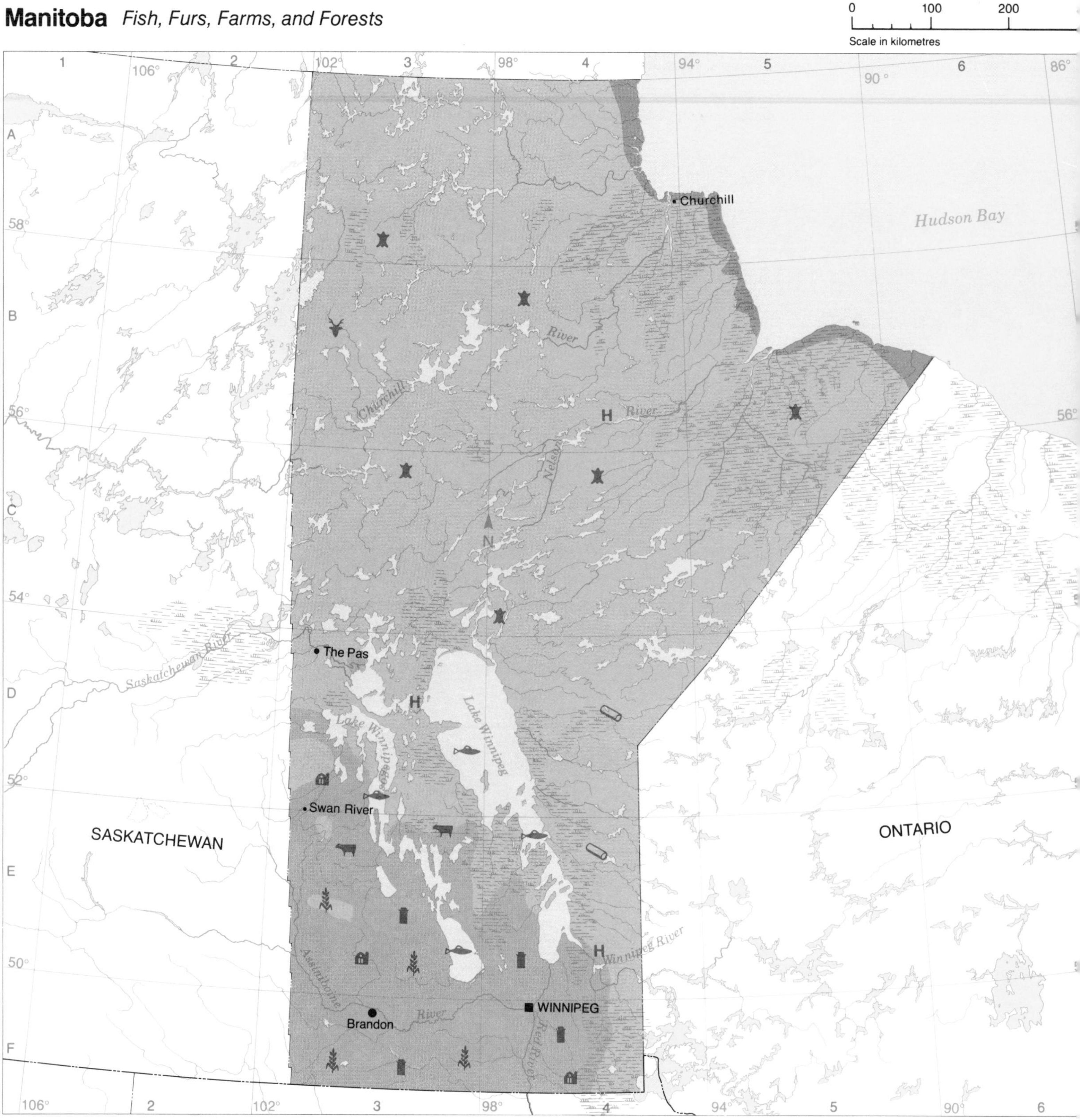

Tundra*

Mainly Forested Land

Mainly Farmland

Mixed Farming*

Dairy Farming*

Grain Farming*

Livestock*

Hunting

Trapping

Logging and Lumbering*

Fishing*

H Hydro-electric Power Plants*

*These terms are explained in the Glossary.

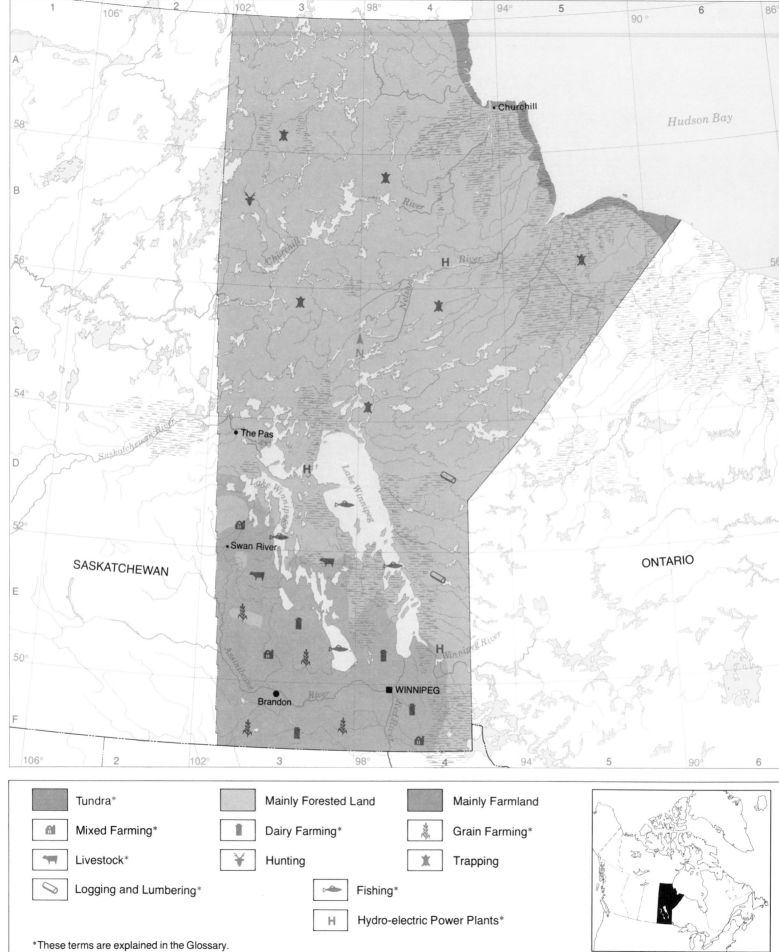

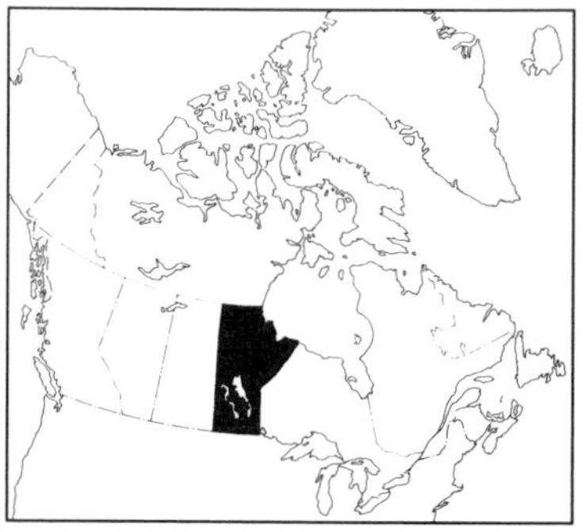

askatchewan *Fish, Furs, Farms, and Forests*

0 100 200 300
Scale in kilometres

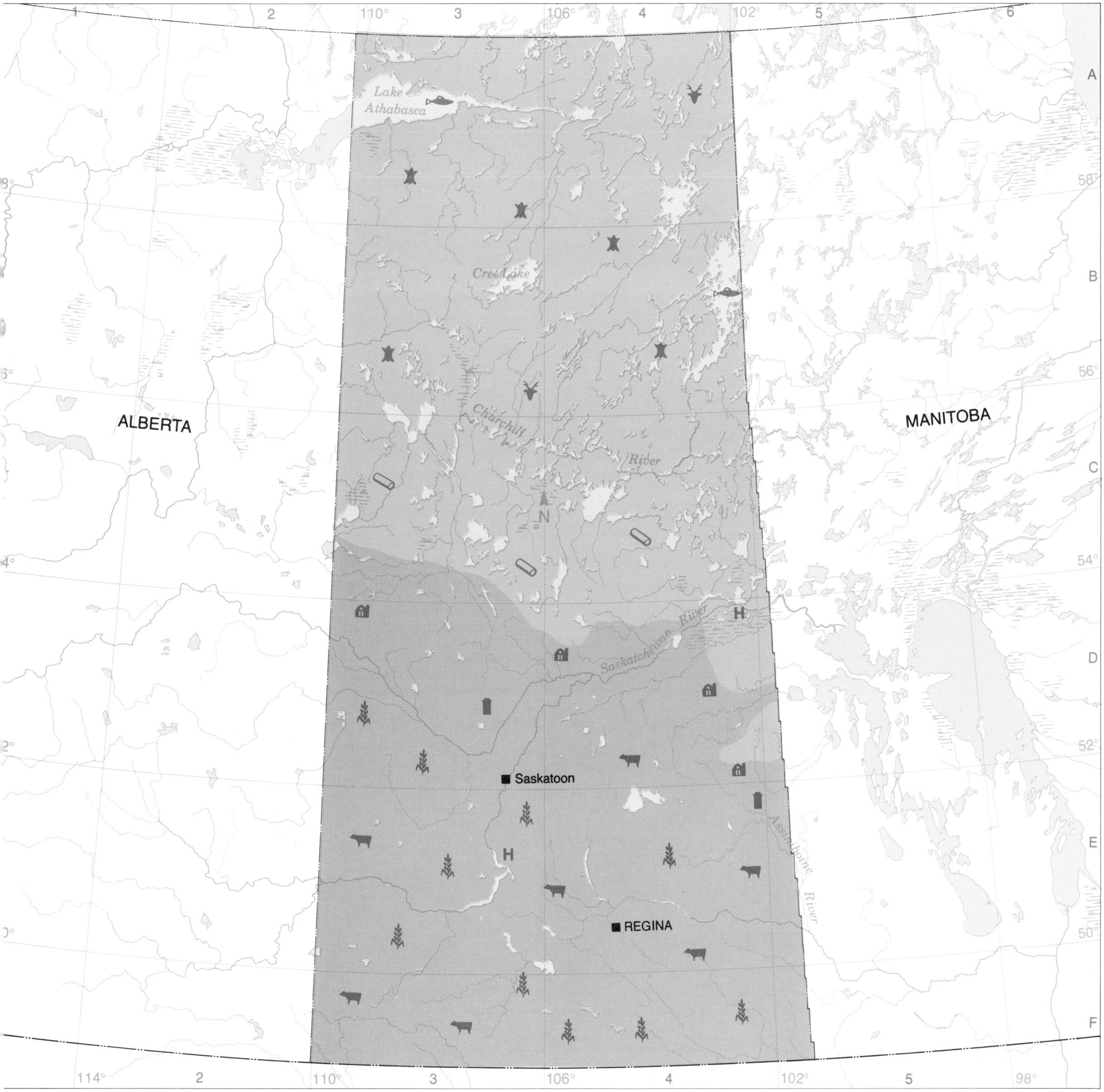

- Mainly Forested Land
- Mainly Farmland
- Mixed Farming*
- Grain Farming*
- Dairy Farming*
- Livestock*
- Hunting
- Trapping
- H Hydro-electric Power Plants*
- Logging and Lumbering*
- Fishing*

*These terms are explained in the Glossary.

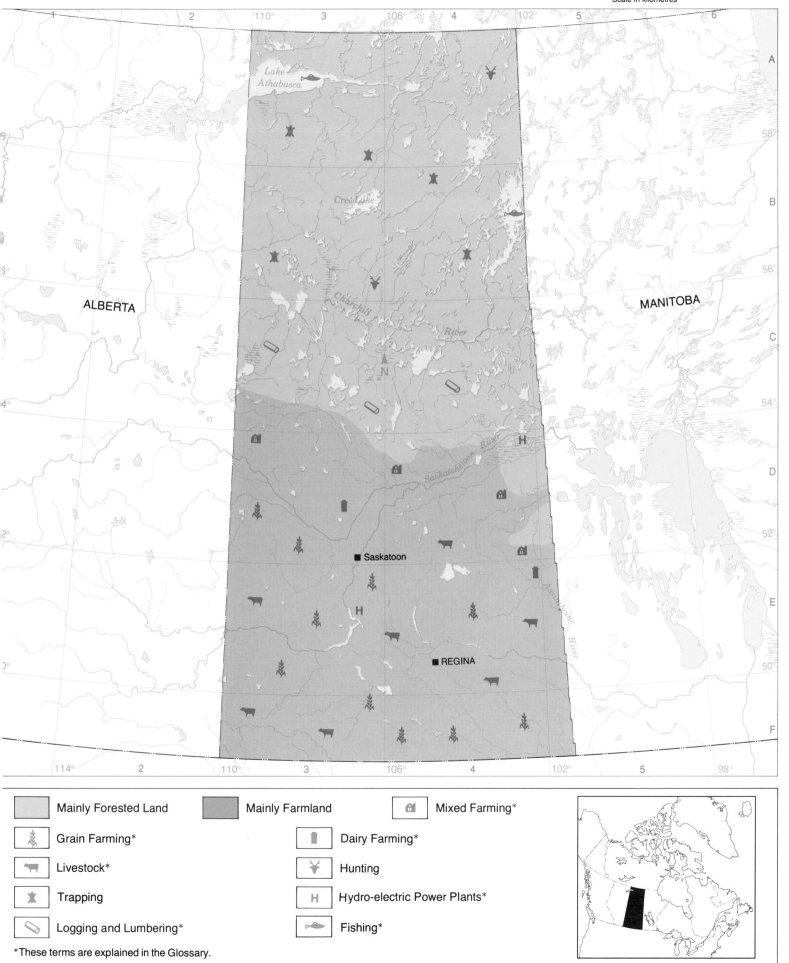

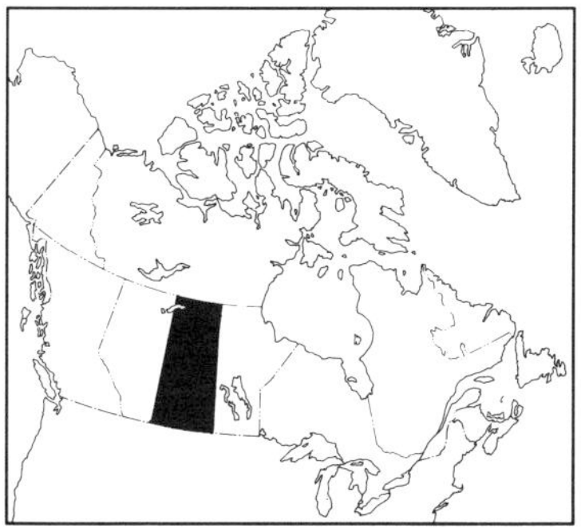

Alberta *Fish, Furs, Farms, and Forests*

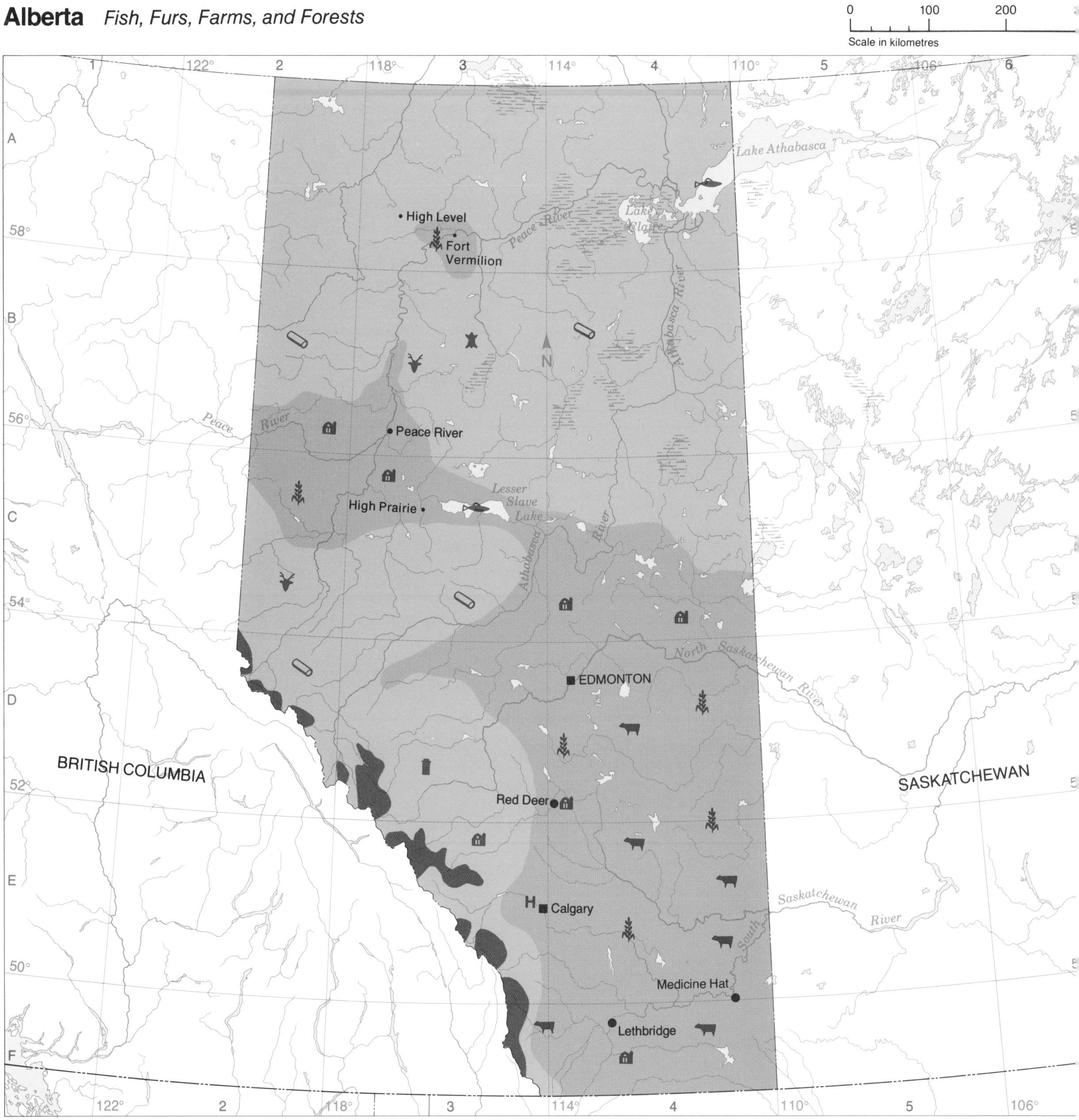

- Alpine Regions*
- Mainly Forested Land
- Mainly Farmland
- Mixed Farming*
- Grain Farming*
- Dairy Farming*
- Livestock*
- Marsh*
- Fishing*
- Hunting
- Trapping
- Logging and Lumbering*
- H Hydro-electric Power Plants*

*These terms are explained in the Glossary.

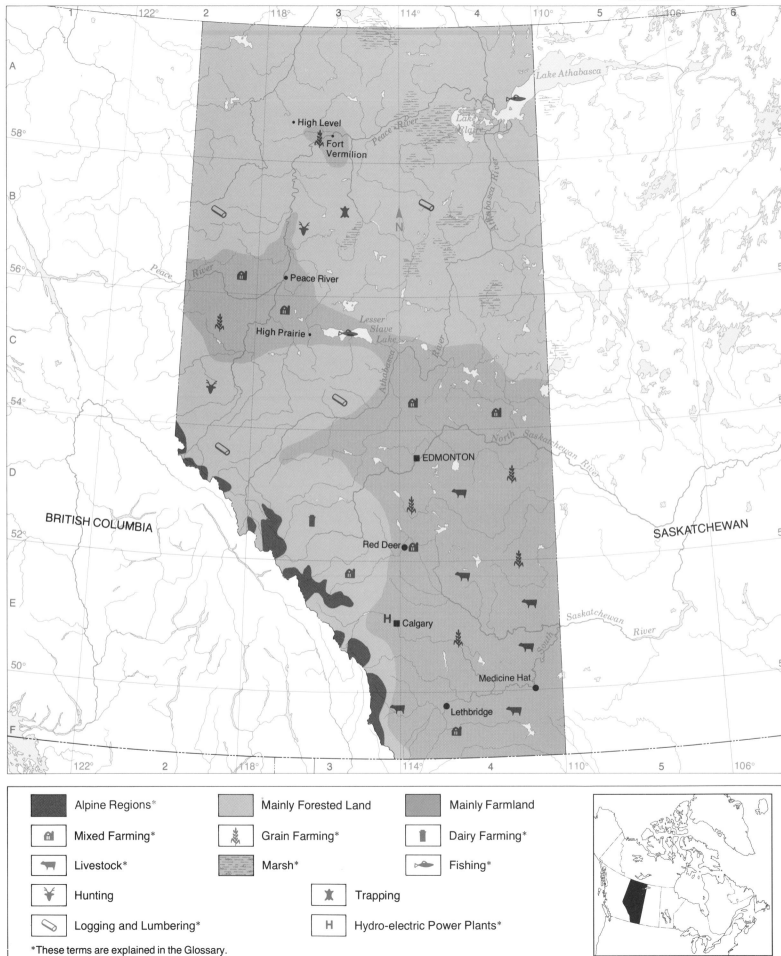

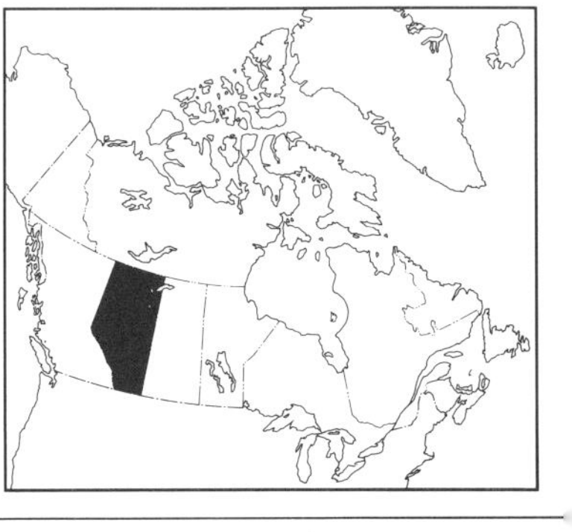

British Columbia *Fish, Furs, Farms, and Forests*

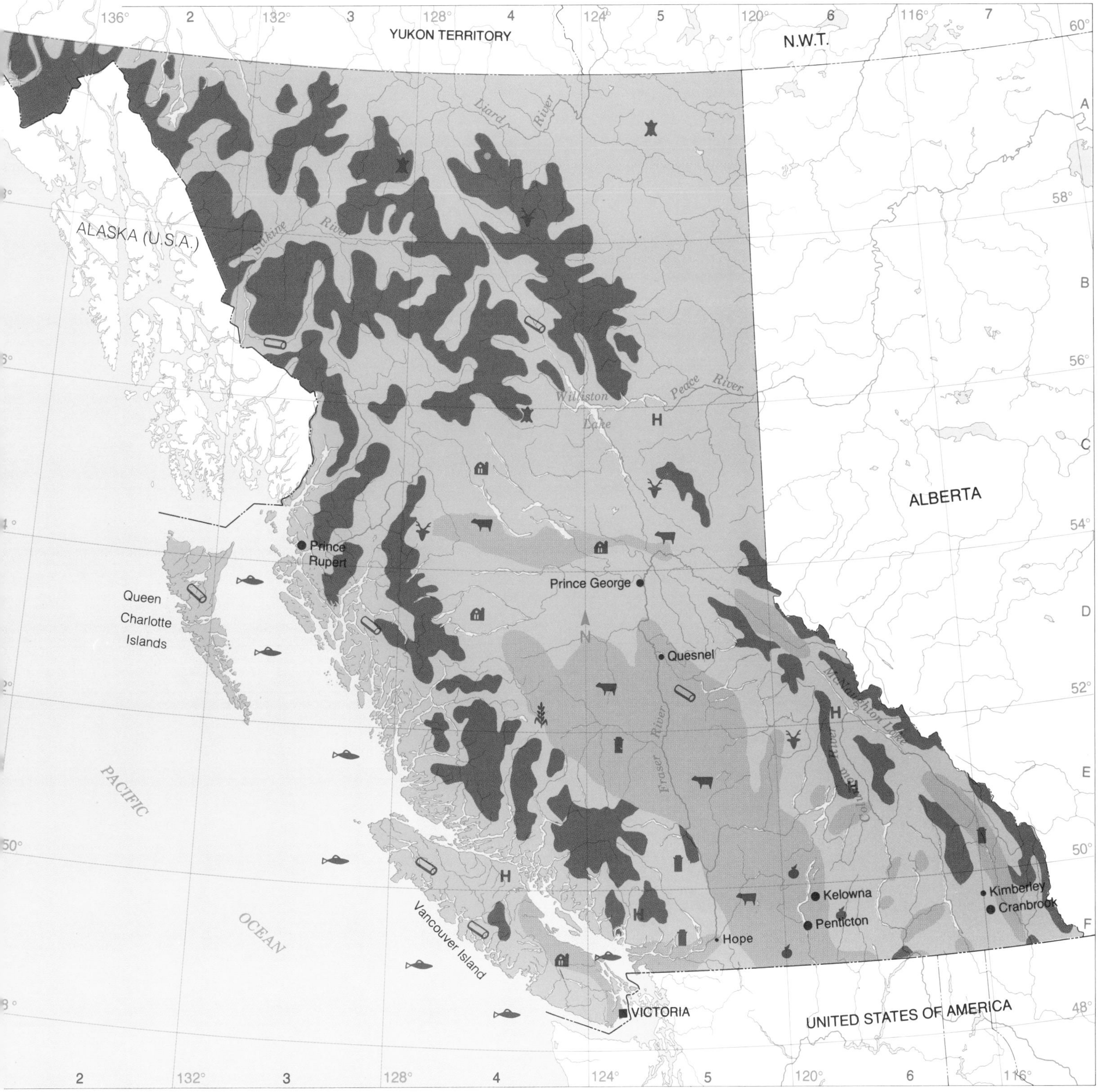

Alpine Regions*
Mainly Forested Land
Mainly Farmland
Mixed Farming*
Livestock*
Dairy Farming*
Grain Farming*
Fruit Farming*
Hunting
Trapping
Fishing*
Logging and Lumbering*
Hydro-electric Power Plants*

*These terms are explained in the Glossary.

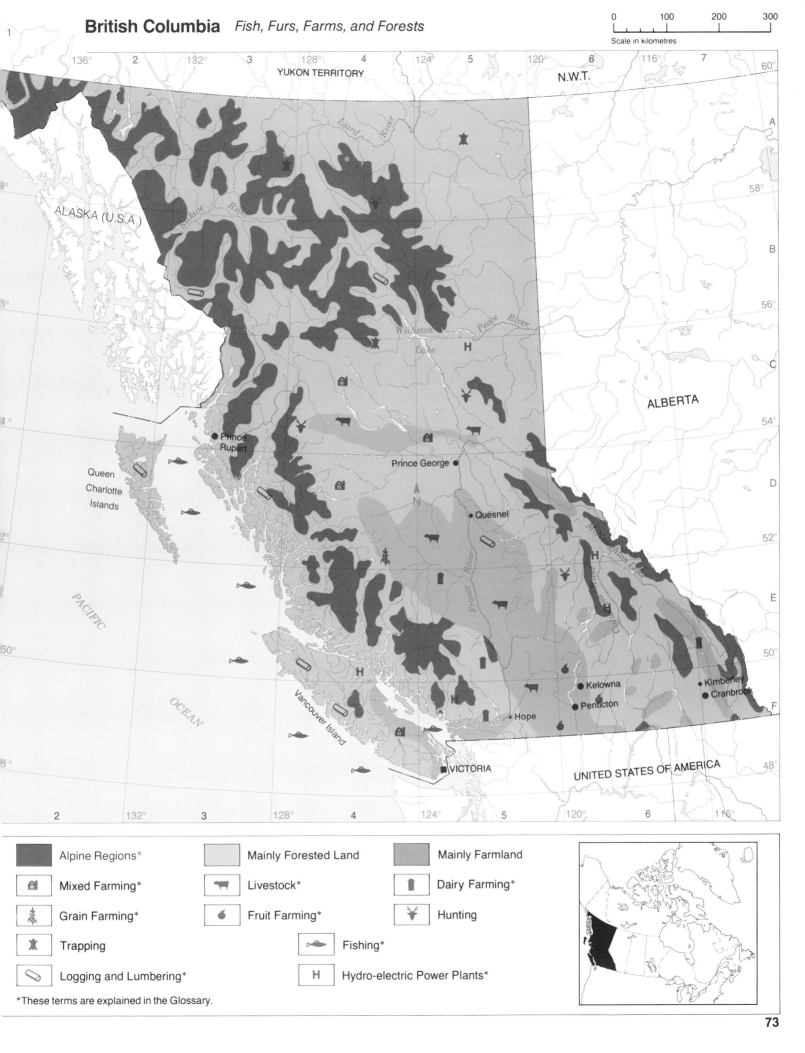

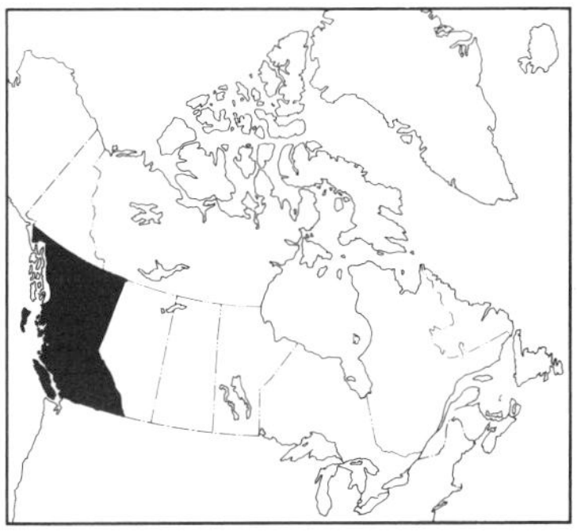

150°
B
1
140°
2
130°
3
120°
4
110°
C
D
E
ARCTIC OCEAN
Melville Island
Banks Island
Beaufort Sea
ALASKA (U.S.A.)
Arctic Circle
65°
Victoria Island
NORTHWEST T
YUKON TERRITORY
Great Bear Lake
Mackenzie River
60°
WHITEHORSE
YELLOWKNIFE
Great Slave Lake
BRITISH COLUMBIA
ALBERTA
2
130°
3
120°
4
110°

Tundra*

Mainly Forested Land

Fishing*

Trapping

*These terms are explained in the Glossary.

Hunting

Logging and Lumbering*

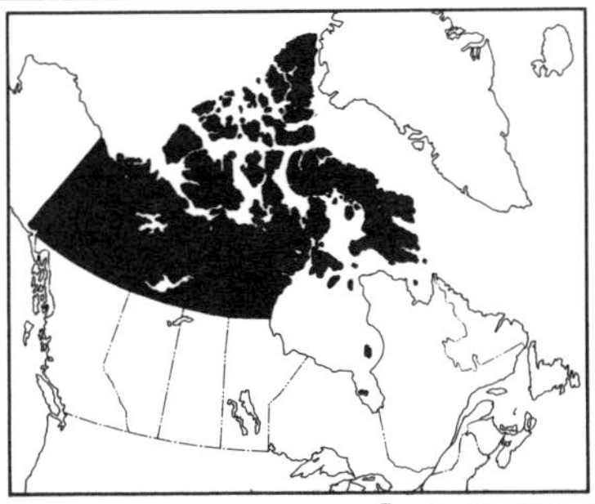

USING LAND AND WATER

MINERALS AND MINERAL FUELS

The maps in this part of the section on Using Land and Water show "crops" that are taken out of mines and wells in the earth. Many of the minerals will be unfamiliar to you. As you read the maps, use the *Glossary*. It describes each of these minerals and tells what it's used for.

1. In what provinces are oil and gas found?
2. How are they transported to other parts of Canada?
3. What is the approximate length of the oil pipeline from Edmonton to Sarnia?
4. What is the approximate length of the gas pipeline from Calgary to Montreal?
5. In what general direction do the pipelines flow?
6. From a quick reading of the maps, which two provinces have more mines than any of the other provinces?
7. List the minerals found in the Atlantic Provinces.
8. In what provinces is gold mined?
9. What is the only province in which potash is mined?
10. Match each mineral in the left-hand column with a place in the right-hand column.

copper	Flin Flon, Man.
iron	Uranium City, Sask.
nickel	Schefferville, Que.
salt	Lindbergh, Alta.
uranium	Revelstoke, B.C.
zinc	Copper Cliff, Ont.

11. Where is each of the following minerals mined and what is it used for?

asbestos	limestone
coal	quartz
lead	silver

anada: Oil and Gas Pipelines

Gas Wells	Oil Wells
Gas Pipelines	Oil Pipelines

Atlantic Canada *Minerals and Mineral Fuels*

0
100
200
Scale in kilometres
LABRADOR
Labrador City
Wabush
QUEBEC
PROVINCE OF NEWFOUNDLAND
ATLANTIC OCEAN
Baie Verte
Buchans
Flat Bay
ST. JOHN'S
St. Lawrence River
QUEBEC
Gulf of St. Lawrence
Bathurst
Newcastle
N.B.
CHARLOTTETOWN
P.E.I.
CAPE BRETON ISLAND
Inverness
Sydney
Minto
Havelock
FREDERICTON
Nappan
Pugwash
Springhill
Pictou
River Denys
Irish Cove
U.S.A.
Bay of Fundy
Milford Station
N.S.
HALIFAX
ATLANTIC OCEAN

Symbol	Mineral	Symbol	Mineral
A	Asbestos*	□	Limestone
C	Copper*	△	Salt
G	Gypsum*	Z	Zinc*
I	Iron*	▲	Coal
●	Lead*		

*Some of the uses of these minerals are explained in the Glossary.

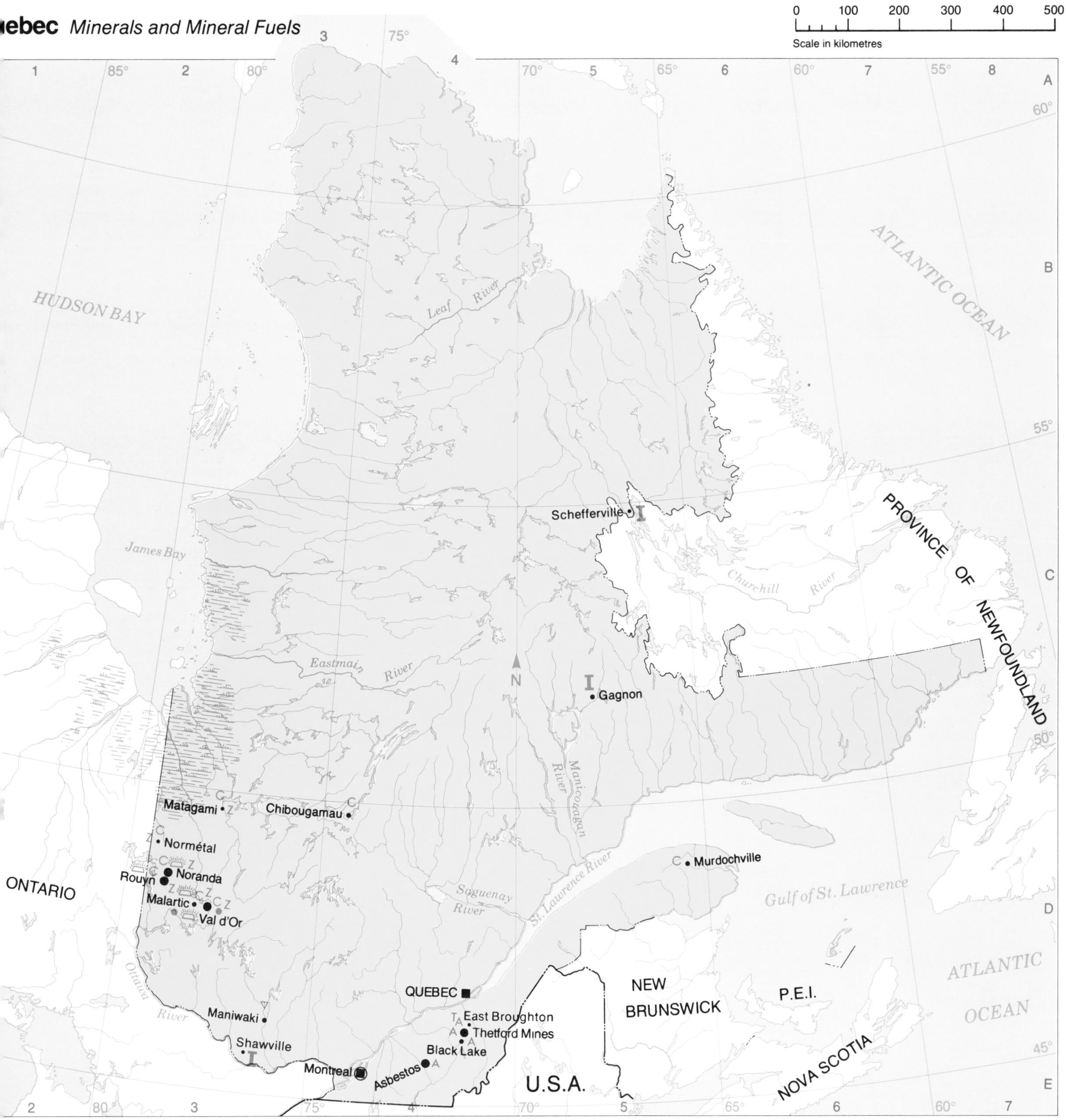
0 100 200 300 400 500
Scale in kilometres
HUDSON BAY
James Bay
Leaf River
Eastmain River
Churchill River
ATLANTIC OCEAN
PROVINCE OF NEWFOUNDLAND
Schefferville
Gagnon
Matagami
Chibougamau
Normétal
Noranda
Rouyn
Malartic
Val d'Or
ONTARIO
Manicouagan River
Saguenay River
St. Lawrence River
Murdochville
Gulf of St. Lawrence
QUEBEC
East Broughton
Thetford Mines
Black Lake
Asbestos
Montreal
Maniwaki
Shawville
Ottawa River
NEW BRUNSWICK
P.E.I.
NOVA SCOTIA
ATLANTIC OCEAN
U.S.A.

A	Asbestos*
C	Copper*
Gold symbol	Gold*
I	Iron*
▽	Quartz*
Z	Zinc*
T	Talc*

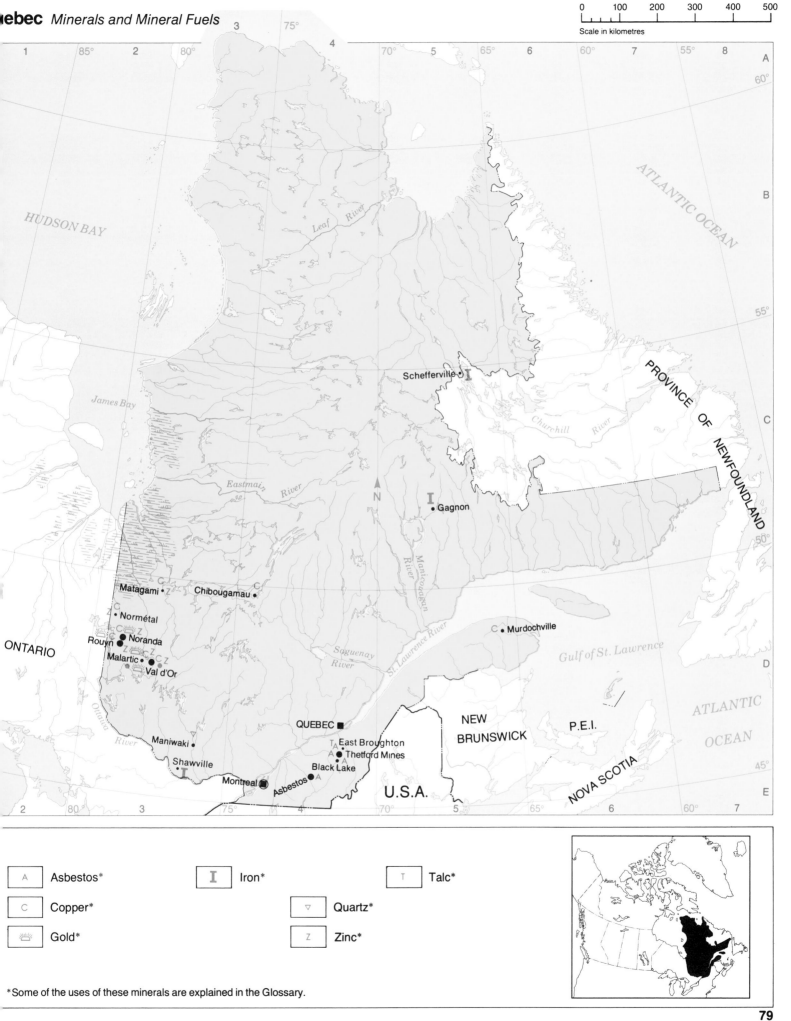

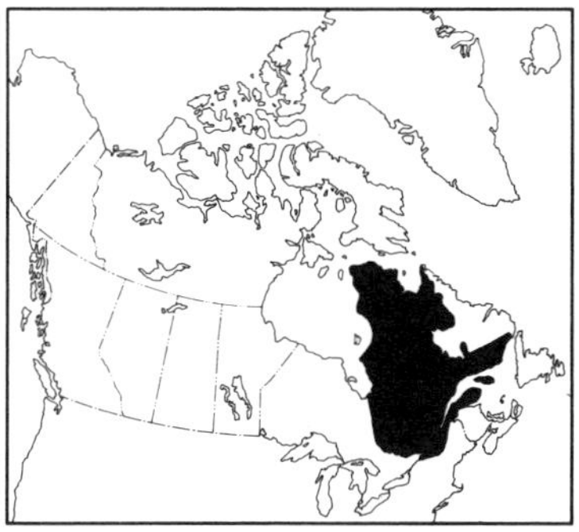

*Some of the uses of these minerals are explained in the Glossary.

Ontario *Minerals and Mineral Fuels*

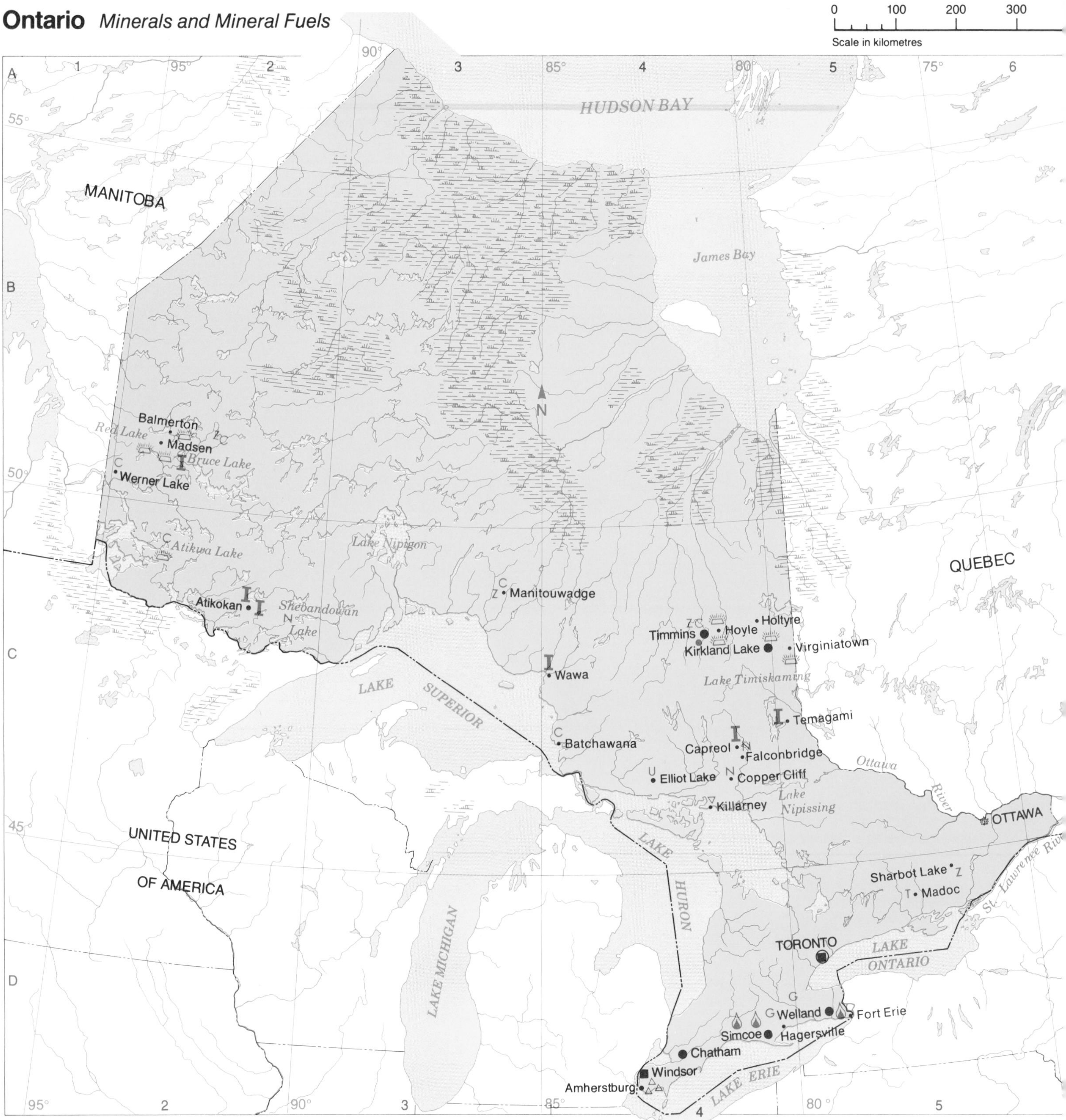
0
100
200
300
Scale in kilometres
HUDSON BAY
James Bay
MANITOBA
QUEBEC
Balmerton
Madsen
Red Lake
Bruce Lake
Werner Lake
Atikwa Lake
Lake Nipigon
Atikokan
Shebandowan Lake
Manitouwadge
Timmins
Hoyle
Holtyre
Kirkland Lake
Virginiatown
Lake Timiskaming
Wawa
Temagami
Batchawana
Capreol
Falconbridge
Elliot Lake
Copper Cliff
Killarney
Lake Nipissing
Ottawa River
OTTAWA
LAKE SUPERIOR
LAKE HURON
LAKE MICHIGAN
UNITED STATES OF AMERICA
Sharbot Lake
Madoc
St. Lawrence River
TORONTO
LAKE ONTARIO
Welland
Fort Erie
Simcoe
Hagersville
Chatham
Windsor
Amherstburg
LAKE ERIE

C Copper*	△ Salt	T Talc*
Gold*	U Uranium*	
G Gypsum*	Z Zinc*	
I Iron*	Gas	
N Nickel*	▽ Quartz*	

*Some of the uses of these minerals are explained in the Glossary.

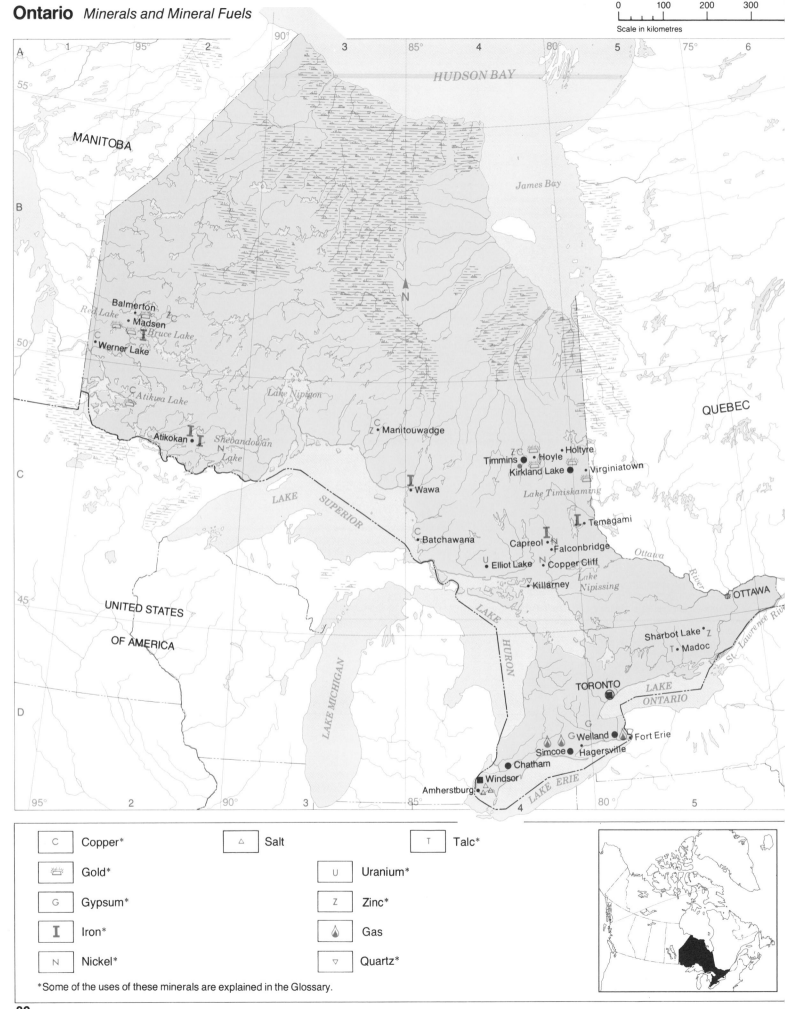

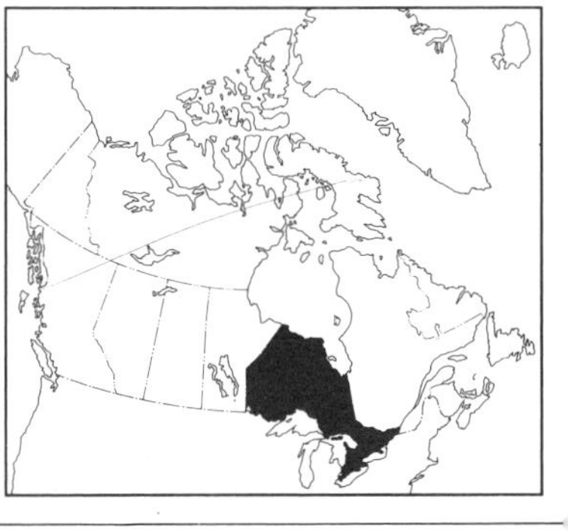

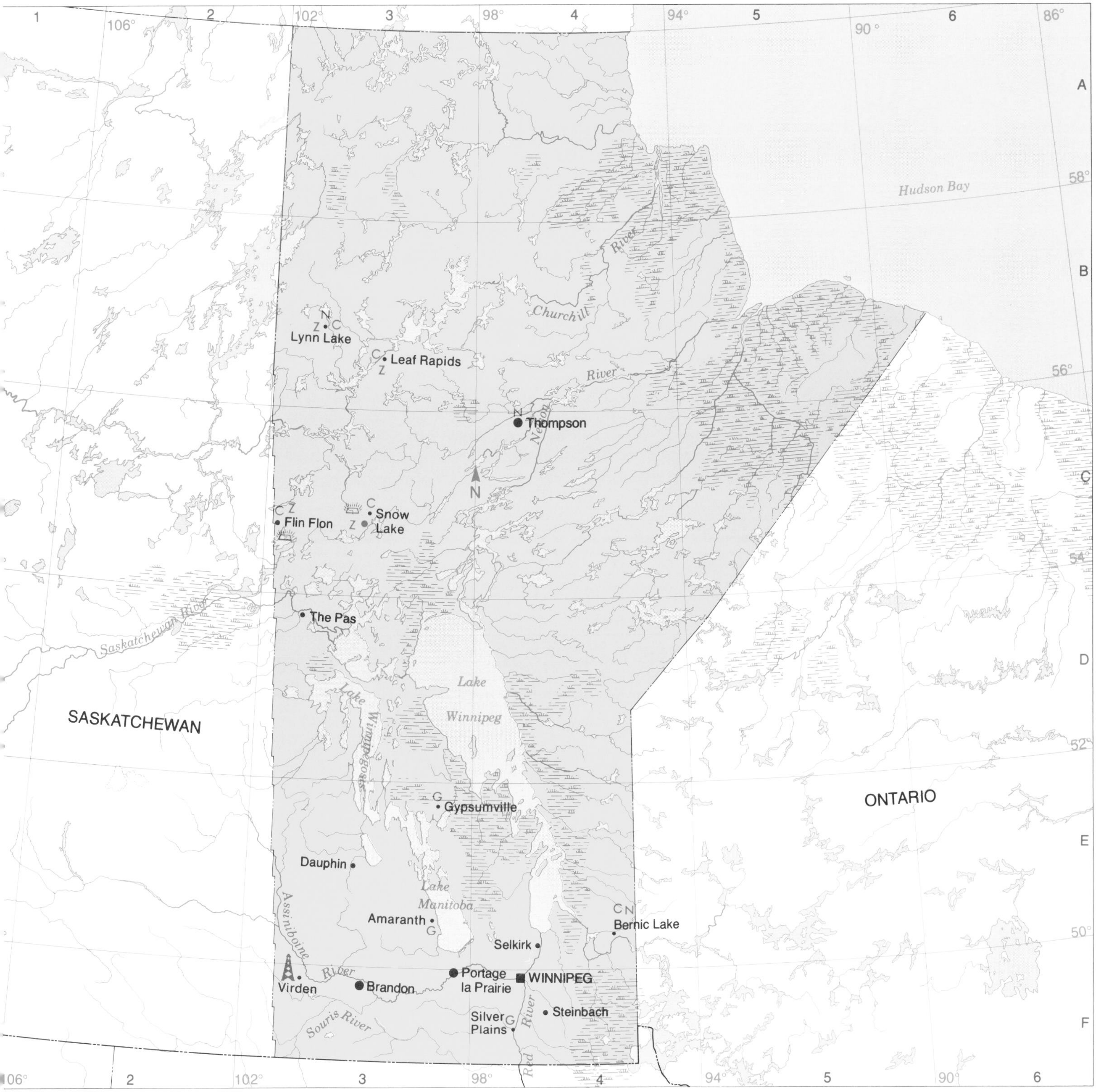
0
100
200
300
Scale in kilometres
Hudson Bay
Churchill
River
River
Nelson
Lynn Lake
Leaf Rapids
Thompson
Flin Flon
Snow Lake
The Pas
Saskatchewan River
Lake Winnipeg
Lake Winnipegosis
SASKATCHEWAN
ONTARIO
Gypsumville
Dauphin
Lake Manitoba
Amaranth
Bernic Lake
Selkirk
Assiniboine
River
Virden
Brandon
Portage la Prairie
WINNIPEG
Steinbach
Silver Plains
Souris River
Red River
106°
102°
98°
94°
90°
86°
58°
56°
54°
52°
50°
A
B
C
D
E
F
1
2
3
4
5
6

C	Copper*	N	Nickel*
(gold symbol)	Gold*	Z	Zinc*
G	Gypsum*	(oil symbol)	Oil

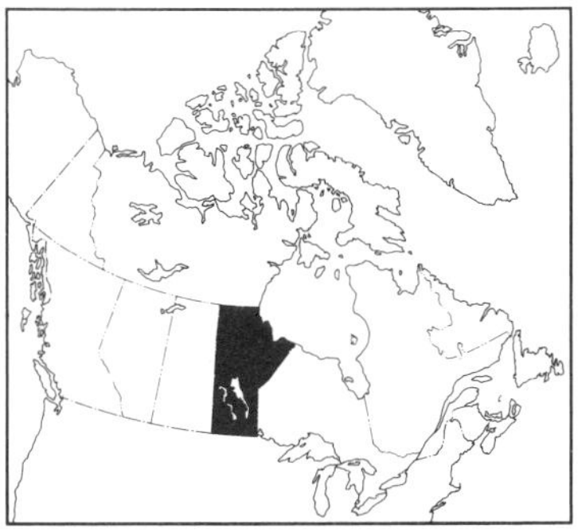

*Some of the uses of these minerals are explained in the Glossary.

Saskatchewan *Minerals and Mineral Fuels*

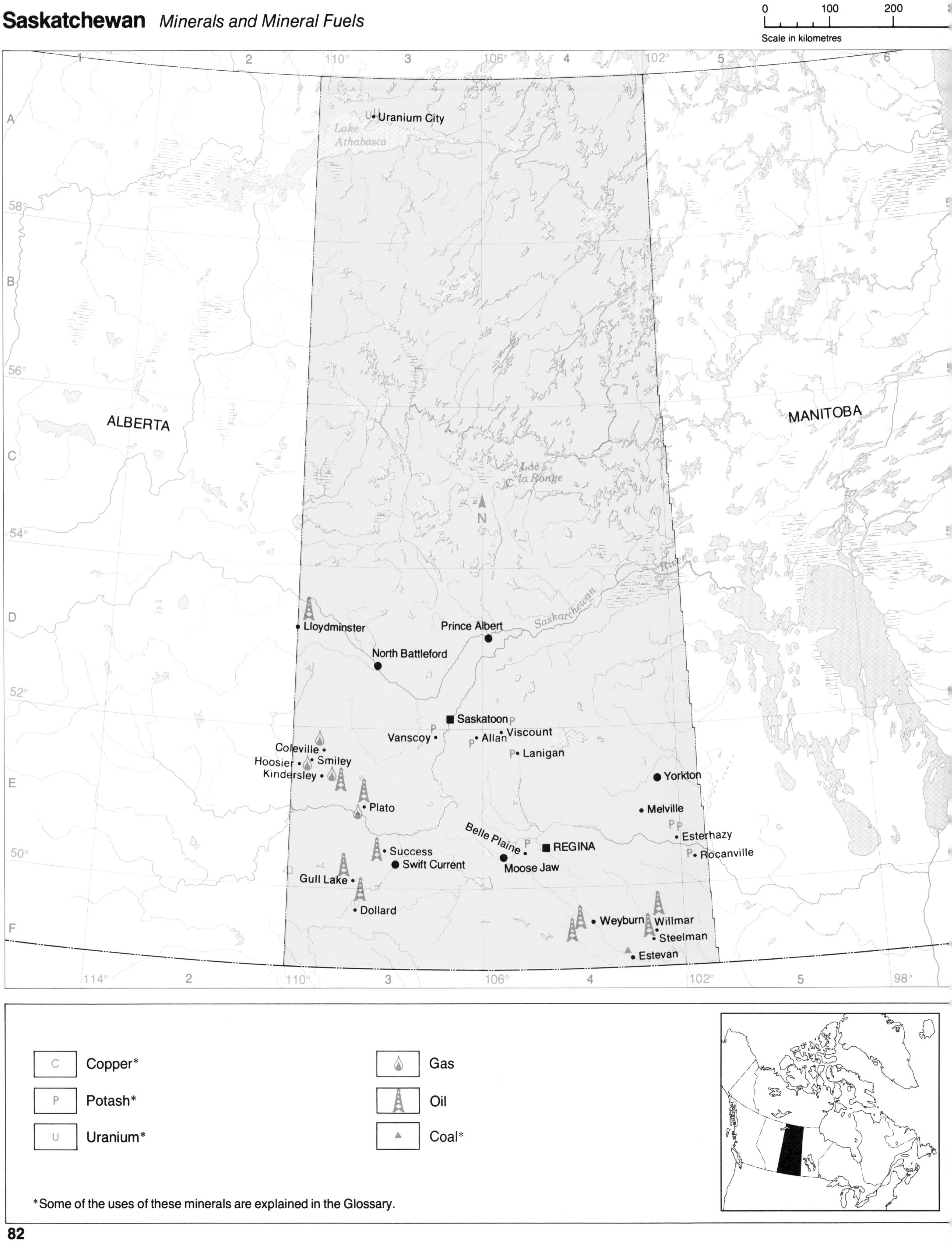

*Some of the uses of these minerals are explained in the Glossary.

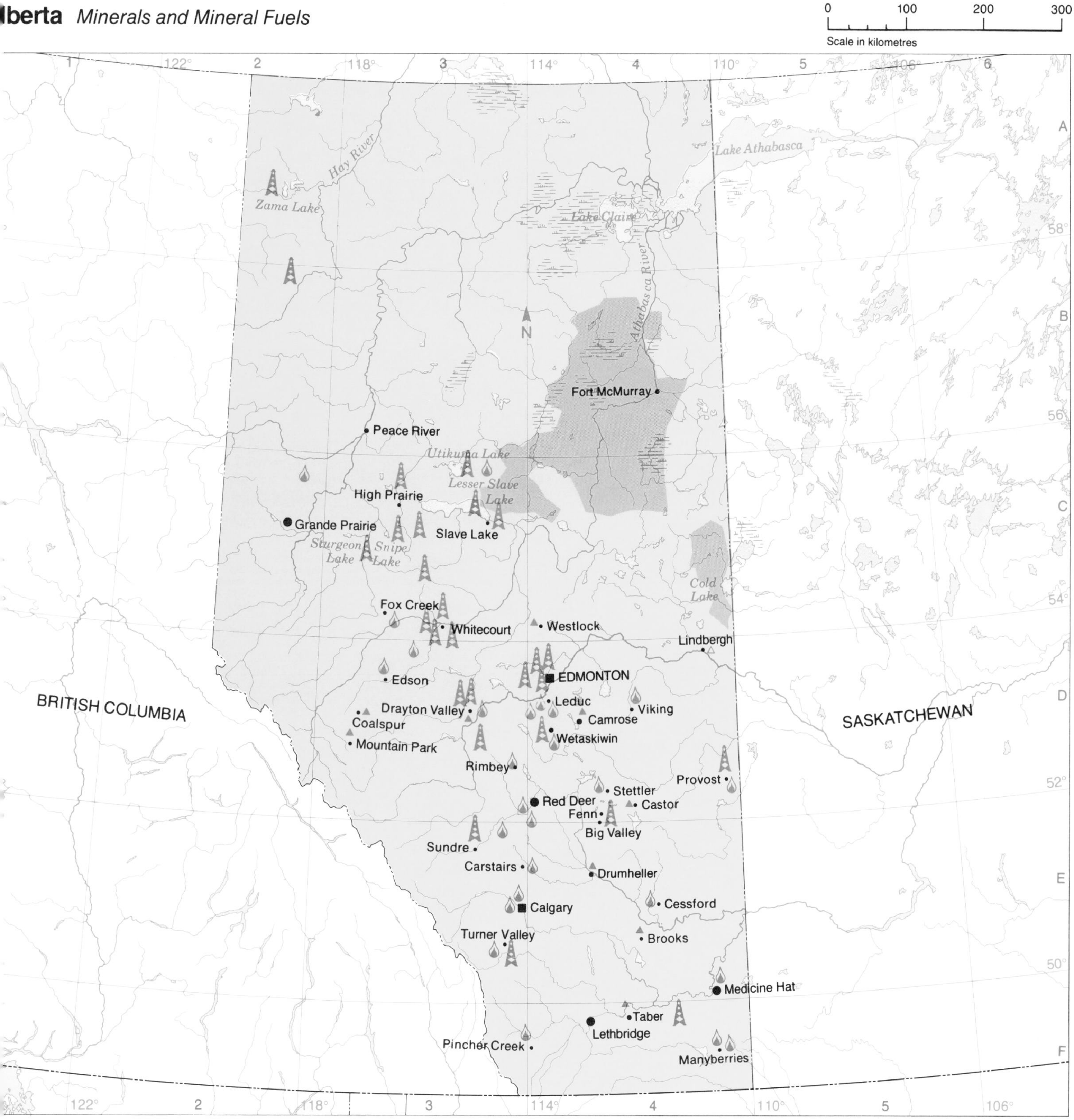
0
100
200
300
Scale in kilometres
Zama Lake
Hay River
Lake Athabasca
Lake Claire
Athabasca River
N
Fort McMurray
Peace River
Utikuma Lake
Lesser Slave Lake
High Prairie
Grande Prairie
Slave Lake
Sturgeon Lake
Snipe Lake
Cold Lake
Fox Creek
Whitecourt
Westlock
Lindbergh
Edson
EDMONTON
BRITISH COLUMBIA
Drayton Valley
Leduc
Viking
Camrose
Coalspur
Mountain Park
Wetaskiwin
SASKATCHEWAN
Rimbey
Provost
Stettler
Red Deer
Castor
Fenn
Big Valley
Sundre
Carstairs
Drumheller
Cessford
Calgary
Turner Valley
Brooks
Medicine Hat
Taber
Lethbridge
Pincher Creek
Manyberries
122°
118°
114°
110°
106°
58°
56°
54°
52°
50°
A
B
C
D
E
F
1
2
3
4
5
6

Coal*

Gas

Tar Sands*

Oil

Salt

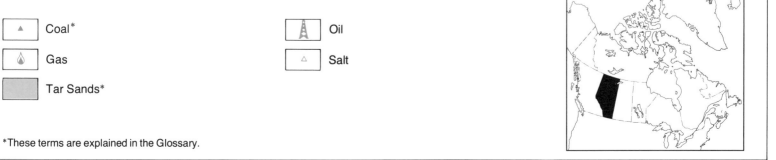

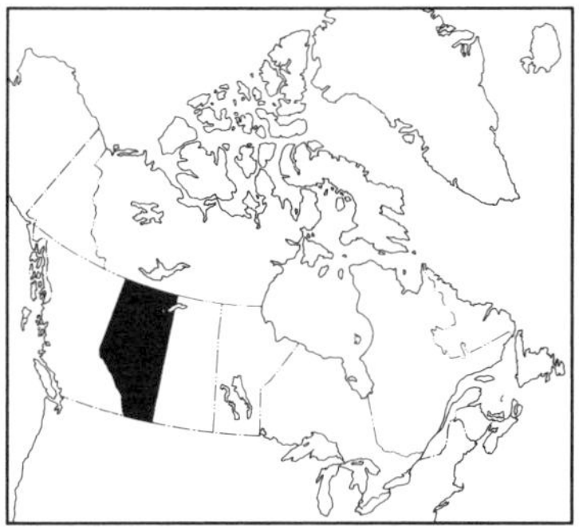

*These terms are explained in the Glossary.

British Columbia *Minerals and Mineral Fuels*

0 100 200
Scale in kilometres
YUKON TERRITORY
NORTHWEST TERRITORIES
ALASKA (U.S.A.)
ALBERTA
UNITED STATES OF AMERICA
PACIFIC OCEAN
Queen Charlotte Islands
Tasu Sound
Queen Charlotte Sound
VANCOUVER ISLAND
Texada Island
Liard River
Peace River
Williston Lake
Babine Lake
Fraser River
Columbia River
Cassiar
Fort Nelson
Fort St. John
Dawson Creek
Stewart
Prince Rupert
Kitimat
Prince George
Benson Lake
Campbell River
Myra Falls
Powell River
Britannia Beach
Vancouver
VICTORIA
River Jordan
Ashcroft
Kamloops
Merritt
Peachland
Kelowna
Penticton
Hope
Oliver
Beaverdell
Grand Forks
Revelstoke
New Denver
Kimberley
Cranbrook
Nelson
Salmo
Trail
N
60° 58° 56° 54° 52° 50° 48°
136° 132° 128° 124° 120° 116°
1 2 3 4 5 6 7
A B C D E F

C Copper*

Gold*

I Iron*

Lead*

N Nickel*

A Asbestos*

Quartz*

Silver*

Z Zinc*

Coal

Gas*

Oil*

*Some of the uses of these minerals are explained in the Glossary.

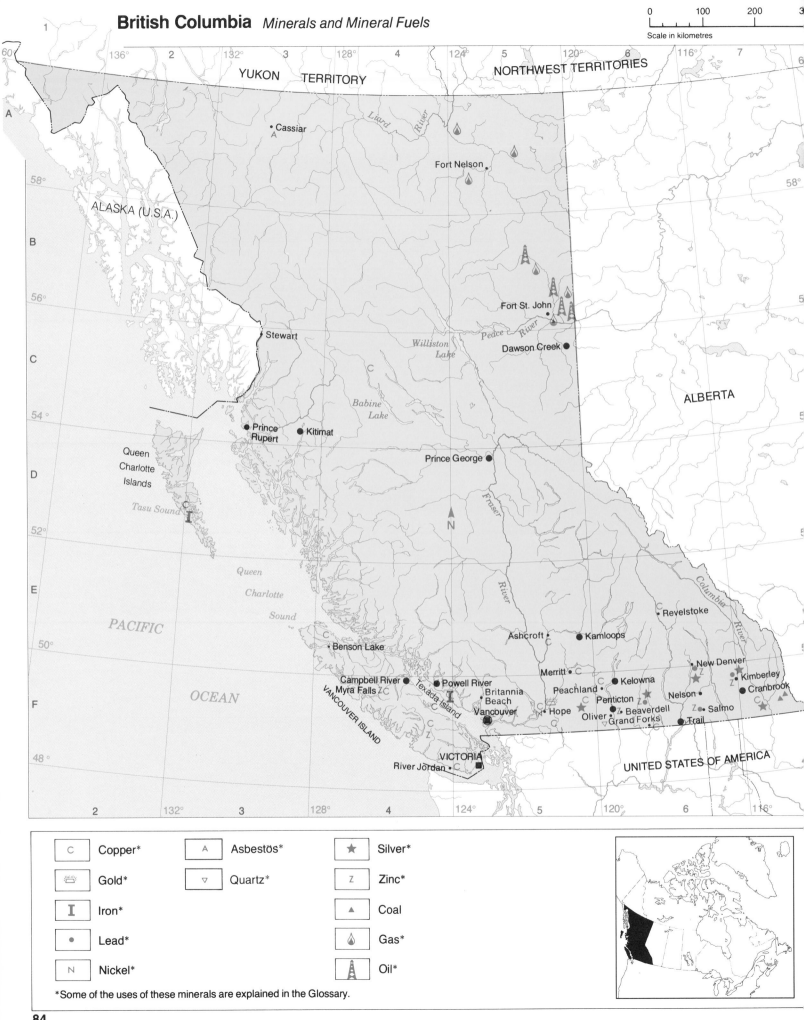

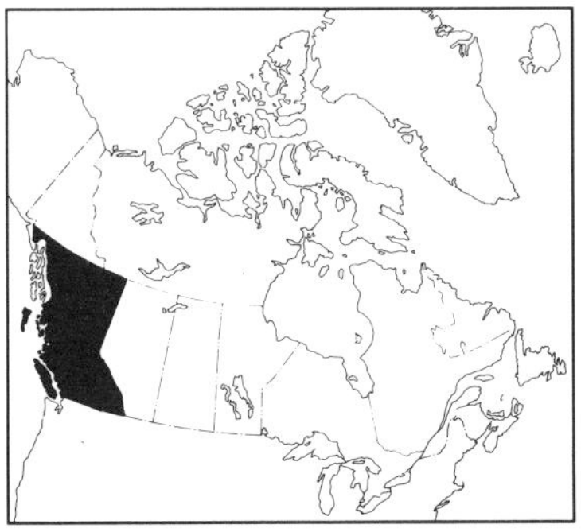

ANUFACTURING—MAKING GOODS

anufacturing is making things in a factory. Goods e things that people use. Fruit, grain, fish, meat, od, furs, and other crops from the land and the ter are goods that can be used in their natural te. Or, they can be made into ketchup, sausages, h sticks, tables, suede jackets, and other manu- ctured goods. Minerals are used to make all kinds manufactured goods, from paper clips to giant nbo jets. They are also used to make the achines that make manufactured goods. Oil and s are used to run both machines like cars and rplanes and also machines that manufacture ods.

e *Glossary* will help you understand unfamiliar rms like "food processing" and "metal refining."

. What goods are manufactured in the Atlantic Provinces?

. What goods are manufactured in Central Canada?

. What goods are manufactured in Western Canada?

. What kind of food is processed in the Atlantic Provinces? At Niagara Falls, Ontario? At Penticton, B.C.?

. What metals are refined at Trail, B.C.?

. In what region of Canada are electrical products manufactured?

. In what province are chemicals manufactured?

. Which region of Canada has the greatest variety of manufacturing?

. List some goods that are manufactured in or near your community.

. Why do you think there are oil refineries at Sarnia, Ontario, and Montreal, Quebec? The *Glossary* and the map on page 77 will help you answer this question.

. Compare the map on page 31 with the maps that show manufacturing. What connection can you make between where most Canadians live and where most manufacturing is carried on? Why do you think this is so?

Atlantic Canada *Manufacturing – Making Goods*

70°
1
68°
2
66°
3
64°
4
62°
B
C
D
E
48°
46°
44°
QUEBEC
QUEBEC
QUE
St. Lawrence River
Atholville
Dalhousie
Chaleur Bay
Gulf of St. Lawrence
N
Edmundston
Bathurst
UNITED STATES
OF AMERICA
Newcastle
NEW BRUNSWICK
Alberton
PRINCE EDWARD ISLAND
FREDERICTON
Moncton
CHARLOTTETOWN
Georgetown
Sussex
Amherst
St. Stephen
Springhill
Saint John
Blacks Harbour
Abercrombie Point
CAPE BRETON ISLAND
Kentville
Port Hawkesbury
Bay of Fundy
Hantsport
SCOTIA
NOVA
HALIFAX
Dartmouth
Sheet Harbour
Lunenburg
Brooklyn
Liverpool
Shelburne
68°
2
66°
3
64°
4
62°
5
60°

Clothing

Food Processing*

Iron and Steel

Motor Vehicles

*These terms are explained in the Glossary.

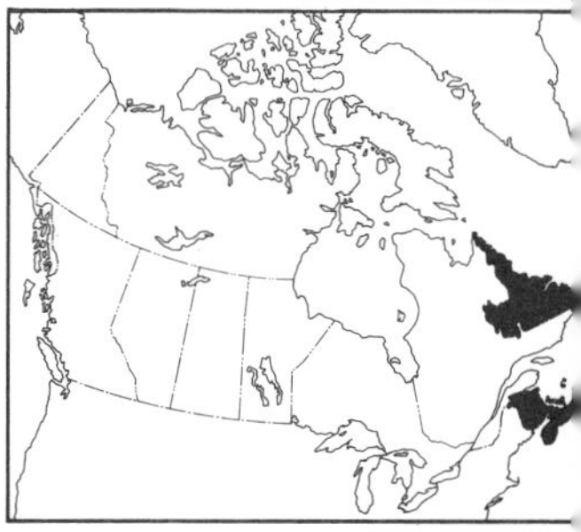

0
100
200
Scale in kilometres
Cape Bauld
ATLANTIC
OCEAN
Notre Dame Bay
Fogo
Bay of Islands
Corner Brook
Grand Falls
ISLAND OF NEWFOUNDLAND
Burgeo
Ramea
Conception Bay
Carbonear
Harbour Grace
ST. JOHN'S
Fortune Bay
Grand Bank
Marystown
Burin
Placentia Bay
Cape Race
ATLANTIC OCEAN
Sable Island (N.S.)
ATLANTIC
OCEAN
PROVINCE OF NEWFOUNDLAND
Labrador City
QUEBEC
N.B.
P.E.I.
N.S.
0 100 200

Shipbuilding and Repair

Oil Refining*

Pulp and Paper*

Lake Nipigon
Red Rock
Thunder Bay
Terrace Bay
Marathon
Kapuskasing
ONTARIO
LAKE SUPERIOR
Sault Ste. Marie
Sudbury
Sturgeon Falls
UNITED STATES OF AMERICA
Georgian Bay
LAKE HURON
LAKE MICHIGAN
Collingwood
Barrie
TORONTO
Oakville
Cambridge
Kitchener
Hamilton
Sarnia
Nanticoke
Chatham
Windsor
LAKE ERIE
S
N
A
B
C
D
E
1
2
3
4
5
6
7
92°
90°
88°
86°
84°
82°
80°
46°
44°
42°

Clothing

Electrical Products*

Farm Machinery

Food Processing*

S Iron and Steel

Metals* and Chemical

Motor Vehicles

*These terms are explained in the Glossary.

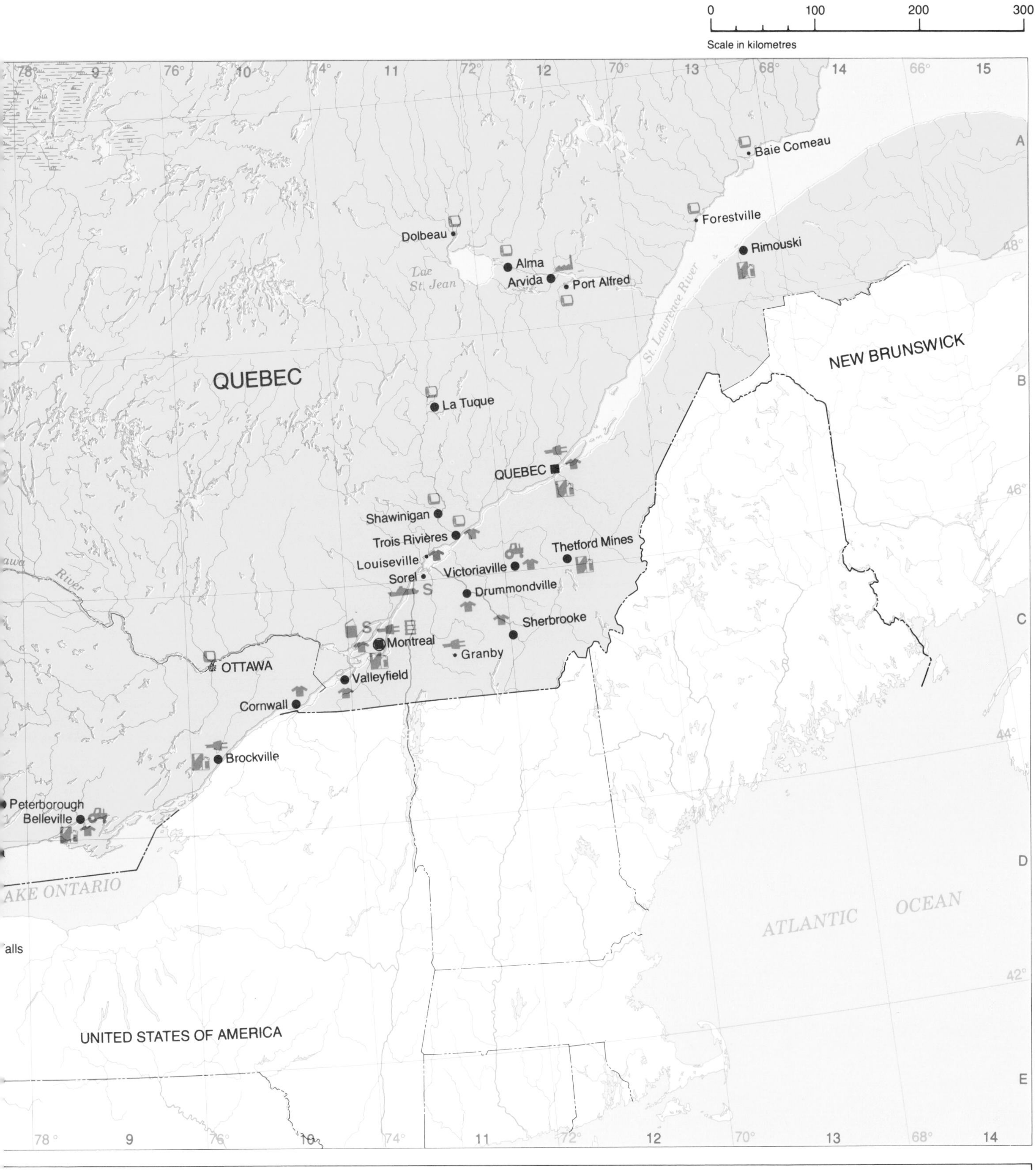

0
100
200
300
Scale in kilometres
QUEBEC
NEW BRUNSWICK
Baie Comeau
Forestville
Rimouski
Dolbeau
Alma
Arvida
Port Alfred
Lac St. Jean
St. Lawrence River
La Tuque
QUEBEC
Shawinigan
Trois Rivières
Louiseville
Sorel
Victoriaville
Thetford Mines
Drummondville
Sherbrooke
Montreal
Granby
OTTAWA
Valleyfield
Cornwall
Brockville
Peterborough
Belleville
AKE ONTARIO
alls
ATLANTIC OCEAN
UNITED STATES OF AMERICA
River

	Oil Refining*		Pulp and Paper*
	Publishing		Shipbuilding and Repair

Western Canada *Manufacturing – Making Goods*

Clothing	Food Processing*
Farm Machinery	Metal Refining*
Oil Refining*	Publishing

*These terms are explained in the Glossary.

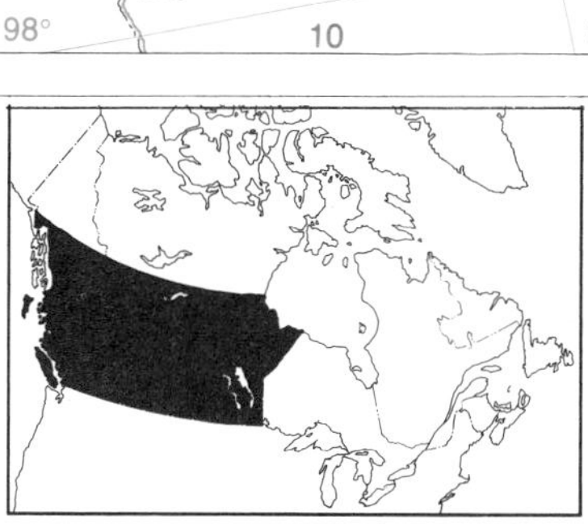

Pulp and Paper*

TRANSPORTATION—MOVING PEOPLE AND GOODS

When we think of transportation, we usually think of cars, trucks, buses, trains, boats, and airplanes. But transportation is moving goods and people, so anything that does that is a means of transportation. What map of Canada in another section of this atlas is also a transportation map? What means of transportation is shown on that map?

What other means of transportation can you think of? Which are particularly well suited to Canada's northern climate?

1. In what direction do the main road and railway lines run?
2. Why are the main roads and railway lines located in southern Canada?
3. Why do you think railway lines were built to Schefferville and to Lynn Lake?
4. What are the main railway centres in Canada?
5. How far is it by ferry from North Sydney, N.S., to Argentia, Nfld.?
6. What are the main ports in the Atlantic Provinces? In British Columbia?
7. Why are there so few road and railway lines in Newfoundland?
8. Why are there so many airports in the Northwest Territories?
9. How do people in the Yukon and the Northwest Territories earn a living?
10. What is the latitude of the southern border of the Yukon and of most of the Northwest Territories?
11. What is the capital of the Northwest Territories? What is its location?
12. From your reading of the physical maps in this atlas, what problems would there be in building railways in Canada?
13. About how long would it take to fly from Montreal to Victoria in a plane travelling at 700 km/h?
14. About how long would it take to drive from Toronto to Vancouver travelling 600 km a day?
15. Imagine you are keeping a diary of a motor trip from Toronto to Vancouver. At the end of each day of the trip, write in your diary the look of the land and the names of towns, cities, rivers, lakes, mountains, and other physical features on your route.

0 200 400 600 800 1000
Scale in kilometres
130° 110° 90° 70°
ARCTIC OCEAN
GREENLAND
Arctic Circle
ALASKA (U.S.A.)
YUKON TERR.
WHITEHORSE
PACIFIC OCEAN
N.W.T.
YELLOWKNIFE
Fort Nelson
B.C.
Prince Rupert
ALTA.
SASK.
Churchill
EDMONTON
Vancouver
MAN.
ONT.
QUE.
Moosonee
Schefferville
Sept Iles
NEWFOUNDLAND
ATLANTIC OCEAN
Channel-Port aux Basques
ST. JOHN'S
Sydney
P.E.I.
N.B.
N.S.
Saint John
HALIFAX
Montreal
OTTAWA
TORONTO
Windsor
UNITED STATES OF AMERICA
110° 100° 90° 80° 70°
40° 50° 60°
N

Roads
Railways

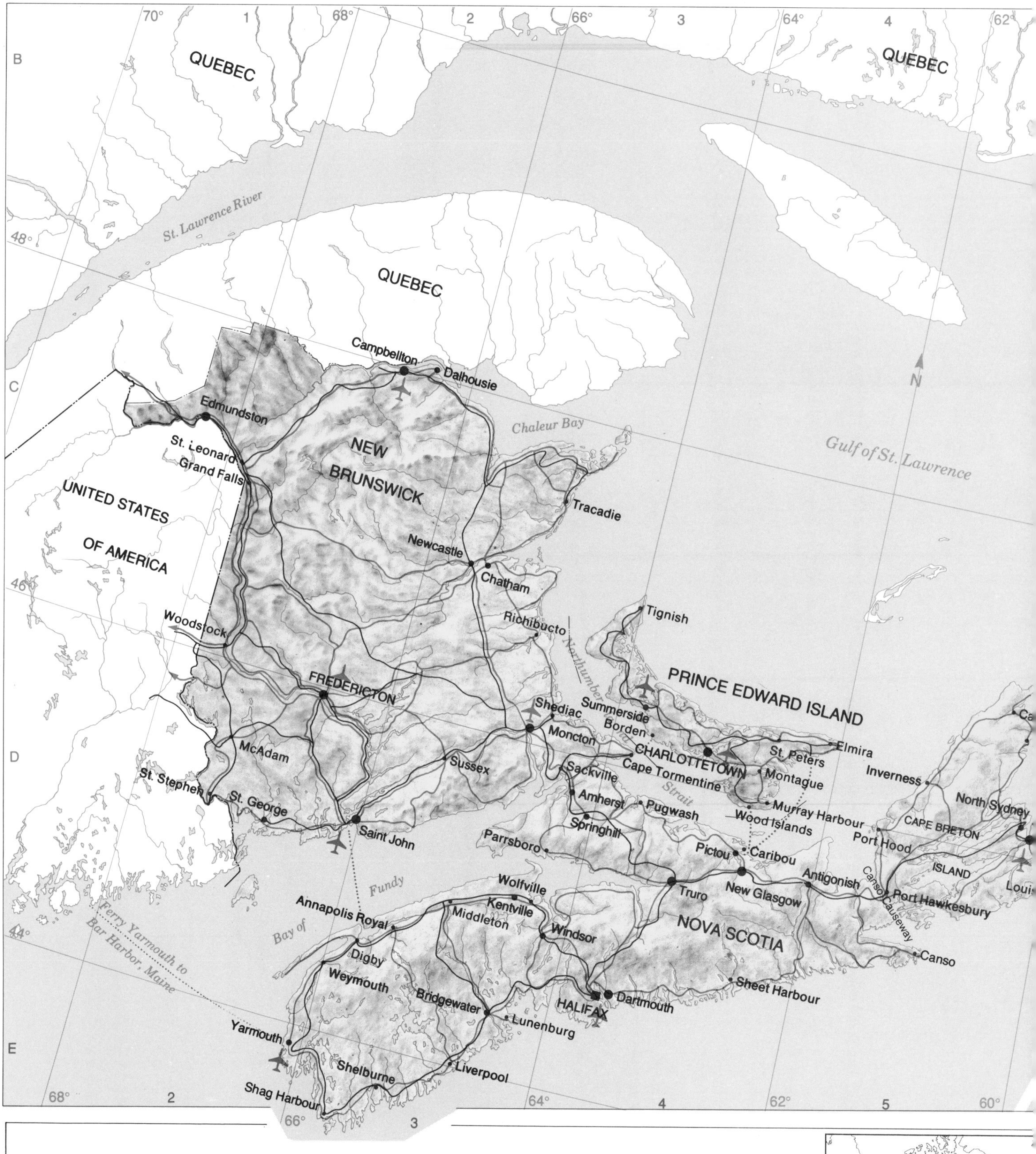
QUEBEC
QUEBEC
QUEBEC
St. Lawrence River
Campbellton
Dalhousie
Edmundston
Chaleur Bay
Gulf of St. Lawrence
St. Leonard
Grand Falls
NEW BRUNSWICK
UNITED STATES OF AMERICA
Tracadie
Newcastle
Chatham
Richibucto
Tignish
Woodstock
Northumberland Strait
PRINCE EDWARD ISLAND
FREDERICTON
Shediac
Summerside
Borden
Moncton
CHARLOTTETOWN
Elmira
St. Peters
McAdam
Sackville
Cape Tormentine
Montague
Inverness
Sussex
St. Stephen
St. George
Amherst
Pugwash
Murray Harbour
Wood Islands
North Sydney
CAPE BRETON ISLAND
Springhill
Port Hood
Saint John
Parrsboro
Pictou
Caribou
Canso Causeway
Antigonish
Port Hawkesbury
Truro
New Glasgow
Fundy
Wolfville
Kentville
Annapolis Royal
Middleton
NOVA SCOTIA
Windsor
Bay of
Canso
Ferry Yarmouth to Bar Harbor, Maine
Digby
Weymouth
Sheet Harbour
Bridgewater
HALIFAX
Dartmouth
Lunenburg
Yarmouth
Shelburne
Liverpool
Shag Harbour
N
70°
68°
66°
64°
62°
60°
48°
46°
44°
1
2
3
4
5
B
C
D
E

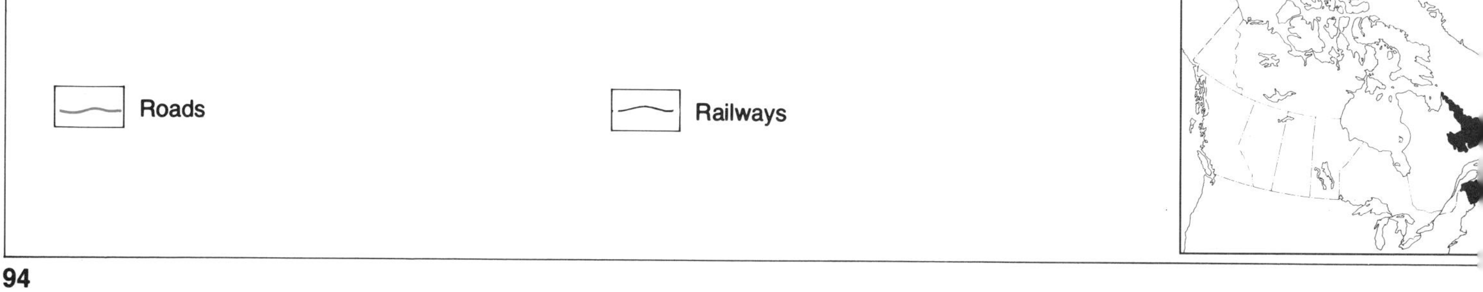
Roads
Railways

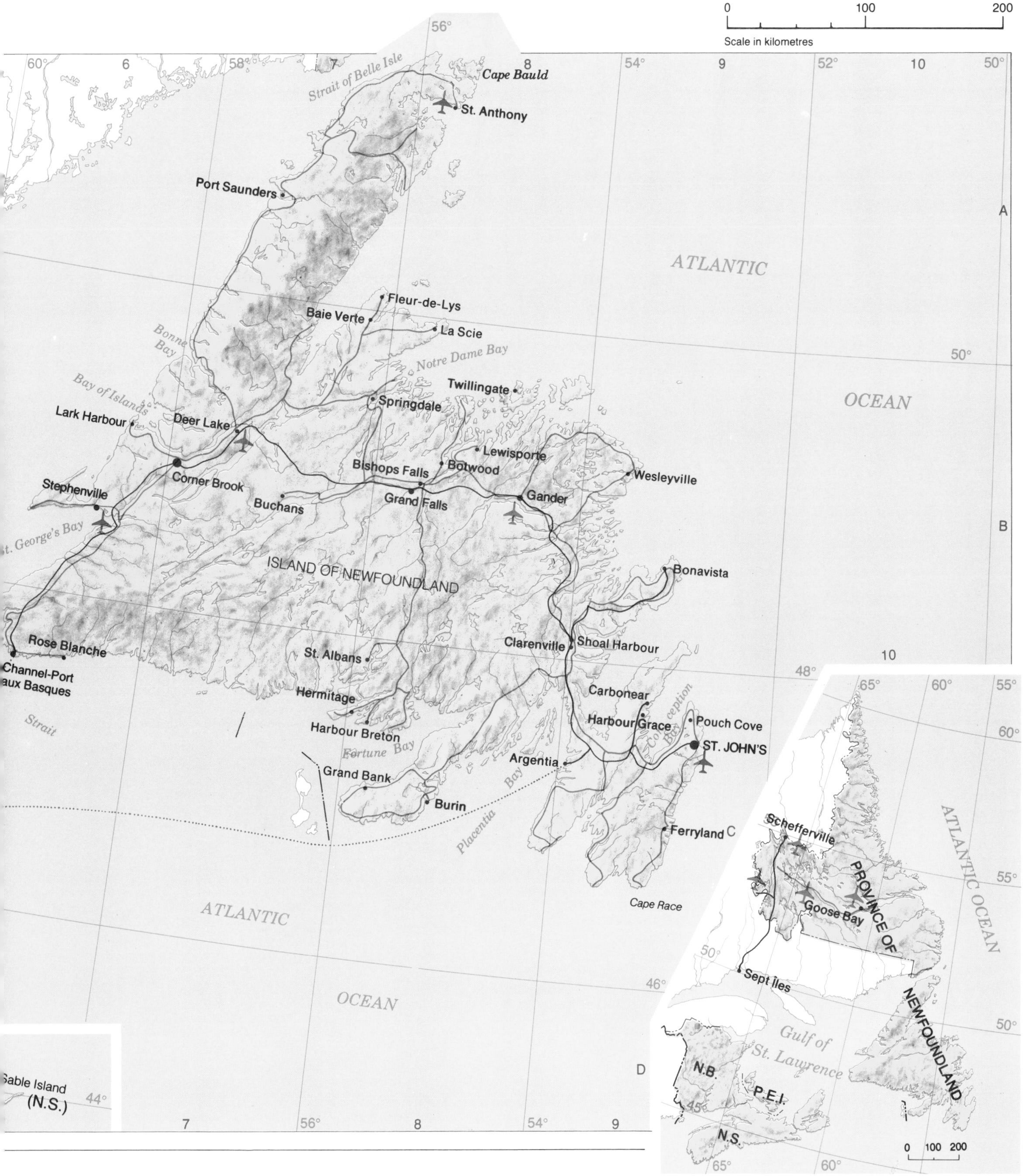

0
100
200
Scale in kilometres
Strait of Belle Isle
Cape Bauld
St. Anthony
Port Saunders
ATLANTIC
Fleur-de-Lys
Baie Verte
La Scie
Bonne Bay
Notre Dame Bay
Bay of Islands
Twillingate
Springdale
OCEAN
Lark Harbour
Deer Lake
Lewisporte
Botwood
Bishops Falls
Wesleyville
Corner Brook
Stephenville
Buchans
Grand Falls
Gander
St. George's Bay
ISLAND OF NEWFOUNDLAND
Bonavista
Rose Blanche
Channel-Port aux Basques
St. Albans
Clarenville
Shoal Harbour
Hermitage
Carbonear
Conception Bay
Harbour Grace
Pouch Cove
ST. JOHN'S
Harbour Breton
Fortune Bay
Argentia
Grand Bank
Burin
Placentia Bay
Ferryland
Cape Race
ATLANTIC
OCEAN
Sable Island (N.S.)
Schefferville
PROVINCE OF NEWFOUNDLAND
Goose Bay
ATLANTIC OCEAN
Sept Îles
Gulf of St. Lawrence
N.B.
P.E.I.
N.S.
0 100 200

Airports

Ferry Routes

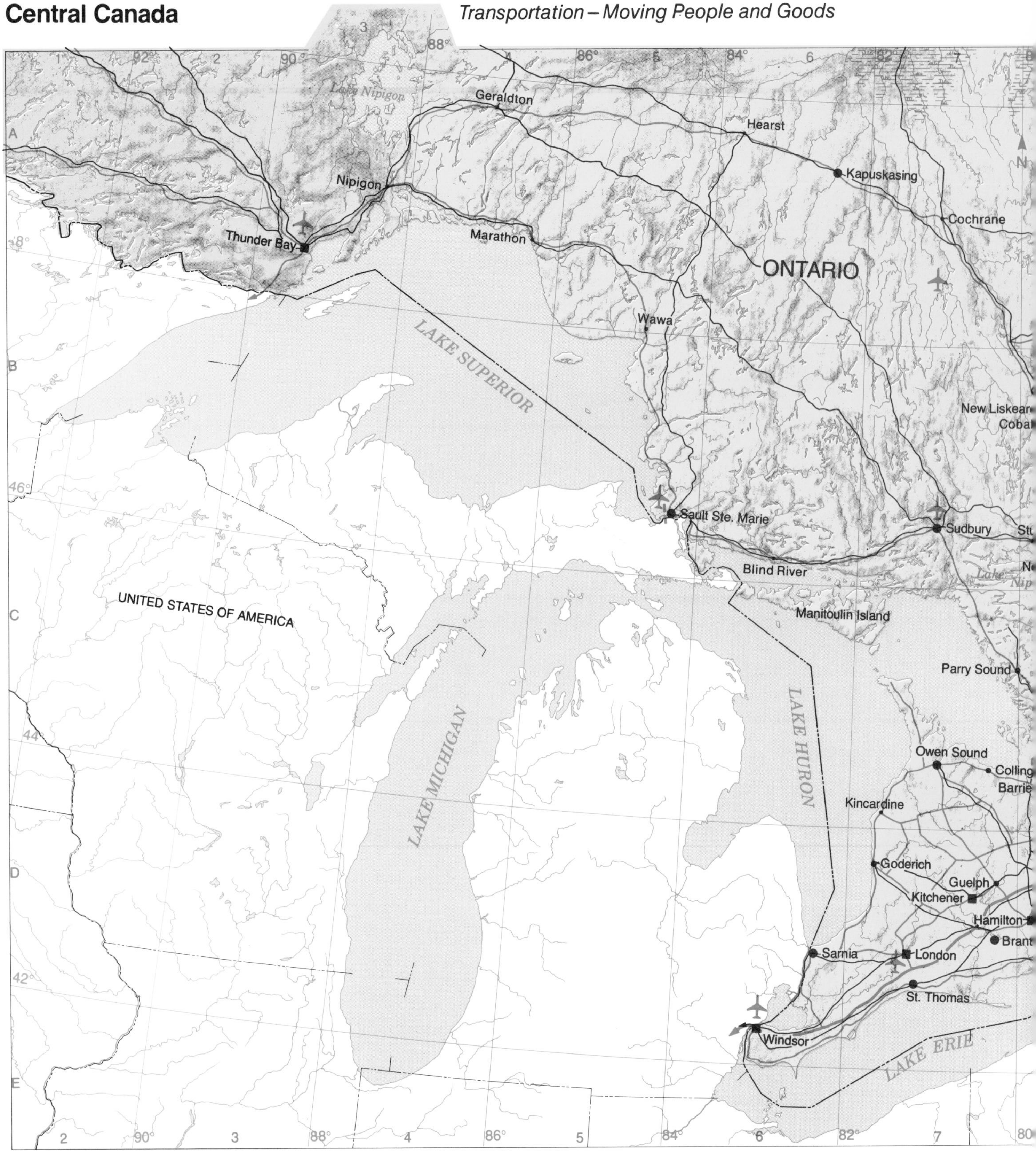

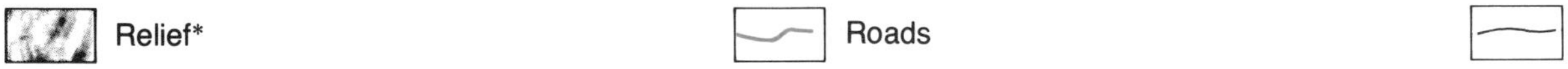

*This term is explained in the Glossary.

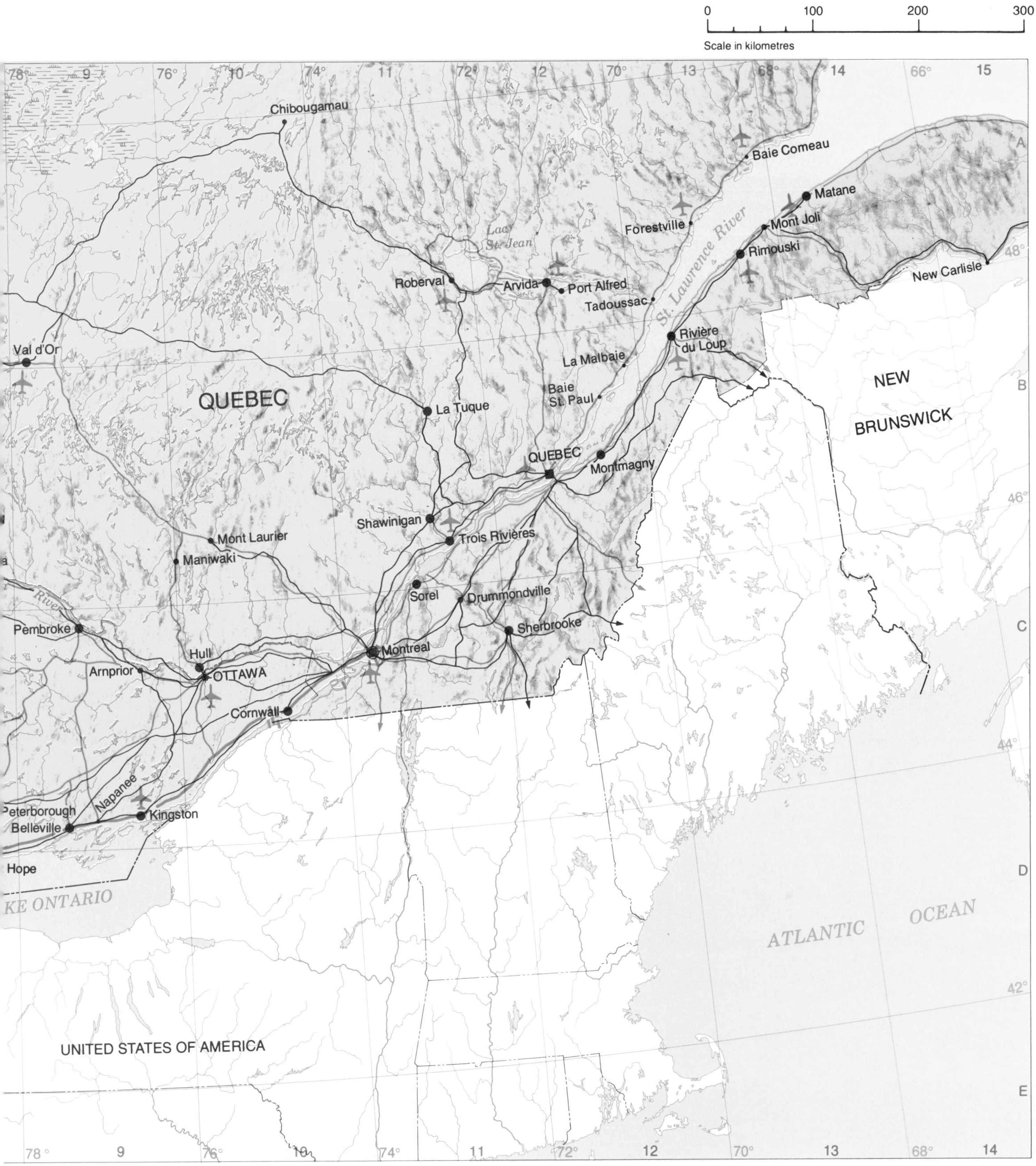
0
100
200
300
Scale in kilometres
QUEBEC
Chibougamau
Baie Comeau
Matane
Mont Joli
Rimouski
Forestville
St. Lawrence River
Lac St. Jean
Roberval
Arvida
Port Alfred
Tadoussac
New Carlisle
Val d'Or
Rivière du Loup
La Malbaie
Baie St. Paul
La Tuque
NEW BRUNSWICK
QUEBEC
Montmagny
Shawinigan
Trois Rivières
Mont Laurier
Maniwaki
Sorel
Drummondville
Sherbrooke
Pembroke
Hull
Montreal
Arnprior
OTTAWA
Cornwall
Napanee
Kingston
Peterborough
Belleville
Hope
KE ONTARIO
ATLANTIC OCEAN
UNITED STATES OF AMERICA
A
B
C
D
E
78°
76°
74°
72°
70°
68°
66°
48°
46°
44°
42°
9
10
11
12
13
14
15

Airports

Seaway Locks

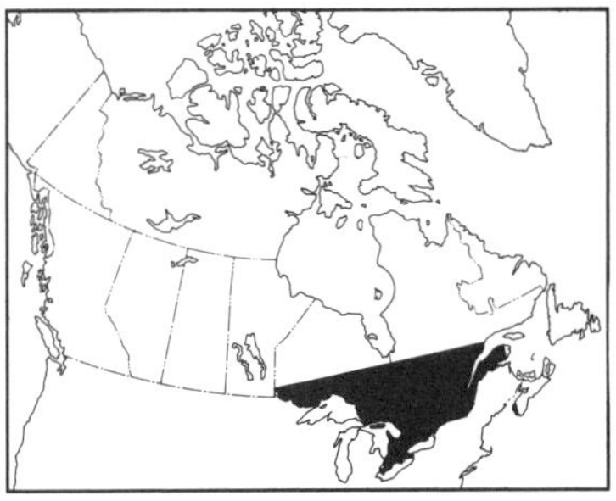

Alaska
Fort Nelson
Mackenzie
High Level
Highway
Peace River
Fort St. John
Dawson Creek
ALASKA (U.S.A.)
Prince Rupert
Skeena
Kitimat
Grande Prairie
Lesser Slave Lake
ALBERTA
Prince George
BRITISH COLUMBIA
Hinton
Jasper
EDMONTON
Williams Lake
100 Mile House
Red Deer
PACIFIC
OCEAN
Fraser River
Golden
Banff
Calgary
Revelstoke
Kamloops
Campbell River
Courtenay
Vancouver Island
Vernon
Kelowna
Parksville
Nanaimo
Vancouver
Princeton
Hope
Penticton
Cranbrook
Fort Macleod
Fernie
Chilliwack
Trail
VICTORIA

Relief*

Roads

Railways

*This term is explained in the Glossary.

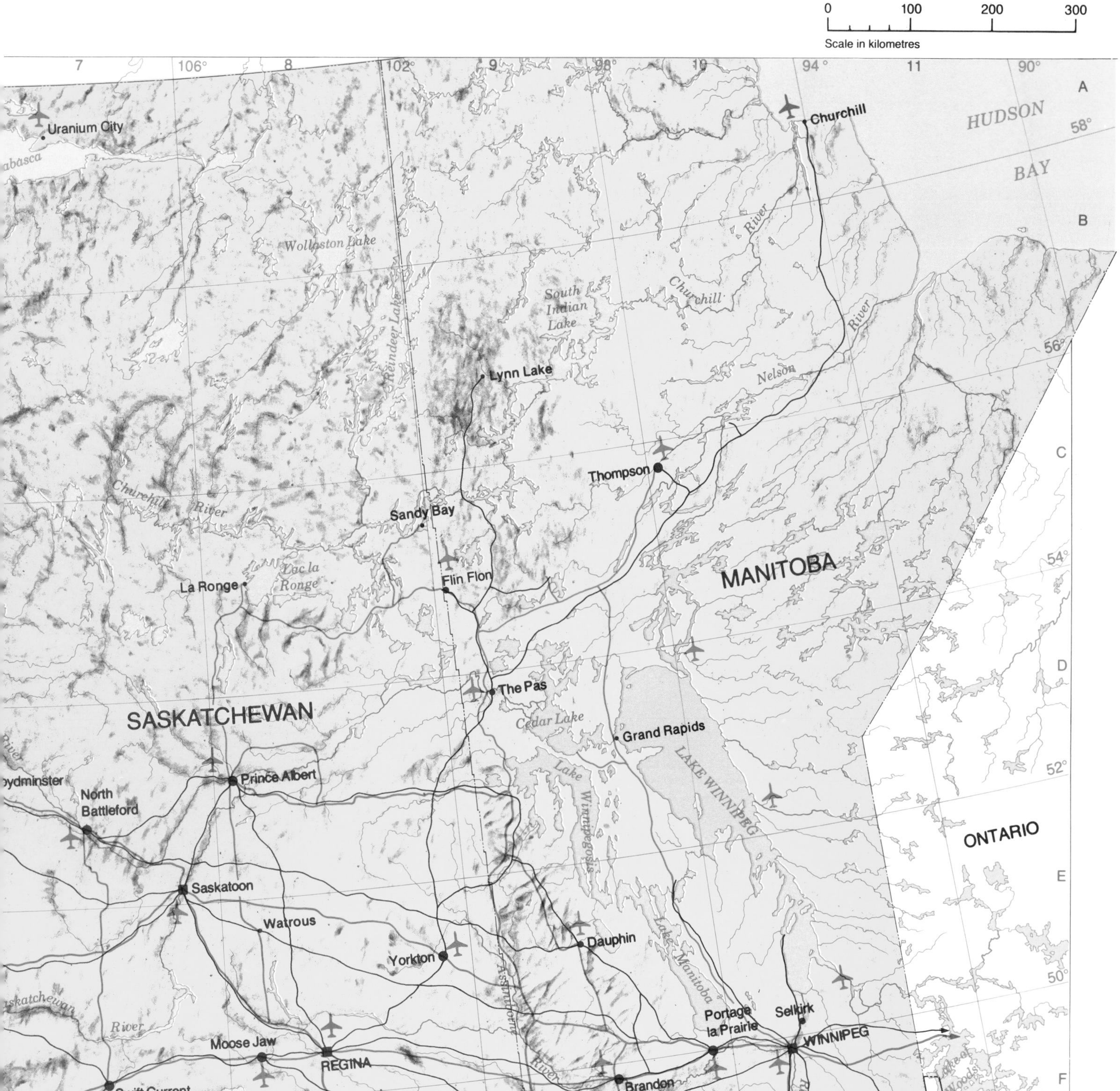
0
100
200
300
Scale in kilometres
7
106°
8
102°
9
98°
10
94°
11
90°
A
B
C
D
E
F
58°
56°
54°
52°
50°
48°
HUDSON BAY
Churchill
Uranium City
Wollaston Lake
South Indian Lake
Churchill River
Reindeer Lake
Nelson River
Lynn Lake
Thompson
Sandy Bay
Churchill River
Lac la Ronge
La Ronge
Flin Flon
MANITOBA
The Pas
SASKATCHEWAN
Cedar Lake
Grand Rapids
LAKE WINNIPEG
Prince Albert
North Battleford
Lake Winnipegosis
ONTARIO
Saskatoon
Watrous
Dauphin
Yorkton
Assiniboine River
Lake Manitoba
Saskatchewan River
Portage la Prairie
Selkirk
WINNIPEG
Moose Jaw
REGINA
Brandon
Swift Current
Weyburn
Assiniboia
Shaunavon
Red River
Lake of the Woods
Estevan
UNITED STATES OF AMERICA
106°
102°
98°
94°

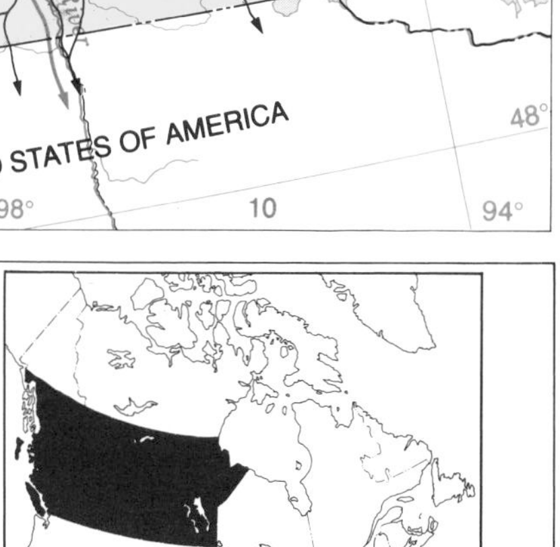

Airports

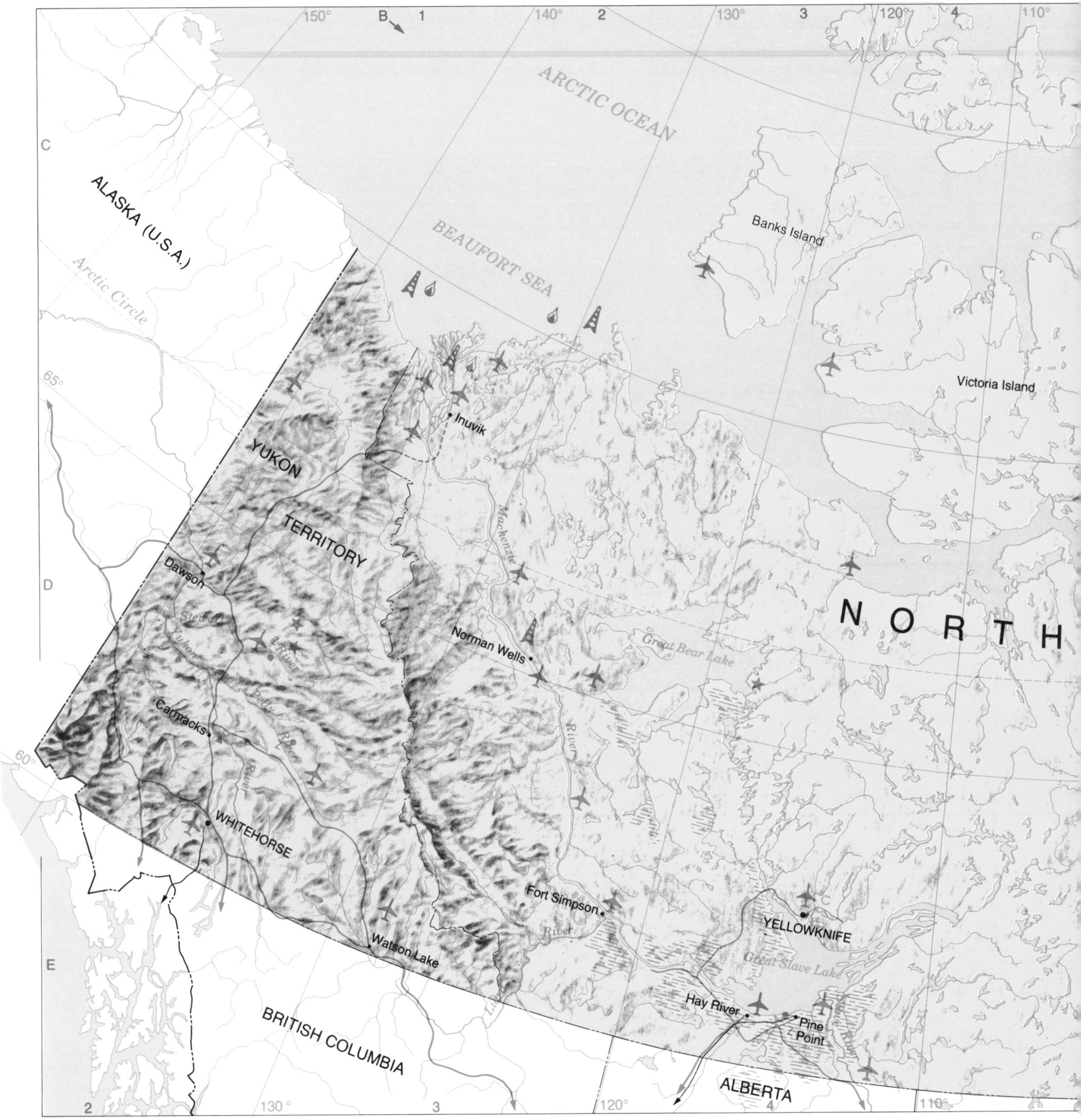
ARCTIC OCEAN
BEAUFORT SEA
ALASKA (U.S.A.)
Arctic Circle
Banks Island
Victoria Island
Inuvik
YUKON
TERRITORY
Dawson
Norman Wells
Great Bear Lake
NORTH
Mackenzie
River
Carmacks
Pelly River
WHITEHORSE
Fort Simpson
YELLOWKNIFE
Great Slave Lake
Watson Lake
Hay River
Pine Point
BRITISH COLUMBIA
ALBERTA
150°
140°
130°
120°
110°
65°
60°
B
1
2
3
4
C
D
E

Zinc*

Coal*

Gold*

Lead*

Silver*

Copper*

Gas

Oil

*See the Glossary for information and explanation.

Roads

Railways

Airports or Landing Strips

Relief*

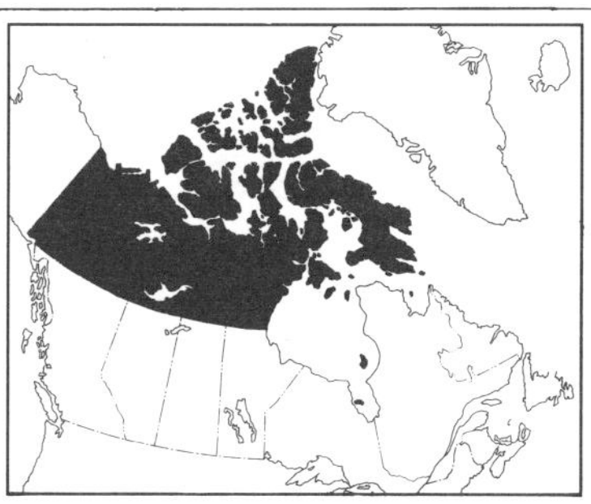

CITIES, TOWNS, AND VILLAGES

If you just look quickly at the People and Places section and the Cities, Towns, and Villages section, you may think that they both show the same kind of information. However, if you look more closely you will see that they are different in a very important way. Compare the maps in this section with those in the People and Places section, and you will see the difference. In which section do the maps show more places? Which section shows more large towns and cities?

The capital cities appear on the maps in *both* sections, but most larger places are not marked on the maps in the Cities, Towns, and Villages section. If they were all shown on the maps in this section, there would not be enough room to mark the smaller towns and villages.

Newfoundland *Cities, Towns, and Villages*

0 100 200
Scale in kilometres

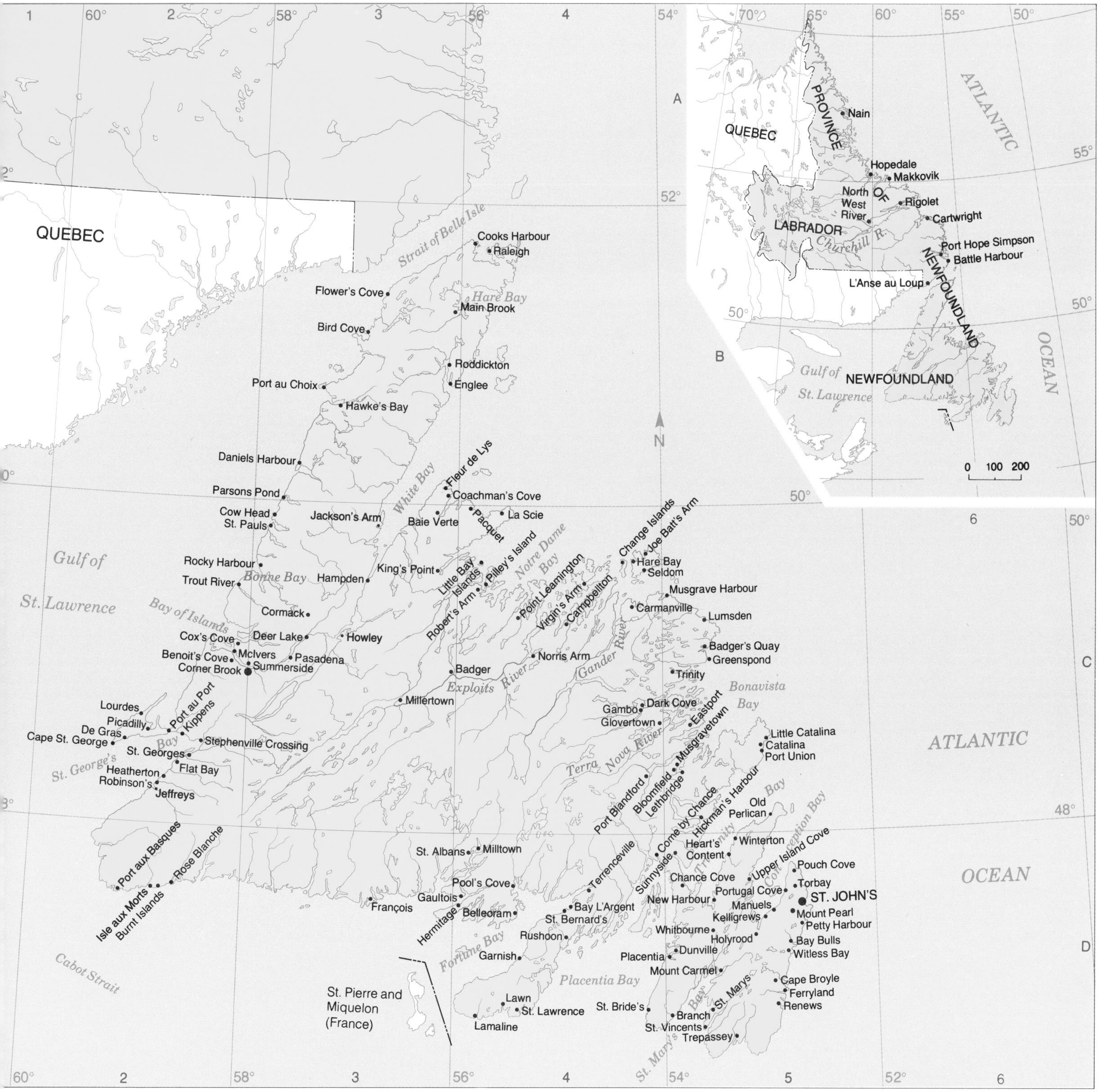

QUEBEC
Strait of Belle Isle
Cooks Harbour
Raleigh
Flower's Cove
Hare Bay
Main Brook
Bird Cove
Roddickton
Englee
Port au Choix
Hawke's Bay
Daniels Harbour
Fleur de Lys
White Bay
Parsons Pond
Coachman's Cove
Cow Head
St. Pauls
Jackson's Arm
Baie Verte
Pacquet
La Scie
Gulf of St. Lawrence
Rocky Harbour
Bonne Bay
Trout River
Hampden
King's Point
Little Bay Islands
Pilley's Island
Notre Dame Bay
Robert's Arm
Point Leamington
Virgin's Arm
Campbellton
Change Islands
Joe Batt's Arm
Hare Bay
Seldom
Musgrave Harbour
Carmanville
Lumsden
Bay of Islands
Cormack
Cox's Cove
Deer Lake
Howley
Benoit's Cove
McIvers
Pasadena
Corner Brook
Summerside
Badger
Norris Arm
Gander River
Badger's Quay
Greenspond
Trinity
Exploits River
Millertown
Bonavista Bay
Gambo
Dark Cove
Glovertown
Eastport
Lourdes
Picadilly
Port au Port
Kippens
De Gras
Cape St. George
Stephenville Crossing
St. Georges
St. George's Bay
Heatherton
Flat Bay
Robinson's
Jeffreys
Terra Nova River
Musgravetown
Little Catalina
Catalina
Port Union
ATLANTIC OCEAN
Port Blandford
Bloomfield
Lethbridge
Come by Chance
Hickman's Harbour
Old Perlican
Trinity Bay
Conception Bay
Port aux Basques
Rose Blanche
Isle aux Morts
Burnt Islands
St. Albans
Milltown
Terrenceville
Sunnyside
Heart's Content
Winterton
Upper Island Cove
Pouch Cove
Torbay
Chance Cove
Portugal Cove
ST. JOHN'S
Pool's Cove
Gaultois
François
Hermitage
Belleoram
Bay L'Argent
St. Bernard's
New Harbour
Manuels
Kelligrews
Mount Pearl
Petty Harbour
Whitbourne
Holyrood
Bay Bulls
Witless Bay
Rushoon
Fortune Bay
Garnish
Placentia
Dunville
Mount Carmel
Cabot Strait
St. Pierre and Miquelon (France)
Placentia Bay
Cape Broyle
Ferryland
Renews
Lawn
St. Lawrence
Lamaline
St. Bride's
Branch
St. Marys
St. Mary's Bay
St. Vincents
Trepassey
N
1 2 3 4 5 6
A B C D
60° 58° 56° 54° 52° 50° 48°
QUEBEC
PROVINCE OF NEWFOUNDLAND
LABRADOR
Nain
Hopedale
Makkovik
North West River
Rigolet
Cartwright
Churchill R.
Port Hope Simpson
Battle Harbour
L'Anse au Loup
Gulf of St. Lawrence
NEWFOUNDLAND
ATLANTIC OCEAN
70° 65° 60° 55° 50°
0 100 200

•	Population under 5 000
•	Population 5 000-10 000
●	Population 10 000-100 000

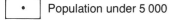

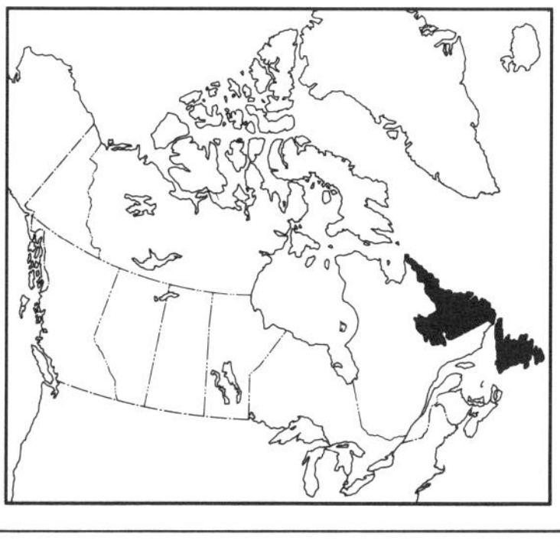

Nova Scotia *Cities, Towns, and Villages*

0
50
100
Scale in kilometres
1
2
3
4
5
6
7
8
A
B
C
D
E
66°
65°
64°
63°
62°
61°
60°
47°
46°
45°
44°
43°
NEWFOUNDLAND
Gulf of
St. Lawrence
Magdalen Islands
(Quebec)
Cabot Strait
NEW
BRUNSWICK
PRINCE
EDWARD
ISLAND
Northumberland
Strait
N
Capstick
Dingwall
Neil Harbour
Ingonish
Petit Etang
Chéticamp
Grand Etang
Belle Cote
Margaree Harbour
Margaree Forks
Inverness
Indian Brook
CAPE BRETON
ISLAND
Big Bras d'Or
Florence
New Waterford
Dominion
Reserve Mines
Port Morien
Sydney River
Mabou
East Bay
Little Narrows
Grand Narrows
Catalone
Louisbourg
Orangedale
Judique
Fort Lawrence
Nappan
Maccan
Athol
Joggins
River Hebert
Wentworth
Oxford
Collingwood
Corner
Wallace
Malagash
Tatamagouche
River John
Lyons Brook
Trenton
Merigomish
Thorburn
Pomquet
Westville
Eureka
Troy
Frankville
Monastery
Port Hastings
Mulgrave
Point Tupper
St. Peters
Louisdale
Petit de Grat
Arichat
Boylston
Apple River
Port Greville
Parrsboro
Great Village
Debert
Belmont
Advocate Harbour
Bible Hill
Hilden
Brookfield
Goshen
Caledonia
Queensport
Canso
Little Dover
Whitehead
Larry's River
New Harbour
Goldboro
Sherbrooke
Canning
Centreville
Port Williams
Grand Pré
Walton
Kennetcook
Berwick
Stewiacke
Shubenacadie
Scotch Village
New Minas
Falmouth
Three Mile Plains
Kingston
Middleton
Bay of Fundy
Lantz
Enfield
Moser River
Port Dufferin
Ecum Secum
Bridgetown
Parker Cove
Granville Ferry
Port Royal
Clementsport
Dalhousie West
New Ross
Mount Uniacke
Fall River
Waverley
Beaverbank
Timberlea
Salmon
River Bridge
Tangier
Musquodoboit Harbour
Porters Lake
Hubbards
HALIFAX
Cow Bay
Herring Cove
Bear River
Hemford
Chester Basin
Western Shore
Whites Lake
Chester
Blandford
Sambro
Terence Bay
Mahone Bay
Little River
Tiverton
Maitland Bridge
Belliveau
Cove
Caledonia
Bridgewater
Freeport
Saulnierville
La Have
Blue Rocks
Riverport
Meteghan
Middlewood
Mavillette
Salmon River
Mill Village
Milton
Beach Meadows
Port Maitland
Carleton
Hebron
Port Mouton
Sable River
Jordon Falls
Wedgeport
Birchtown
Pubnico
Lockeport
Lower Wood Harbour
Barrington Passage
Clark's Harbour
ATLANTIC
OCEAN
Sable Island

•	Population under 5 000
•	Population 5 000-10 000
■	Population over 100 000

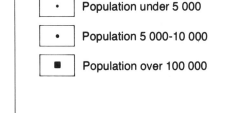

Prince Edward Island *Cities, Towns, and Villages*

0 20 40 60 80
Scale in kilometres

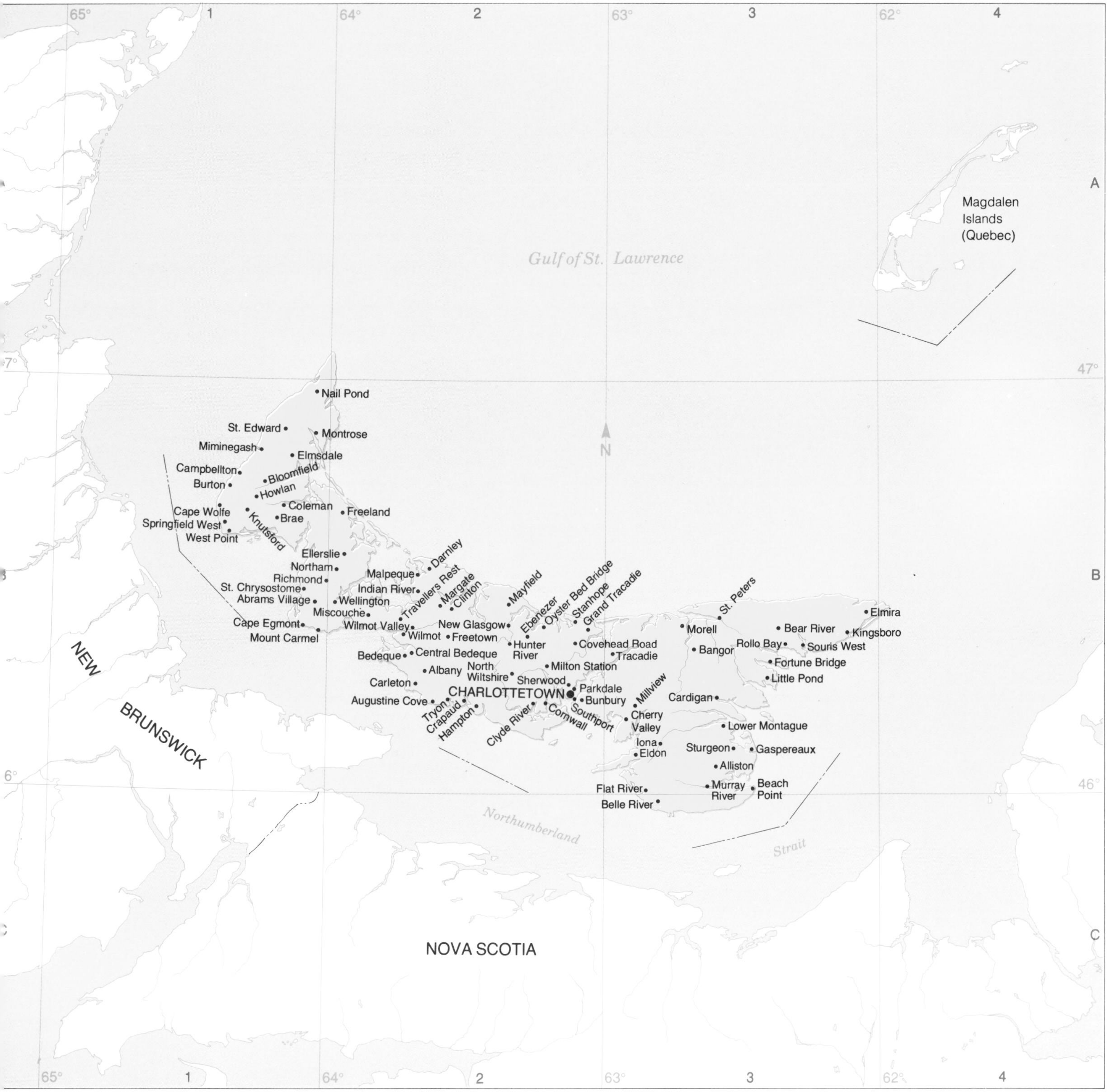

65°
64°
63°
62°
47°
46°
1
2
3
4
A
B
C
Gulf of St. Lawrence
Magdalen Islands (Quebec)
N
Nail Pond
St. Edward
Montrose
Miminegash
Elmsdale
Campbellton
Bloomfield
Burton
Howlan
Coleman
Cape Wolfe
Freeland
Springfield West
Brae
West Point
Knutsford
Ellerslie
Northam
Darnley
Malpeque
Richmond
Travellers Rest
Indian River
Margate
St. Chrysostome
Clinton
Abrams Village
Wellington
Mayfield
Miscouche
Ebenezer
Oyster Bed Bridge
Stanhope
Grand Tracadie
St. Peters
Cape Egmont
Wilmot Valley
New Glasgow
Mount Carmel
Wilmot
Freetown
Hunter River
Covehead Road
Tracadie
Morell
Bear River
Elmira
Kingsboro
Bangor
Rollo Bay
Souris West
Fortune Bridge
Little Pond
Bedeque
Central Bedeque
Albany
North Wiltshire
Milton Station
Sherwood
Carleton
Parkdale
CHARLOTTETOWN
Bunbury
Millview
Cardigan
Augustine Cove
Tryon
Crapaud
Hampton
Clyde River
Cornwall
Southport
Cherry Valley
Lower Montague
Iona
Eldon
Sturgeon
Gaspereaux
Alliston
Flat River
Murray River
Beach Point
Belle River
Northumberland Strait
NEW BRUNSWICK
NOVA SCOTIA

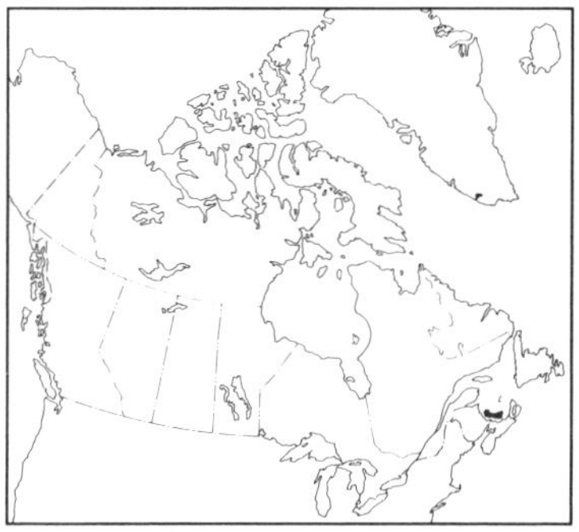

Population under 5 000

Population 10 000-100 000

New Brunswick *Cities, Towns, and Villages*

0 50 1
Scale in kilometres

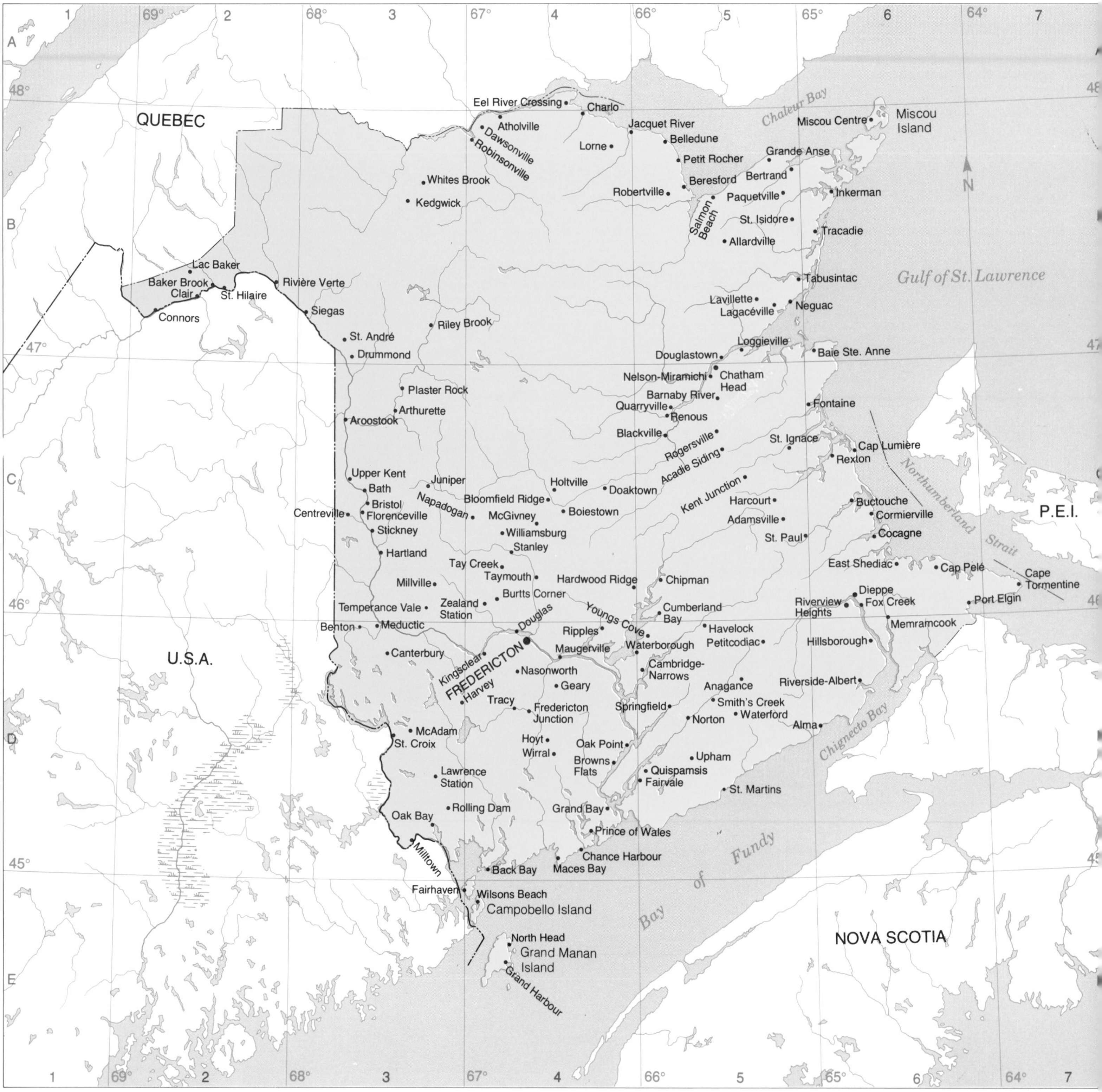

QUEBEC
U.S.A.
NOVA SCOTIA
P.E.I.
Miscou Island
Chaleur Bay
Gulf of St. Lawrence
Northumberland Strait
Chignecto Bay
Bay of Fundy
Campobello Island
Grand Manan Island
N
69°
68°
67°
66°
65°
64°
48°
47°
46°
45°
1
2
3
4
5
6
7
A
B
C
D
E
Eel River Crossing
Charlo
Atholville
Dawsonville
Robinsonville
Jacquet River
Belledune
Lorne
Petit Rocher
Grande Anse
Miscou Centre
Bertrand
Beresford
Robertville
Paquetville
Inkerman
Salmon Beach
St. Isidore
Tracadie
Allardville
Whites Brook
Kedgwick
Lac Baker
Baker Brook
Clair
St. Hilaire
Connors
Rivière Verte
Siegas
Tabusintac
Laville tte
Lagacéville
Neguac
Riley Brook
St. André
Drummond
Loggieville
Douglastown
Baie Ste. Anne
Nelson-Miramichi
Chatham Head
Barnaby River
Quarryville
Renous
Fontaine
Plaster Rock
Arthurette
Aroostook
Blackville
Rogersville
Acadie Siding
St. Ignace
Cap Lumière
Rexton
Upper Kent
Bath
Juniper
Holtville
Doaktown
Kent Junction
Harcourt
Buctouche
Cormierville
Bristol
Florenceville
Centreville
Napadogan
Bloomfield Ridge
McGivney
Boiestown
Adamsville
Cocagne
Stickney
Williamsburg
Stanley
St. Paul
Hartland
Tay Creek
Taymouth
East Shediac
Cap Pelé
Cape Tormentine
Millville
Hardwood Ridge
Chipman
Burtts Corner
Dieppe
Fox Creek
Riverview Heights
Port Elgin
Temperance Vale
Zealand Station
Douglas
Youngs Cove
Cumberland Bay
Memramcook
Benton
Meductic
Ripples
Havelock
Hillsborough
Maugerville
Waterborough
Petitcodiac
Canterbury
Kingsclear
FREDERICTON
Nasonworth
Cambridge-Narrows
Geary
Harvey
Tracy
Fredericton Junction
Springfield
Anagance
Smith's Creek
Riverside-Albert
Norton
Waterford
Alma
McAdam
St. Croix
Hoyt
Wirral
Oak Point
Browns Flats
Upham
Lawrence Station
Quispamsis
Fairvale
St. Martins
Rolling Dam
Grand Bay
Oak Bay
Prince of Wales
Milltown
Chance Harbour
Back Bay
Maces Bay
Fairhaven
Wilsons Beach
North Head
Grand Harbour

•	Population under 5 000
•	Population 5 000-10 000
●	Population 10 000-100 000

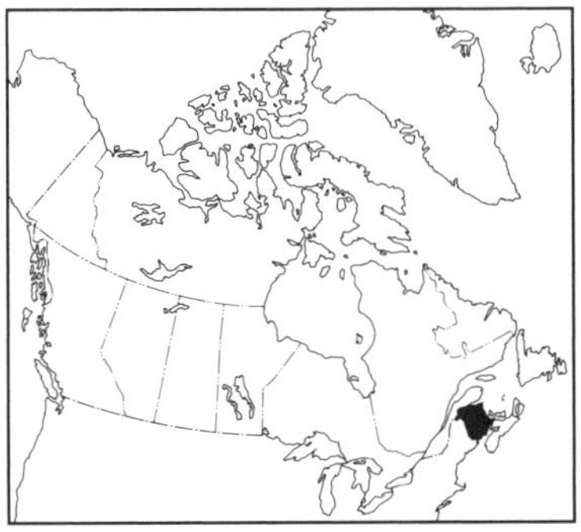

uebec *Cities, Towns, and Villages*

0 100 200 300 400 500
Scale in kilometres
1 2 3 4 5 6 7 8
A B C D E
85° 80° 75° 70° 65° 60° 55°
60° 55° 50° 45°
Hudson
Bay
James
Bay
Ungava
Bay
N
NEWFOUNDLAND
ONTARIO
Schefferville
Havre St. Pierre
Chute aux Outardes
Baie Trinité
Hauterive
Grandes Bergeronnes
River
Lawrence
Gulf of
St. Lawrence
Duparquet
Amos
Evain
Senneterre
Barraute
Cadillac
Notre Dame du Nord
Belleterre
Ville Marie
Temiscaming
Normandin
St. Félicien
St. Prime
St. Gédéon
Lac Bouchette
Kénogami
Jonquière
Bagotville
St. Siméon
Luceville
Bic
L'Isle Verte
Clermont
St. Pascal
Causapscal
Carleton
Chandler
Newport
Bonaventure
Magdalen
Islands
Tourville
Beauport
QUEBEC
Montmorency
Sillery
Lauzon
St. Tite
St. Gabriel de Brandon
Shawinigan Sud
Lac Etchemin
St. Georges Ouest
Disraeli
Danville
Ferme Neuve
Mont Laurier
Maniwaki
Fort Coulonge
Bryson
Gatineau
Pointe Gatineau
St. Émile
Lachute
Thurso
Mascouche
Ste. Thérèse
Repentigny
Montréal Nord
St. Hubert
Farnham
Dorval
Longueuil
Huntingdon
Lacolle
U.S.A.
N.B.
P.E.I.
N.S.
ATLANTIC
OCEAN

•	Population under 5 000
•	Population 5 000-10 000
●	Population 10 000-100 000
■	Population over 100 000

Ontario *Cities, Towns, and Villages*

0 100 200 300
Scale in kilometres

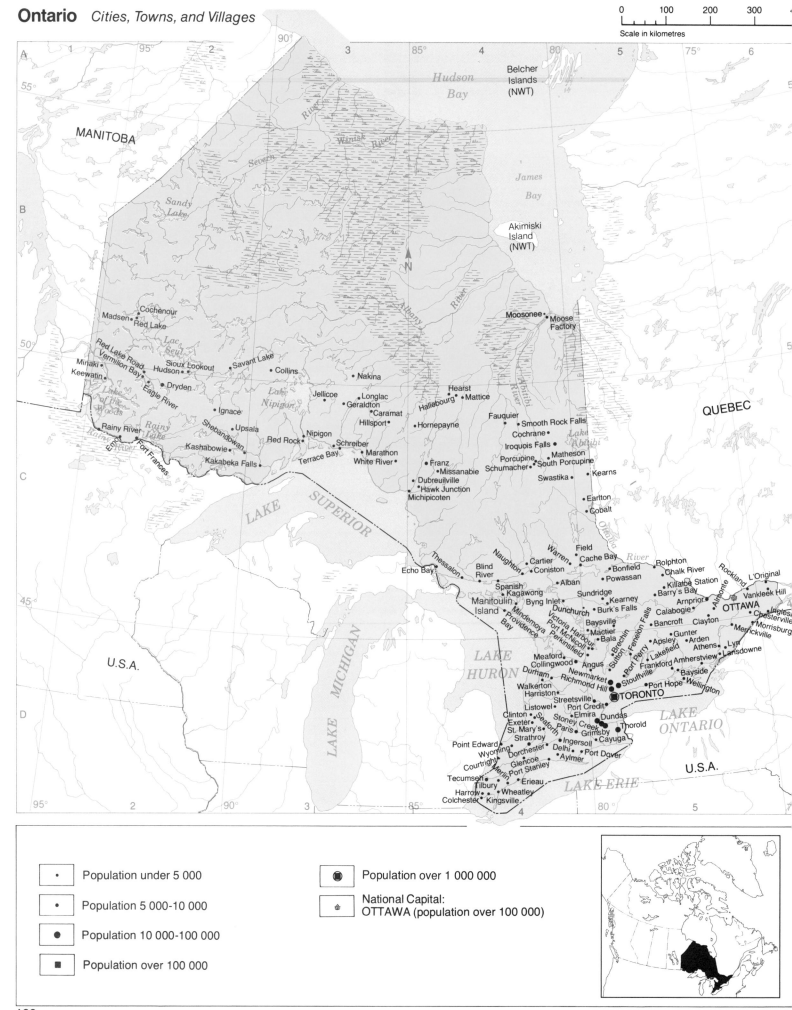

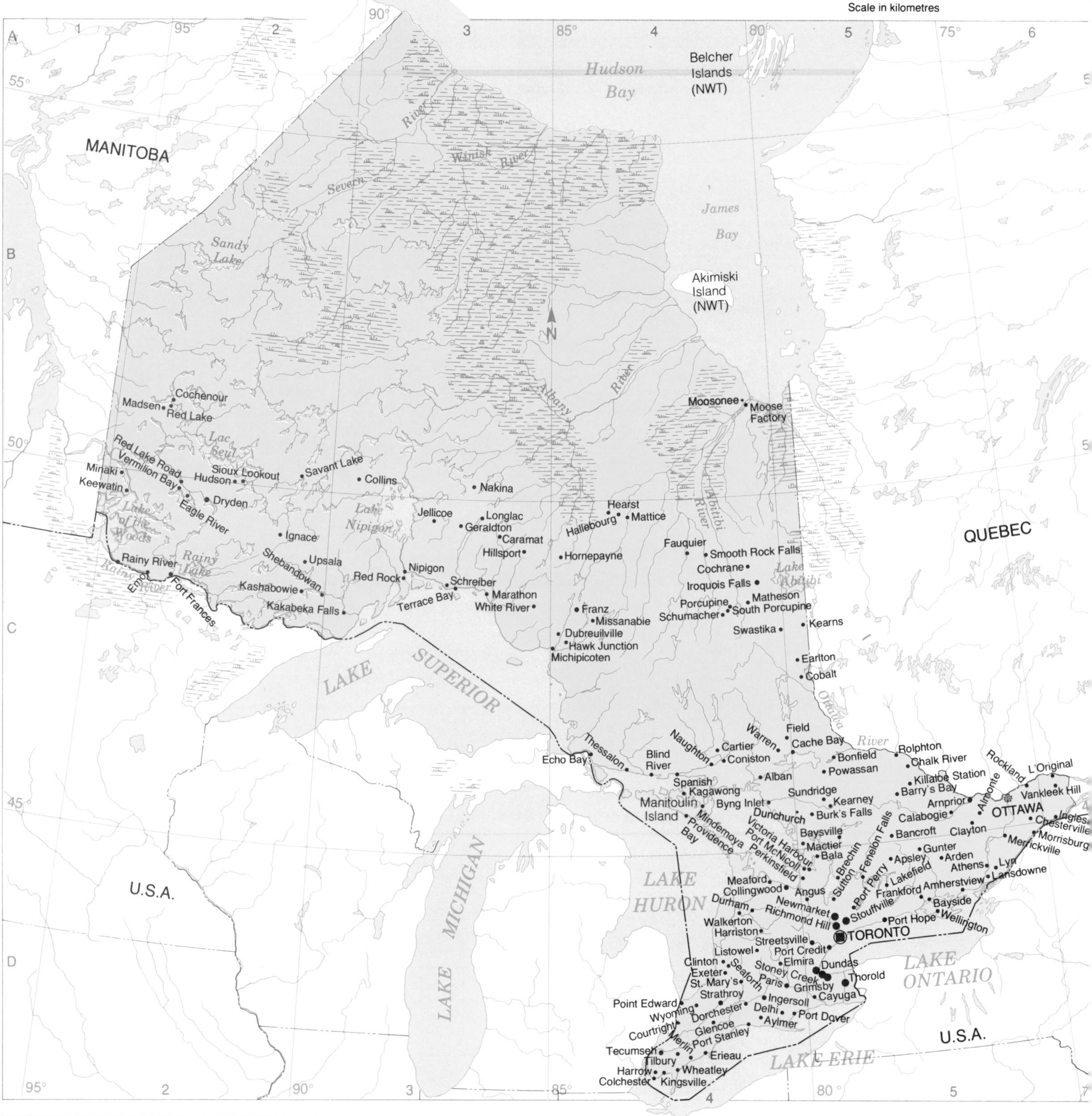

MANITOBA
QUEBEC
U.S.A.
U.S.A.
Hudson Bay
James Bay
Belcher Islands (NWT)
Akimiski Island (NWT)
Severn River
Winisk River
Albany River
Abitibi River
Ottawa River
Sandy Lake
Lac Seul
Lake of the Woods
Rainy Lake
Rainy River
Lake Nipigon
Lake Abitibi
LAKE SUPERIOR
LAKE MICHIGAN
LAKE HURON
LAKE ONTARIO
LAKE ERIE
Manitoulin Island
N
A B C D
1 2 3 4 5 6
95° 90° 85° 80° 75°
55° 50° 45°
Cochenour
Madsen
Red Lake
Red Lake Road
Vermilion Bay
Minaki
Keewatin
Sioux Lookout
Hudson
Savant Lake
Collins
Nakina
Dryden
Eagle River
Ignace
Upsala
Shebandowan
Rainy River
Emo
Fort Frances
Kashabowie
Kakabeka Falls
Red Rock
Nipigon
Schreiber
Terrace Bay
Marathon
White River
Jellicoe
Longlac
Geraldton
Caramat
Hillsport
Hornepayne
Hearst
Hallebourg
Mattice
Fauquier
Smooth Rock Falls
Cochrane
Iroquois Falls
Matheson
Porcupine
South Porcupine
Schumacher
Swastika
Kearns
Franz
Missanabie
Dubreuilville
Hawk Junction
Michipicoten
Moosonee
Moose Factory
Earlton
Cobalt
Field
Warren
Cache Bay
Naughton
Cartier
Coniston
Bonfield
Powassan
Rolphton
Chalk River
Thessalon
Echo Bay
Blind River
Spanish
Kagawong
Alban
Sundridge
Kearney
Byng Inlet
Dunchurch
Burk's Falls
Mindemoya
Providence Bay
Victoria Harbour
Port McNicoll
Perkinsfield
Baysville
Mactier
Bala
Brechin
Sutton
Fenelon Falls
Port Perry
Stouffville
Killaloe Station
Barry's Bay
Rockland
L'Original
Vankleek Hill
Almonte
Arnprior
OTTAWA
Calabogie
Ingleside
Chesterville
Morrisburg
Merrickville
Bancroft
Clayton
Gunter
Apsley
Lakefield
Arden
Athens
Lyn
Lansdowne
Amherstview
Frankford
Bayside
Wellington
Port Hope
Meaford
Collingwood
Angus
Newmarket
Richmond Hill
Durham
Walkerton
Harriston
TORONTO
Streetsville
Port Credit
Listowel
Elmira
Dundas
Clinton
Seaforth
Exeter
St. Mary's
Stoney Creek
Paris
Grimsby
Thorold
Cayuga
Strathroy
Ingersoll
Point Edward
Wyoming
Dorchester
Delhi
Port Dover
Courtright
Glencoe
Aylmer
Port Stanley
Merlin
Tecumseh
Erieau
Tilbury
Wheatley
Harrow
Colchester
Kingsville

Population under 5 000

Population 5 000-10 000

Population 10 000-100 000

Population over 100 000

Population over 1 000 000

National Capital:
OTTAWA (population over 100 000)

Manitoba *Cities, Towns, and Villages*

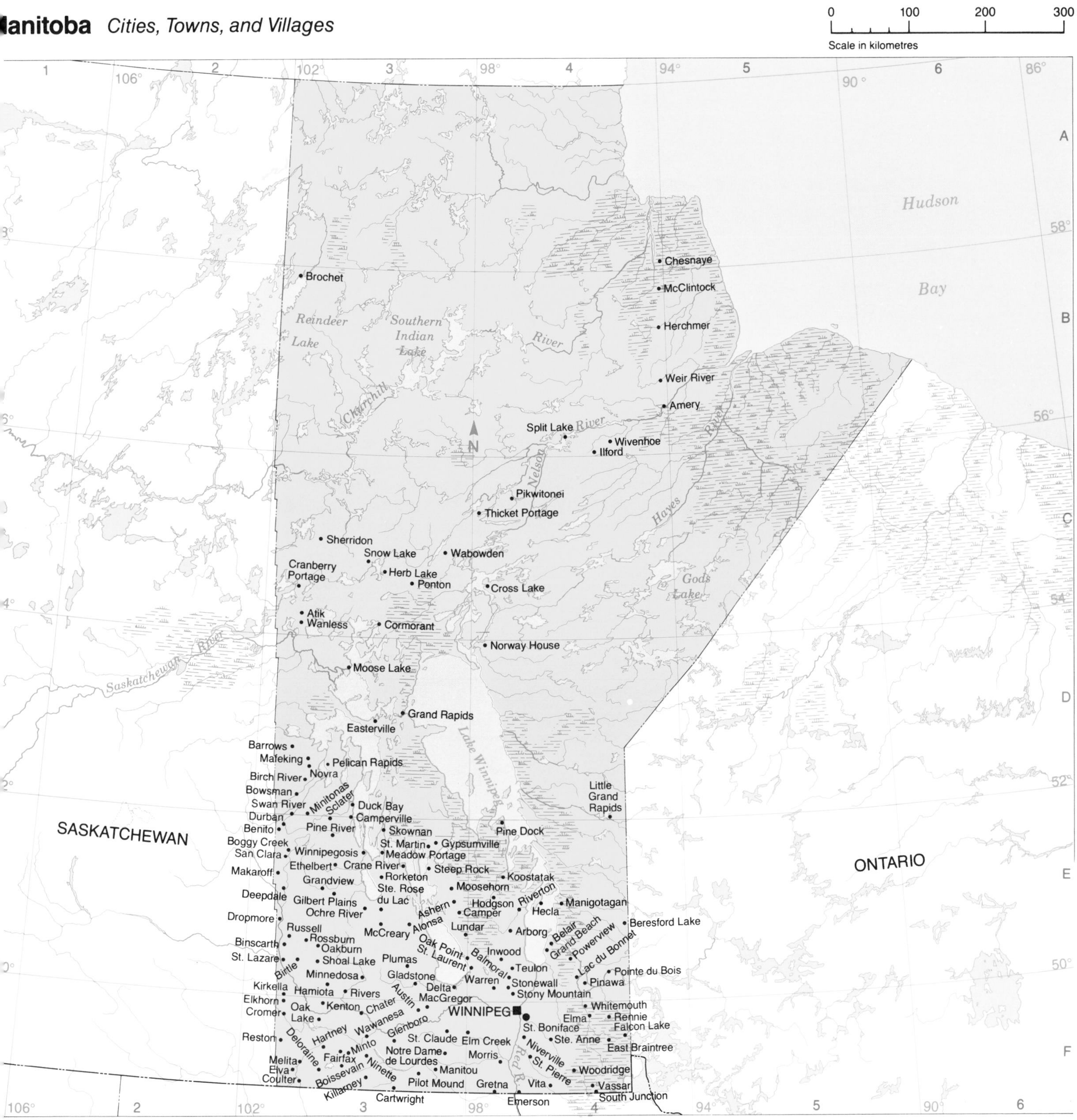

0 100 200 300
Scale in kilometres
1
2
3
4
5
6
106°
102°
98°
94°
90°
86°
58°
56°
54°
52°
50°
A
B
C
D
E
F
Hudson
Bay
Chesnaye
McClintock
Herchmer
Weir River
Amery
Brochet
Reindeer
Lake
Southern
Indian
Lake
Churchill
River
Split Lake
Nelson
River
Wivenhoe
Ilford
Hayes
River
Pikwitonei
Thicket Portage
Sherridon
Snow Lake
Wabowden
Cranberry
Portage
Herb Lake
Ponton
Cross Lake
Gods
Lake
Atik
Wanless
Cormorant
Norway House
Saskatchewan
River
Moose Lake
Grand Rapids
Easterville
Lake Winnipeg
Barrows
Mafeking
Pelican Rapids
Birch River
Novra
Bowsman
Minitonas
Sclater
Swan River
Duck Bay
Durban
Camperville
Benito
Pine River
Skownan
Pine Dock
Little
Grand
Rapids
SASKATCHEWAN
ONTARIO
Boggy Creek
San Clara
Winnipegosis
St. Martin
Gypsumville
Meadow Portage
Makaroff
Ethelbert
Crane River
Steep Rock
Rorketon
Koostatak
Grandview
Ste. Rose
du Lac
Moosehorn
Deepdale
Gilbert Plains
Ochre River
Ashern
Hodgson
Camper
Riverton
Hecla
Manigotagan
Dropmore
Russell
Rossburn
Oakburn
McCreary
Alonsa
Lundar
Arborg
Belair
Grand Beach
Powerview
Lac du Bonnet
Beresford Lake
Binscarth
St. Lazare
Birtle
Shoal Lake
Plumas
Oak Point
St. Laurent
Balmoral
Inwood
Teulon
Pointe du Bois
Minnedosa
Gladstone
Warren
Stonewall
Stony Mountain
Pinawa
Kirkella
Hamiota
Rivers
Delta
Austin
MacGregor
Elkhorn
Oak
Lake
Kenton
Chater
Cromer
WINNIPEG
Whitemouth
Elma
Rennie
Reston
Deloraine
Hartney
Wawanesa
Glenboro
St. Claude
Elm Creek
St. Boniface
Ste. Anne
Falcon Lake
Minto
Fairfax
Notre Dame
de Lourdes
Morris
Red R.
Niverville
St. Pierre
East Braintree
Melita
Elva
Coulter
Boissevain
Ninette
Manitou
Woodridge
Killarney
Pilot Mound
Gretna
Vita
Vassar
Cartwright
Emerson
South Junction
N

- Population under 5 000
- Population 10 000-100 000
- Population over 100 000

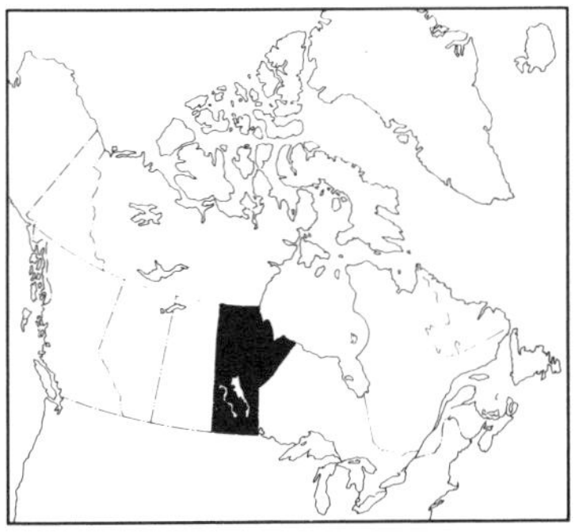

Saskatchewan *Cities, Towns, and Villages*

0 100 200
Scale in kilometres

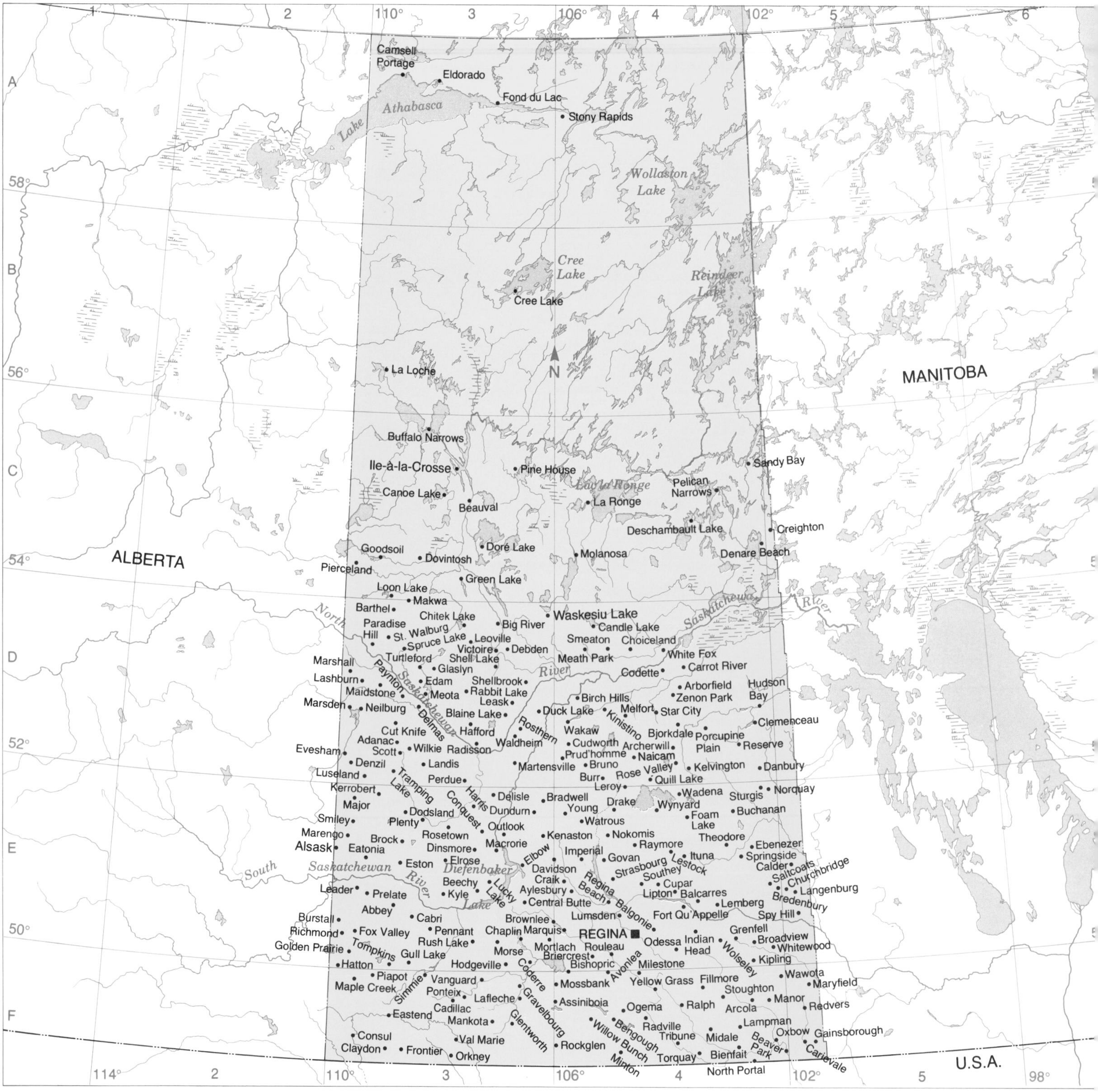

ALBERTA
MANITOBA
U.S.A.
Camsell Portage
Eldorado
Lake Athabasca
Fond du Lac
Stony Rapids
Wollaston Lake
Cree Lake
Cree Lake
Reindeer Lake
La Loche
N
Buffalo Narrows
Ile-à-la-Crosse
Pine House
Sandy Bay
Lac la Ronge
Pelican Narrows
Canoe Lake
La Ronge
Beauval
Deschambault Lake
Creighton
Goodsoil
Doré Lake
Dovintosh
Molanosa
Denare Beach
Pierceland
Green Lake
Loon Lake
Makwa
Barthel
Chitek Lake
Big River
Waskesiu Lake
Paradise Hill
St. Walburg
Candle Lake
Spruce Lake
Leoville
Smeaton
Choiceland
Victoire
Debden
Marshall
Turtleford
Shell Lake
Meath Park
White Fox
Lashburn
Glaslyn
Carrot River
Paynton
Edam
Shellbrook
Codette
Maidstone
Meota
Rabbit Lake
Arborfield
Hudson Bay
Marsden
Neilburg
Leask
Birch Hills
Zenon Park
Blaine Lake
Duck Lake
Melfort
Star City
Delmas
Hafford
Clemenceau
Cut Knife
Rosthern
Kinistino
Wakaw
Bjorkdale
Porcupine Plain
Adanac
Waldheim
Cudworth
Reserve
Evesham
Scott
Wilkie
Radisson
Archerwill
Prud'homme
Naicam
Denzil
Landis
Martensville
Bruno
Rose Valley
Kelvington
Danbury
Luseland
Tramping Lake
Perdue
Burr
Quill Lake
Kerrobert
Leroy
Norquay
Major
Harris
Delisle
Bradwell
Wadena
Sturgis
Conquest
Dundurn
Young
Drake
Wynyard
Buchanan
Smiley
Dodsland
Plenty
Outlook
Watrous
Foam Lake
Marengo
Brock
Rosetown
Kenaston
Nokomis
Theodore
Alsask
Eatonia
Dinsmore
Macrorie
Raymore
Ebenezer
Imperial
Springside
South Saskatchewan River
Eston
Elrose
Elbow
Govan
Itunu
Calder
Lake Diefenbaker
Davidson
Strasbourg
Lestock
Saltcoats
Beechy
Craik
Southey
Churchbridge
Leader
Prelate
Kyle
Lucky Lake
Aylesbury
Regina Beach
Cupar
Langenburg
Lipton
Balcarres
Central Butte
Lemberg
Bredenbury
Abbey
Balgonie
Burstall
Cabri
Brownlee
Lumsden
Fort Qu'Appelle
Spy Hill
Richmond
Fox Valley
Pennant
Chaplin
Marquis
REGINA
Grenfell
Broadview
Golden Prairie
Tompkins
Rush Lake
Mortlach
Rouleau
Odessa
Indian Head
Wolseley
Whitewood
Gull Lake
Morse
Briercrest
Avonlea
Hatton
Hodgeville
Bishopric
Milestone
Kipling
Piapot
Vanguard
Coderre
Mossbank
Yellow Grass
Fillmore
Wawota
Maple Creek
Simmie
Ponteix
Gravelbourg
Stoughton
Maryfield
Laflèche
Assiniboia
Ogema
Ralph
Manor
Eastend
Cadillac
Arcola
Redvers
Mankota
Glentworth
Radville
Lampman
Consul
Val Marie
Willow Bunch
Bengough
Tribune
Midale
Oxbow
Gainsborough
Claydon
Frontier
Orkney
Rockglen
Minton
Torquay
Bienfait
Beaver Park
Carievale
North Portal
North Saskatchewan River
Saskatchewan River
58°
56°
54°
52°
50°
110°
106°
102°
114°
98°
A
B
C
D
E
F
1
2
3
4
5
6

•	Population under 5 000
■	Population over 100 000

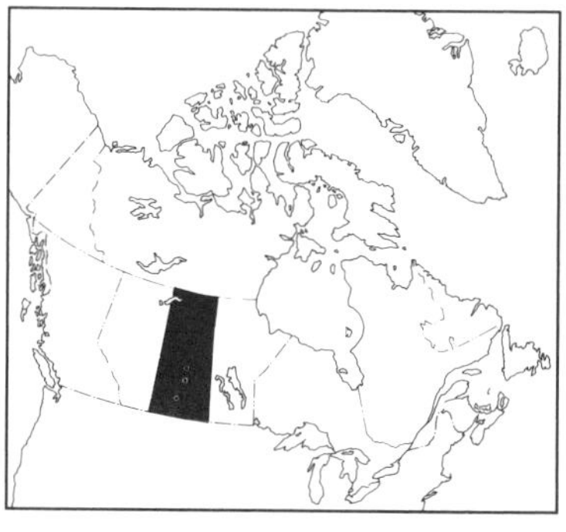

lberta *Cities, Towns, and Villages*

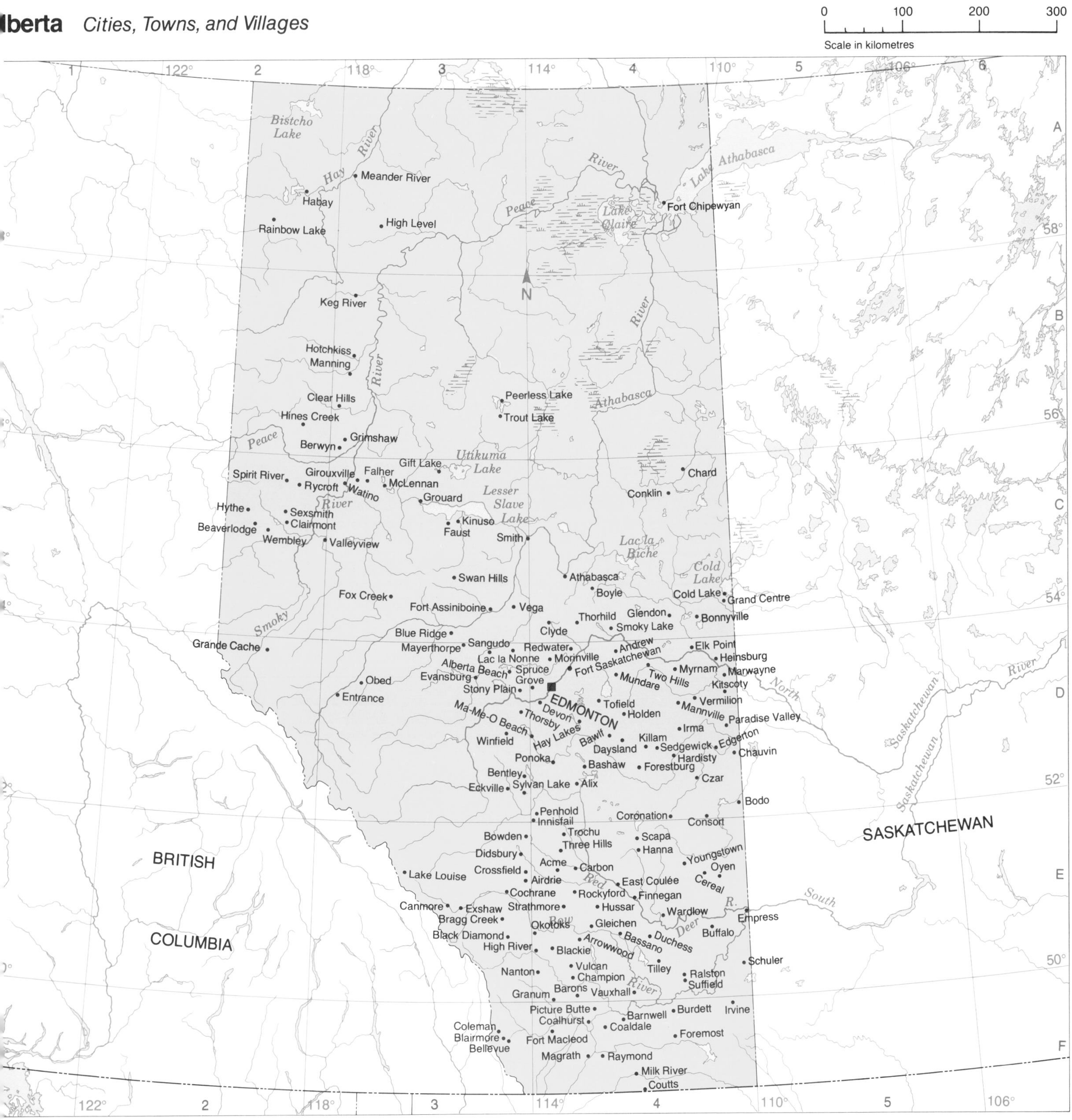

0
100
200
300
Scale in kilometres
122°
118°
114°
110°
106°
58°
56°
54°
52°
50°
1
2
3
4
5
6
A
B
C
D
E
F
N
Bistcho Lake
Hay River
Peace River
Lake Athabasca
Lake Claire
Athabasca River
Utikuma Lake
Lesser Slave Lake
Lac la Biche
Cold Lake
Smoky River
Wapiti River
North Saskatchewan River
South Saskatchewan River
Red Deer R.
Bow River
BRITISH COLUMBIA
SASKATCHEWAN
EDMONTON
Meander River
Habay
Rainbow Lake
High Level
Fort Chipewyan
Keg River
Hotchkiss
Manning
Peerless Lake
Trout Lake
Clear Hills
Hines Creek
Berwyn
Grimshaw
Gift Lake
Spirit River
Girouxville
Falher
Rycroft
McLennan
Grouard
Hythe
Sexsmith
Clairmont
Beaverlodge
Wembley
Valleyview
Kinuso
Faust
Smith
Chard
Conklin
Swan Hills
Athabasca
Boyle
Fox Creek
Fort Assiniboine
Vega
Cold Lake
Grand Centre
Thorhild
Glendon
Smoky Lake
Bonnyville
Clyde
Blue Ridge
Grande Cache
Mayerthorpe
Sangudo
Redwater
Andrew
Elk Point
Lac la Nonne
Morinville
Fort Saskatchewan
Heinsburg
Alberta Beach
Spruce Grove
Myrnam
Marwayne
Evansburg
Obed
Mundare
Two Hills
Kitscoty
Stony Plain
Entrance
Tofield
Vermilion
Devon
Holden
Mannville
Paradise Valley
Ma-Me-O Beach
Thorsby
Hay Lakes
Bawlf
Irma
Killam
Edgerton
Winfield
Daysland
Sedgewick
Chauvin
Ponoka
Hardisty
Bashaw
Forestburg
Bentley
Czar
Eckville
Sylvan Lake
Alix
Bodo
Penhold
Innisfail
Coronation
Consort
Trochu
Bowden
Scapa
Three Hills
Hanna
Didsbury
Youngstown
Acme
Carbon
Oyen
Lake Louise
Crossfield
Airdrie
East Coulée
Cereal
Cochrane
Rockyford
Finnegan
Canmore
Exshaw
Strathmore
Hussar
Wardlow
Empress
Bragg Creek
Okotoks
Gleichen
Black Diamond
Bassano
Duchess
Buffalo
High River
Arrowwood
Blackie
Schuler
Vulcan
Nanton
Champion
Tilley
Ralston
Suffield
Granum
Barons
Vauxhall
Picture Butte
Barnwell
Burdett
Irvine
Coalhurst
Coaldale
Coleman
Blairmore
Bellevue
Fort Macleod
Foremost
Magrath
Raymond
Milk River
Coutts

• Population under 5 000	● Population 10 000-100 000
• Population 5 000-10 000	■ Population over 100 000

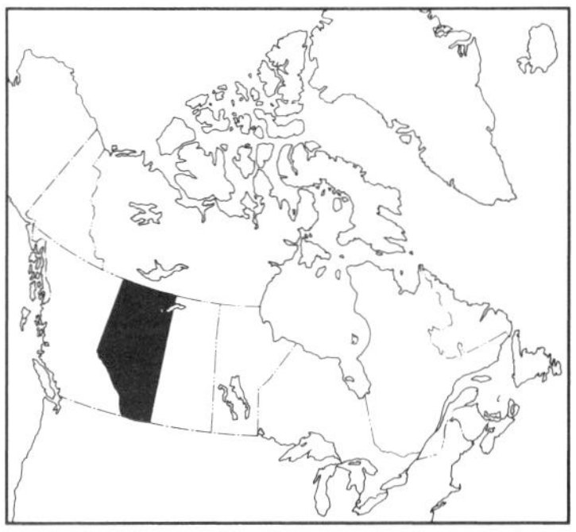

British Columbia *Cities, Towns, and Villages*

0 100 200
Scale in kilometres

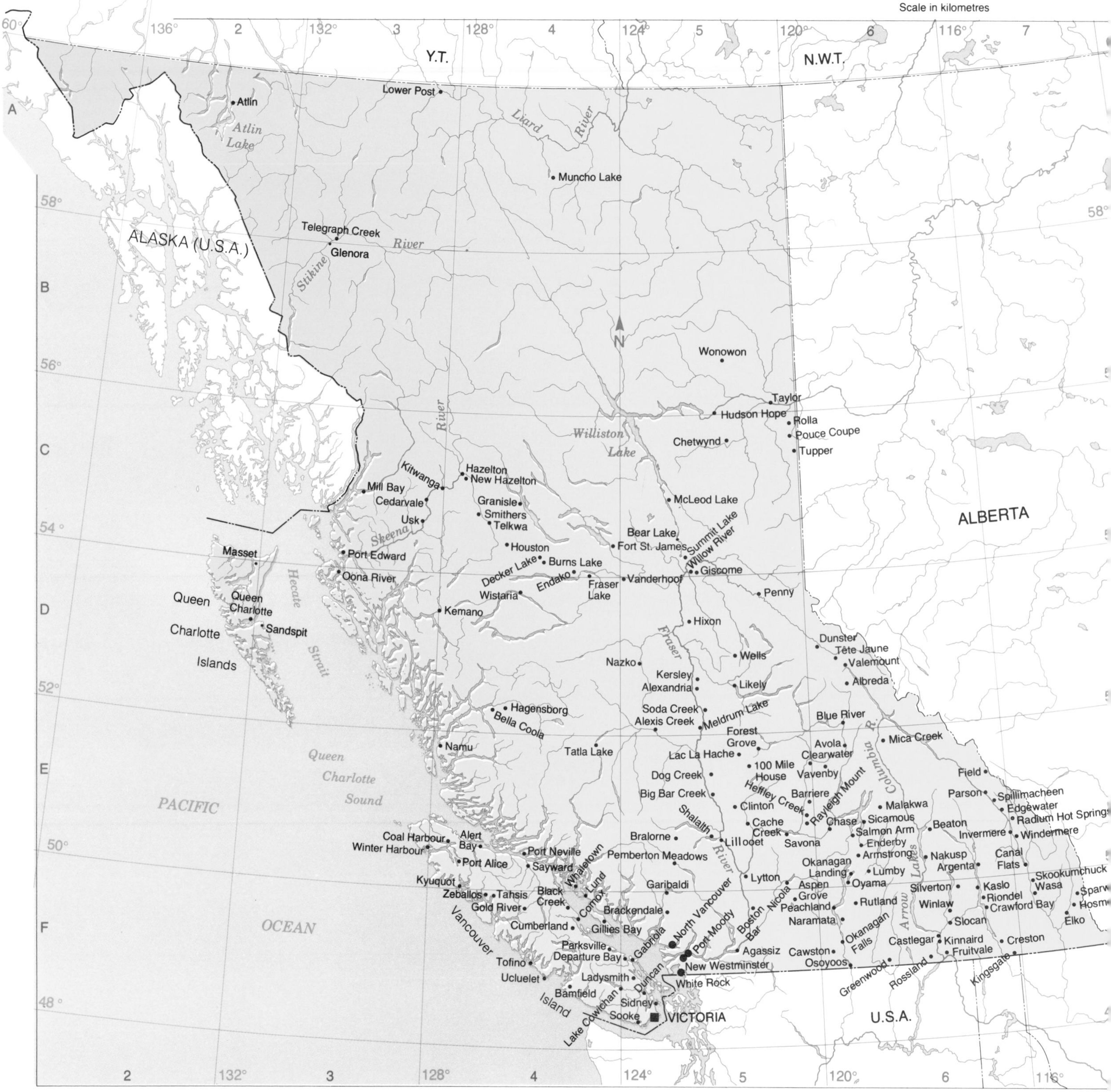

Y.T.
N.W.T.
ALASKA (U.S.A.)
ALBERTA
U.S.A.
PACIFIC
OCEAN
Queen Charlotte Islands
Hecate Strait
Queen Charlotte Sound
Vancouver Island
Atlin
Atlin Lake
Lower Post
Liard River
Muncho Lake
Telegraph Creek
Glenora
Stikine River
Wonowon
Taylor
Hudson Hope
Rolla
Pouce Coupe
Tupper
Chetwynd
Williston Lake
Skeena
River
Kitwanga
Hazelton
New Hazelton
Mill Bay
Cedarvale
Granisle
Smithers
Telkwa
Usk
McLeod Lake
Bear Lake
Summit Lake
Willow River
Fort St. James
Giscome
Houston
Burns Lake
Decker Lake
Endako
Fraser Lake
Vanderhoof
Wistaria
Penny
Masset
Port Edward
Oona River
Queen Charlotte
Sandspit
Kemano
Hixon
Fraser
Dunster
Tête Jaune
Valemount
Wells
Nazko
Kersley
Alexandria
Likely
Albreda
Hagensborg
Bella Coola
Soda Creek
Alexis Creek
Meldrum Lake
Blue River
Namu
Tatla Lake
Forest Grove
Lac La Hache
Avola
Clearwater
Mica Creek
Columbia R.
100 Mile House
Vavenby
Dog Creek
Big Bar Creek
Heffley Creek
Barriere
Raleigh Mount
Field
Parson
Spillimacheen
Edgewater
Radium Hot Springs
Clinton
Malakwa
Cache Creek
Sicamous
Chase
Beaton
Invermere
Windermere
Shalalth
Bralorne
Lillooet
Savona
Salmon Arm
Enderby
Armstrong
Coal Harbour
Alert Bay
Winter Harbour
Port Neville
Port Alice
Sayward
Whaletown
Pemberton Meadows
River
Okanagan Landing
Nakusp
Argenta
Canal Flats
Lumby
Lytton
Aspen Grove
Oyama
Skookumchuck
Kyuquot
Zeballos
Tahsis
Black Creek
Lund
Comox
Garibaldi
Silverton
Kaslo
Wasa
Riondel
Sparwood
Hosmer
Gold River
Brackendale
North Vancouver
Nicola
Peachland
Rutland
Winlaw
Crawford Bay
Elko
Cumberland
Gillies Bay
Port Moody
Boston Bar
Naramata
Arrow Lakes
Slocan
Okanagan Falls
Castlegar
Kinnaird
Creston
Parksville
Gabriola
Agassiz
Cawston
Fruitvale
Departure Bay
Tofino
New Westminster
Osoyoos
Greenwood
Rossland
Kingsgate
Ucluelet
Ladysmith
Duncan
White Rock
Bamfield
Lake Cowichan
Sidney
Sooke
VICTORIA

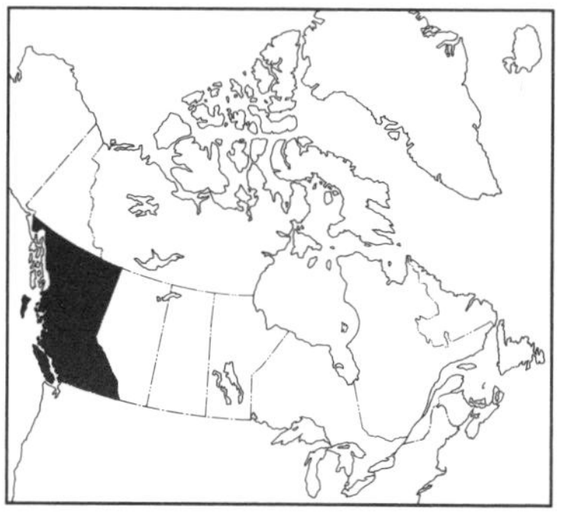

· Population under 5 000	● Population 10 000-100 000
• Population 5 000-10 000	■ Population over 100 000

GLOSSARY
&
GAZETTEER

GLOSSARY

Alpine Regions. In parts of Alberta and British Columbia, trees cannot grow because of the high mountains. Above a certain altitude, the air is too cold and the soil is too thin to allow trees to grow.

Asbestos. Asbestos is a mineral that is made up of string-like fibres. These fibres do not catch fire and burn, as most fibres do. So, asbestos is used to make things fireproof. Firefighters' suits, roof shingles, and floor tiles are some things that are made from asbestos. Canada produces about 40 per cent of the world's asbestos, mostly from the Province of Quebec.

Chemicals. Salt, water, air, rocks, oil, plants are all natural substances that you know. Workers in the chemical industry take natural substances like these and make chemicals from them. For example, electricity is used to make salt into chlorine gas and caustic soda. Chlorine is used to make bleaches, and caustic soda is used to change animal and vegetable fat into soap. Drugs, paints, plastics, nylon, synthetic rubber, fertilizers, insecticides, and jet fuel are just a few of the thousands of products made by the chemical industry.

Coal. Coal is black rock which can be used in many ways. Coal itself is used to heat buildings. The tar that is removed from coal is used in making many things — plastic, detergent, vitamin pills, and even perfume. The gas from coal is used to make dyes, fertilizers, and weedkillers. Coal that is specially baked is called "coke." Coke is used in the making of iron and steel. The maps in the section on minerals and mineral fuels show where coal is mined in Canada.

Copper. Copper is a reddish-orange metal that has three important properties. First, it does not rust, so it's a good metal to use for water pipes. Second, copper is a soft metal, so it can be shaped easily to make pots, bowls, jewellery, and all kinds of thing Third, electricity passes through it easily, so copp is used to make wiring for lamps, irons, and other things that use electricity. Canada produces about 10 per cent of the world's copper. What Canadian coin is made with copper?

Dairy Farming. Dairy farming means raising an keeping cattle to produce milk and cream. In the places where dairy farming is shown on a map, th farmers earn their living from producing and selling dairy products. They may also raise a few pigs or chickens, but their main work is dairy farming

Electrical Products. Electrical products in this atlas are any products that have anything to do with electricity. This includes wires, cables, and other products that send out electricity. It also includes any products that use electricity — light bulbs, record players, TV sets, stoves and other electrical appliances.

Fishing. In this atlas, fishing means catching anc selling fish only — salmon, cod, herring, etc. It doe not include lobster fishing, which is shown separately. The most important fish in the fishing industry in British Columbia is salmon. The most important fish in the Atlantic Provinces is cod.

Food Processing. Food processing means taking any crops from land or water and changing them into the tins, boxes, or packages of food you buy at a store. Tomatoes, for example, are processed into canned tomatoes, tomato juice, tomato soup, ketchup, spaghetti sauce, chili sauce. Fish is canned, frozen, smoked, or pickled. Wheat is processe into flour and cereals. Flour is further processed with other foods to make breads, cakes, pies, cookies, crackers, cake mixes, etc.

Fruit Farming. The main crops of fruit farms in Canada are apples, peaches, cherries, and grapes. Fruit farmers sell their crops both to supermarket d also to factories, where they are processed into ple sauce, grape juice, canned peaches, cherry pie ling, etc.

ld. Gold is a soft metal that is easy to work with d shape. It is used to make medals, coins, jewel- y, and other ornaments. Gold has another impor- nt property. It does not tarnish easily. Objects of ld that were buried in tombs thousands of years o have been found in perfect condition. Canada is e third-largest producer of gold in the world. ost of it is mined in Ontario.

ain Farming. The main grains grown in Can- a are wheat, barley, and rye. Grain farming is pecially important in the Prairie Provinces.

ypsum. Gypsum is a mineral. When it is heated, becomes a fine, white powder that is used in aking plaster and paint. Gypsum is found in ery province except Prince Edward Island. Nova otia is the largest producer of gypsum in North nerica.

ydro-electric Power Plants. In hydro-electric wer plants, the force of fast falling water is used drive machines that change the energy of the fal- g water into electrical energy. For this reason, dro-electric plants are located near falling water fast-flowing rivers.

on. Iron is a mineral. Rock that contains this neral is called *iron ore*. When iron ore, coke, and nestone are "cooked" together in a blast furnace, ey produce the metal iron. Iron is a hard, cheap, d useful metal. It is used to make fire hydrants, ing pans, railings, and many other things that ed to last a long time. However, its most impor- nt use is to make steel, which is a mixture of iron d other minerals and metals. Steel is even harder an iron and can also be shaped more easily to ake many things—from tiny safety pins to huge yscrapers and airplanes. Canada is the sixth- gest producer of iron in the world.

Lead. Lead is a dense, heavy metal. It is hard for anything to go through lead. Water can't get through it, so lead is used to make water pipes. Sound waves can't get through, so lead is used in making soundproof materials. One of the most important uses of lead is to make batteries. Canada is the fourth-largest lead producer in the world.

Limestone. Limestone has many uses because there are many varieties of limestone. Marble is one variety of limestone. It is used to make statues, table tops and counters, and pillars and floors in important buildings. Chalk is another variety of limestone. It is used to make putty, plaster, and—chalk. Lime is made by grinding limestone into a powder. Lime is used in making glass, china, and water softeners. To find out how limestone is used in making iron, look up *Coal* and *Iron* in the *Glossary*. Limestone is quarried in every province except Saskatchewan.

Livestock. Any animals that are used in farming are livestock. This includes cattle, sheep, chickens, and other animals that produce milk, cream, wool, eggs, etc., which farmers sell. It includes cattle, pigs, sheep, and other animals that are raised to be slaughtered for their meat. It also includes horses, oxen, and other animals that help farmers in their work. In this atlas, livestock are shown only where farmers earn their living from raising and selling livestock for their meat. This kind of farming is usually called *ranching*.

Logging and Lumbering. When trees are cut down and sawn into logs, the logs can be used for lumber or pulp and paper. Logs from some trees, like oak, cherry, Douglas fir, and pine, are sawn into lumber for houses, furniture, fences, shutters, etc. To find out about the pulp and paper industry, look up *Pulp and Paper* in the *Glossary*.

Marsh. Marsh is soft, wet land that is covered at times by water.

Metal Refining. When silver, copper, and other metals are mined, they are not ready for use. They are in hunks of rock. Metal refining is preparing the metal so that it can be used. This includes taking the metals out of the rock, separating metals that are mixed together in the rock, removing chemicals and other impurities that will weaken or damage the metal.

Minerals and Metals. Minerals make up all the rock materials on the earth. In this atlas, a mineral is anything that is taken from the earth by mining. Metals, like copper, iron, lead, gold, silver, etc., are metallic minerals. Asbestos, gypsum, limestone, potash, quartz, talc, sand, and gravel are non-metallic minerals. Oil, gas, and coal are mineral fuels.

Mixed Farming. In mixed farming, the farmer grows crops and also raises animals.

Nickel. Nickel is a hard, shiny metal that does not rust or tarnish easily. So it is used to coat other metals. The metal handles on refrigerators, stoves, and other appliances are coated with nickel to keep them shiny. The metal bumpers and trim on automobiles are coated with nickel to help prevent rusting. Nickel is added to iron to make steel harder. Canada leads the world in the production of nickel.

Oil Refining. The oil that flows from an oil well is actually petroleum. Oil refining turns petroleum into gasoline, diesel fuel, jet fuel, heating oil, asphalt, weedkiller, insect sprays, and many other useful products. The chemicals from petroleum are used to make plastic, nylon and other synthetic materials, and many other useful products. The chemicals from oil are called *petrochemicals*.

Potash. Potash is a mineral that is important in farming. It is used as a fertilizer to increase the size and quality of crops. Small amounts of potash are also used in making drugs, soaps, and dyes. All th potash mined in Canada comes from one province —Saskatchewan.

Pulp and Paper. Logs from softwood trees, like spruce and other evergreens, are ground into woo pulp. Pulp is used to make paper. Canada's most important paper production is newsprint. Newsprint is Canada's second-largest export.

Quartz. Quartz is a mineral that is found in man rocks. Sand and sandstone are usually formed fro quartz. Sandstone is an important building material. Sand is used to make glass and china.

Relief. Relief is simply the ups and downs of the earth's surface. In this atlas, the relief marked on map shows where the land is higher than the lan around it.

Sea Level. The flat surface of the sea when it is calm (no wind) and still (no tide). Heights of land and depths of seas and oceans are measured starting from sea level.

Silver. Silver, like gold, is a valuable metal. However, unlike gold, silver tarnishes easily. Silver is used to make jewellery, ornaments, medals, trays bowls, tableware (knives, forks, etc.), and coins. Because silver is so expensive, Canadian dimes ar quarters now contain more nickel than silver. Canada is the fourth-largest producer of silver.

Talc. Talc is a very soft mineral. It is white, pale green, or grey in color. Talc can be ground to mak talcum powder and face powder. It can also be cut in slabs. Slices of talc are used to line furnaces an stoves because it holds heat in. Roofing materials contain talc for the same reason.

ar Sands. In the valley of the Athabasca and eace rivers in Alberta, there are large amounts of ind that contain oil. These are the Alberta Tar ands. Oil is important to produce gasoline, heat-ıg fuel, chemicals, and other products. So far, get-ng the oil out of the sand is difficult and xpensive. Someday, the Alberta Tar Sands could roduce all the oil Canada needs.

undra. The tundra is a region across the northern ırt of Canada. Large parts of the tundra are flat, wampy land called *muskeg*. It is very cold here for ıost of the year, although a few days in summer ıay be quite warm. The ground is usually frozen, nd even in the summer, only the top 300 cm of the round thaws out. This is a treeless region. Only mosses, low berry bushes, and a few other plants can grow here. The few people who live in the tundra live by hunting, fishing, and trapping.

Uranium. Uranium is a metal. Its main uses are for atomic energy and atomic weapons. Atomic energy from uranium is used to make electricity and nuclear submarines. Canada is a leading producer of uranium.

Zinc. Zinc is a metal with many uses. It is used to coat iron and steel to prevent them from rusting. It is used in making dry-cell batteries. Zinc dust is added to paint to make it last longer. Canada is the second-largest producer of zinc in the world.

GAZETTEER

How to Use the Gazetteer

The name of each space on the maps in this atlas is a number + a letter. This is how the spaces are named.

Notice the numbers going across the top and bottom of the map. *Each number is between two meridians of longitude.* The number 1 is between 114°W and 118°W. All the places that are located between these two lines of longitude are in column 1. Move your finger down column 1. Peerless Lake and High Prairie and Calgary are in column 1. Find these places.

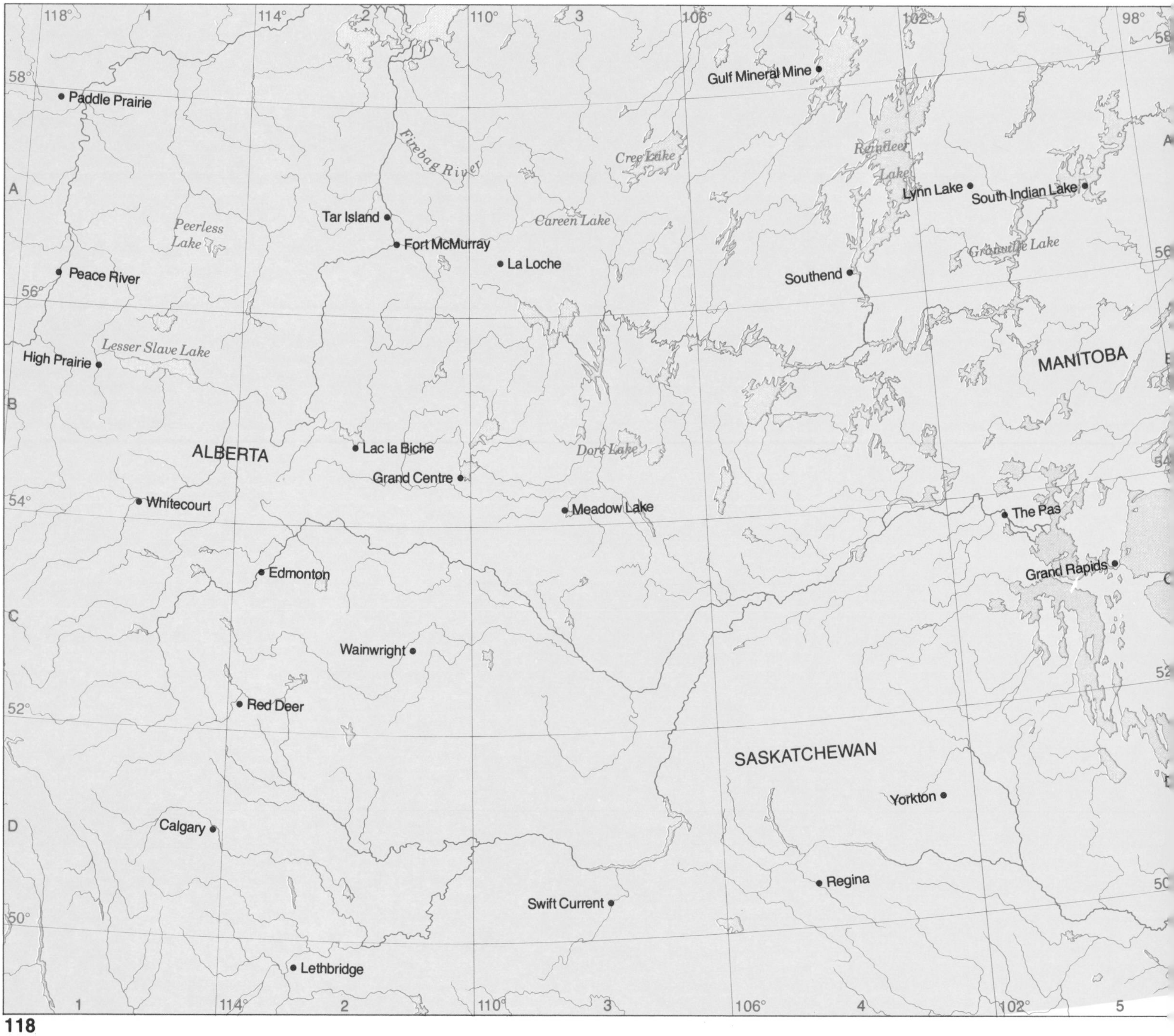

The number 2 is between 110°W and 114°W. All the places that are located between these two lines of longitude are in column 2. Move your finger down column 2. Fort McMurray and Edmonton and Tar Island are in column 2. Find these places.

- Between which two lines of longitude is column 3? Name some places in column 3.
- What column is between 102°W and 106°W? Name some places in this column.

Now notice the letters going down both sides of the map. *Each letter is between two parallels of latitude*. The letter A is between 56°N and 58°N. All the places that are located between these two lines of latitude are in row A. Move your finger along row A. Peace River and Firebag River and Reindeer Lake are in row A. Find these places.

The letter B is between 54°N and 56°N. All the places that are located between these two lines of latitude are in row B. Move your finger along row B. Whitecourt and Lesser Slave Lake and High Prairie are in row B. Find these places.

- Between which two lines of latitude is row C? Name some places in row C.
- What row is between 50°N and 52°N? Name some places in this row.

You can see that each column and each row is divided into spaces. **The name of each space is the number of the column + the letter of the row.**

The space that is in column 2 and row C is 2C. The space that is in column 3 and row B is 3B. The space that is in column 4 and row D is 4D.

To find a space on a map, this is what you do. Let's say you want to find 2C. First, find column 2 and row C. Then, move one finger down column 2 and another finger along row C. The space where your fingers meet is 2C. To find 3B, move one finger down column 3 and another finger along row B. The space where your fingers meet is 3B.

Find these spaces on the map — 4D, 3A, 2B.

- Red Deer is in 2C. Find Red Deer. Name one other place in 2C.
- Meadow Lake is in 3B. Find Meadow Lake. Name one other place in 3B.
- Regina is in 4D. Find Regina. Name one other place in 4D.
- Grand Rapids is in 5C. Find Grand Rapids. Name one other place in 5C.
- Lac la Biche is in 2B. Find Lac la Biche. Name one other place in 2B.

The *Gazetteer* lists all the maps on which a place is shown. It also tells the name of the space in which the place is located on each map. This is how places are listed.

Look at the entry for George River, Que. It tells you that George River is shown on the map on page 50, in space 5B. Turn to page 50 in the atlas and find George River.

George River, Que., **50** — 5B

Look at the entry for Georgetown, P.E.I. Georgetown is shown on two maps. On the map on page 36, it is located in space 3B. On the map on page 86, it is located in space 4C. Find each of these maps in the atlas and locate Georgetown.

Georgetown, P.E.I., **36** — 3B; **86** — 4C

Georgian Bay is shown on four maps, on pages 40, 41, 51, and 88. Name the space in which it is located on each of these maps. Find the maps in the atlas and locate Georgian Bay on each of them.

Georgian Bay, Ont., **40** — 4C; **41** — 1A; **51** — 4C; **88** — 7C

THE GAGE MAP AND GLOBE SKILLS SERIES

CANADA AND YOU: An Introductory Workbook of Map and Globe Skills, written by Ulrike Tuschek Davis and illustrated by Jody Bergsma Andrews
(0-7715-8203-X)

CANADA, THE WORLD, AND YOU: A Workbook of Map and Globe Skills, written and illustrated by Ulrike Tuschek Davis
(0-7715-8204-8)

THE WORLD AND YOU: A Workbook of Map and Globe Skills. IN PREPARATION.

GAGE SCHOOL ATLAS OF CANADA: A Skills-Building Atlas, by G. Cluett, N. Scrimger, and J. K. Smith.
(0-7715-8263-3)